2-6-14

Elaine Lewis

D0760620

# I Will Never Forget

*A Daughter's Story of Her Mother's Arduous*
*and Humorous Journey through Dementia*

## ELAINE C. PEREIRA

iUniverse, Inc.
Bloomington

To my genuinely wonderful daughters, Christie and Angie,
and my amazing husband and friend, Joseph

# Contents

# Acknowledgments

I am blessed to have many great friends who supported me in my endeavor to write *I Will Never Forget*. This is a story that needed to be told, and, inspired by many casual remarks like "You should write a book," I did. To all of you, my coworkers and golf friends especially, I thank you for the many years of genuine, sympathetic listening and reading through the endless pages of my therapeutic e-mails in which I detailed a family in various stages of crises.

A special acknowledgment goes to my cousins Mike Ward, Maggie (Margaret) Bolas, and Jan Blum and their mother, my aunt Dee (Delores) Ward. They have provided me with genuine love and concern through all of our personal losses.

I thank my girlfriends Patricia Roy and Valerie Sfreddo, who have accompanied me for years through every step of every journey, especially the drama and loss of my mother. I also appreciate Barbara Ruga, who provided amazing clarity when I needed it the most, and Delle Morrison, who has always cared and asked about my mom as well as me.

Thank you to Margene Fuller, who graciously provided beautiful details of my mom as a young adult foraging her own dreams, and to Judy Savoy, director of resident services at Friendship Village in Kalamazoo, who patiently validated Mom's gradual, painful decline and allowed me the time I needed to get on board as well.

It is my husband, Joseph, who handed me his handkerchief when I emptied the Kleenex box again; who cradled me when I slid to the floor, overcome with emotions; who laughed so I would not cry; who loved and admired my mom, and me, and selflessly stepped up on our behalf.

And my daughters, Christie A. Thomas and Angela L. Morrison, loved their grandmother and me unconditionally, graciously set aside their very busy lives for us when we needed it the most, and wrote me the most treasured words of love and support, which I Will Never Forget.

I thank you all.

The author, Elaine C. Pereira, is donating a percentage of the proceeds to help fund Alzheimer's research and support programs. To learn more about Alzheimer's disease, go to http://www.alz.org.

Photography by Jen Prouty
www.jenprouty.com

# A Note from the Author

*I Will Never Forget* is a true story that needed to be told. My mother—Betty, as she preferred—was a genuinely wonderful woman who was no different from all great moms. She was kind, intelligent, energetic, and talented. In many ways, I emulate her, except I have a shorter fuse and a stronger voice.

My mother remained resolutely strong for her unborn little girl—me—while simultaneously mourning the tragic death of her infant son, David. Later, she grieved the sudden death of her daughter-in-law, Wendie. Finally, Mom endured heartbreaking loss again, when both Dad and her other son, Jerry, passed away within the same year. Through it all, however, my mom projected amazing personal strength and resolve.

In writing *I Will Never Forget*, I wanted to share my experiences as a caregiver who often blindly navigated dementia's unpredictable haze. Anyone affected by dementia can learn from my unwitting mistakes, recognize the insidious nature of memory decline, and take comfort in knowing he or she is not alone.

Although clearly mystified by my mother's goofy behaviors and irrational thinking, I did not appreciate the devastation of her disease. Mom's subtle ability to mask the truth clouded my vision and prolonged my ignorance until an explosion of events brought me clarity. As Mom's dementia advanced, destroying her persona, I built a repertoire of more effective responses and management techniques on my mom's behalf.

*I Will Never Forget* is the heartwarming and sometimes heartbreaking story of Betty Ward as seen through the eyes of her little girl. It is also the painfully honest, poignant portrayal of Betty as she faces her devastating but also humorous journey through dementia accompanied by her daughter.

# CHAPTER 1

## Christmas Clues and Catastrophes

December 1960

It was a week before Christmas. The tree was in its usual beautiful splendor, although at eight years old, I definitely cared more about what was under the tree than on it. My dad was at work, my older brother Jerry was off somewhere with his friends, and Mom was in the basement doing laundry. With the spies out of the way, I seized the opportunity to investigate my presents.

I huddled under the tree in the back and pressed hard on the top of a box with my name on it. The tissue paper was white, maybe two or three layers thick. The box was light—wide but not very deep. I shook it, but the sounds were vague and did not reveal anything about its contents. Bummer! I tried to remember what I might have put on my Christmas list that could be in a box of this shape and size, but I was stumped. I had to take more serious steps to uncover the prize inside. I pressed down on the top of the box and tried to see if I could unveil any clues.

Something reddish blurred under my fingertips, but I couldn't make anything out. I slid my finger slowly to the right and pressed down firmly again. This time, a bluish mark like an *l* or an *I* came through. I kept going to reveal green and yellow marks but nothing very helpful. Hmm. I went back to the red line on the left side and pressed down with the index fingers of both

1

hands. Maybe doubling up would help. It was working, although the paper and box top were crinkling under the pressure of my fingertips. I kept pushing the paper out to the left and the right while also pushing down, and then there it was: an *L*. So I had an *L* and an *1* or an *I*; of course, it was an *I. LI* ..., I pondered. *Life! The game. Cool.* It wasn't on my list, but my mom had great gift ideas and I was sure it would be fun. So I had figured out one of the presents; now on to the next. Santa had nothing on me!

Subsequent Christmases weren't much different as far as my being the present detective. Sometimes I figured out my brother Jerry's gifts too, but I don't think I ever told. I was not disappointed on those Christmas mornings that there were fewer surprises than there could have been. The compulsion to discover the mystery intrigued me and occupied some of my time during Christmas vacation. Unbeknownst to me, however, my mom was getting suspicious and had observed me clandestinely. She was a pretty good sleuth, too—like mother like daughter. She started to add weight, like a soup can, or sound, such as a box of paper clips, to the packages to throw me off. She was very ingenious.

Finally, one Christmas experience cured me of these Grinch-like investigations. It was Christmas 1962, when I was ten, that I set out on what would be my last mission to reveal gift secrets. One of the boxes under the tree especially attracted my curiosity. It was beautifully wrapped and shaped like a shoe box. I picked it up. It was very light. Certainly there were no soup cans in this box. It also made very little sound when I gently shook it, but I could detect a soft chime. I knew my mom was getting more creative with her packaging, so I wasn't surprised that I was stumped initially.

Since I didn't know that she was already wise to my antics, I didn't realize that she was intentionally trying to trick me. Over the next couple of days, I became increasingly curious about this box. Nothing before had stymied me like this one. I really started to get annoyed and was determined to reveal its contents. The size and shape of the box did not yield any clues. The paper was not transparent enough to read through; in fact, it was heavy, not thin like tissue paper. My gentle shaking turned into rattling, and then I heard it—the unmistakable sound of broken glass. I had broken the gift! I was crushed, and so was the present.

I really didn't know what to do next. If I told my mom, I would give away all of my mischievous secrets. If I didn't tell her, then on Christmas morning I would open up a broken something and Mom would know that it hadn't been broken when she wrapped it. I set the box down and walked away. I had to think. Finally I decided to fess up. I picked up the box from underneath the tree, carried it to my mom, and confessed the truth—well, sort of the truth. I confessed *my version* of the truth.

I told her I had been shaking the box gently, omitting the details of my vigorous rattling, and then had heard broken glass. She was very calm. As I discovered later, she had planted this gift to once and for all stop my present spying. But she did not reveal for several years that she had been wise to my antics for some time. The broken gift turned out to be an inexpensive, very lightweight Christmas ornament. I don't remember what the wrapping paper looked like, but she had intentionally wrapped the box in that paper because she knew I would be attracted to it. Her hope was that I would be so curious about the featherweight box that I might possibly shake it until the gift broke.

Her plan worked. I had done *exactly* what she thought I would. Did she really know me that well? I should never have underestimated her—not then and not later. By the time she revealed her hand and told me of her scheme, I was an adult. She enjoyed her well-deserved moment of triumph retelling the story from her point of view.

Mom made Christmas magical, festive, and fun for our family. Some of the creative enjoyment evolved slowly over the years. She started putting generic clues on certain gifts, like, "Keep Warm" on a sweater or box of socks or "Yum," which usually adorned goodies like chocolate. They were vague but cute. Gradually her proliferation of tags evolved into clue masterpieces, especially when I was a mom and reintroduced the tradition to my family. Each creative "word of art" could take hours to draft. The clues often rhymed, and they were truthful but intentionally very misleading. Sometimes the clues launched treasure hunts, taking the gift recipient all over the house before revealing the present, usually because it was too cumbersome to wrap. Nothing was off limits. We used Scrabble-like clues and made-up crossword puzzles. We did it all and did it masterfully. Our trademark shenanigans persisted for years, tapering off only for the faint of heart who married into our crazy Christmas clue family.

## Christmas 2009

My mom arrived at our house in New Boston, in southeastern Michigan, by sedan limo from her place in Kalamazoo, about two hours west. It was December 23, two days before Christmas. I would have been willing to drive both ways to pick her up and return her home, but she had been insisting for years that it took too much time away from our holiday preparations. She had stopped driving, sort of voluntarily but after lots of drama, in the fall of 2009. Mom had flown over on a few occasions at Christmastime but had experienced flight delays and cancellations. Even if flying had been uneventful for her, Mom was no longer able to handle the chaos of airport travel.

My husband, Joe, had recommended that we try a sedan service in lieu of flying. It was a great idea—perfect, in fact. I wish I had thought of it. It was so much better than the airlines and about the same cost. They were prompt and carried cell phones. For as flawless as this arrangement seemed to us, for some reason my mom grumbled about traveling by limo and sitting in the backseat.

"They're *supposed* to chauffer you," my husband had explained to her with a chuckle. "In a cab, you sit in the back and enjoy the ride over."

She grunted, but strangely she had also started to ramble sometimes about taking a cab to Grand Rapids, an hour north of Kalamazoo, and picking up a flight there.

"Grand Rapids is a bigger airport than podunk Kalamazoo, so maybe their flights won't be canceled," she argued.

My mom used a lot of words like *podunk*, as well as one-liners, quotes, and proverbs for everything. Joe and I both tried to understand her clearly flawed thinking.

"Mom, it would take more time and more money—the cost of the cab and a flight—plus it would take you at least four hours instead of two. Why would you take a cab to Grand Rapids for one hour when you could be halfway to our house?"

She had no logical response because there wasn't one. I couldn't seem to get through to her. Her reasoning, or lack of it, actually, puzzled me. I had been noticing intermittent memory issues, flawed judgment, and strange remarks for some time. Then, at other times, she was spot on. I avoided any further confrontation about her goofy cab/flight plan. When she said she would "look into it," I just said, "Okay. Let me know what you find out." She never did.

My stepson, Chris; his wife, Ali; and our newest grandchild, Mia, then eleven weeks old, were also coming for the holidays. My daughter Angie and her husband, Ryan, were visiting her in-laws in Traverse City in northern Michigan. My other daughter, Christie; son-in-law, Chris; and twenty-one-month-old grandson, Isaac, would also be celebrating the holidays with us, making for a festive and fun family group.

My mom was planning to stay at my house for three nights, December 23–26. The first clue that things were a little amiss was when I saw her rummaging through her suitcase. She was "looking for something" but couldn't tell me what. I saw that she had packed six bras and maybe eight pair of underwear but no extra socks. *No problem*, I figured. *She can borrow some of mine.* Okay, so she was a little off on the undies. Also, she had pajamas but no robe. Robes, especially winter ones, were a little bulky to pack, so I loaned one to her, as well as some extra socks.

Then I noticed that her sweater was uncharacteristically dirty. At first I assumed it was stained permanently, but as I scratched my finger over the discolored streak, I realized something brownish was sloughing off in my hand—chocolate.

"Mom," I said gently, "this is a little dirty. Maybe I can wash it for you?"

"Sure. You can do my laundry anytime," she answered.

As the designated laundry fairy, I was on a mission to search for and rescue her dirty clothes. The slacks she was wearing were soiled too. *This is so not my mom*, I thought. She was a meticulous dresser and never would have gone anywhere with grubby clothes except out in the yard. I organized a laundry coup and started snatching her pants and sweater after she got ready for bed.

A week earlier, I had actually e-mailed her a checklist of what to pack, but she claimed that she couldn't print from the computer center at Friendship Village because "it's their paper." My parents had moved into Friendship Village, a senior independent-living facility, in 1999. I had suspected for some time that the problem was that she couldn't remember *how* to print or even *to* print, rather than a lack of permission to use the paper. I had even bought her a package of printing paper to use as she needed since she had mentioned this issue before. Packing for a short trip to my house was not a new experience for her, nor a difficult one, but clearly she had made several errors. It would not be long before I would be impressed that she had done this well rather than this poorly.

Christmas Day was delightful with bubbly, twenty-one-month-old Isaac ripping paper off the presents and sticking bows on his shirt, plus it was our first opportunity to meet eleven-week-old baby Mia.

My mom was a very generous person but had stopped shopping some time before, so Joe and I weren't expecting to have anything to open, nor was it necessary. Typically she wrote checks for her granddaughters and either mailed them before the holidays or handed them out in person if she was going to see them. She usually gave checks to Joe and me as well.

After dinner and dessert, we gathered back in the living room on Christmas evening. My mom was sitting on the couch next to her granddaughter Christie. Mom was rifling through her purse like she had done with her suitcase, "looking for something" that she couldn't identify. I watched her somewhat disorganized and purposeless searching. She took her wallet out and then put it back in. She took it out again, set it in her lap, and then drove her hand back into the black purse like a child grabbing for a handful of candy. Next, she took out her checkbook, opened it, stared at it, and put it back in her purse. When she took out a clearly used Kleenex and put it back in, I walked over to intervene.

"How are you doing, Mom? Have you had a nice day?" I asked. "I'm glad you're here with us." I carefully confiscated the dirty tissue and cupped it in my hand to dispose of later.

"I'm looking for my checkbook," she said. "I can't find it." She was definitely frustrated and moving her hands more quickly but randomly.

"I think it's in your purse. Is that it?" I offered as I pointed directly at the edge of her lavender checkbook cover embossed with Garfield and Odie.

She didn't answer me as she removed it for a second time and opened it up. I noticed that there were two checkbook packs but no check register. I sat on the armrest of the couch while she ruffled through the pages so I could see clearly.

"Did you send a check to Angie this year? I know you don't really shop much anymore."

"Yes. Well, no. I don't think so. I'm going to." Her reply was choppy. "I didn't write one for you and Joe either."

"You don't have to give us a check, Mom. We're just glad you came," I said as she pulled out a pen and attempted to start writing a check to us anyway.

"What's the date?" she asked, seriously unable to recall it. I suppressed an inappropriate chuckle.

"December 25," I answered.

She smiled as she looked up at me and said sheepishly, "Of course," as she shook her head.

*Well*, I thought, *at least that piece is intact.*

Chris was going to put Isaac to bed, so the little guy made the rounds, doling out hugs and kisses. Ali had already taken baby Mia upstairs. Meanwhile, my mom had managed to finish writing a check to Joe and me and handed it to me. It was for fifty-five dollars. *What a strange amount*, I thought, but I thanked her anyway of course. It was painful to watch. I tried to help her by asking questions, hoping I could really do something purposeful.

"Did you send a check to Angie?" I asked again. I knew she had not given one to Christie and Chris so far, so I suspected that she had not mailed one out to Angie either.

"No. I don't think so. Not yet."

Christie was watching her grandmother as intently as I was. Mom had pulled a blank Christmas card from her purse. I thought it was fortuitous that she had planned ahead to bring cards. She tried over and over to address the card with Christie's name. First, she spelled it with a *K*. She scratched that out and wrote it with a *y* ending rather than an *ie*. I could see Christie's furled brow and soft pout reflect how sad she felt inside to see her grandma struggling. I rested my chin in my hand, fanned my fingers apart to camouflage my own facial expressions of disappointment. Mom put the card down and stared at her checkbook, poring over it as if she was hoping for some inspiration and direction on what to do next. She apparently attempted to write numbers, but they were indecipherable, resembling random scratch marks. I wanted to do something to help her, but my previous offers had been ignored and I didn't want to frustrate her more.

Then Mom turned her head and looked at me with a very tense expression on her face. She said she couldn't think and needed to "figure it out." From there, she went upstairs. I waited about a half hour before I went up to see how she was doing. She had Christmas cards out—one labeled "Joe and Elaine," one labeled "Angie" but without her husband's name—and was attempting to write another one to Christie as I slowly walked in. She had written another check to us for 150 dollars and checks with odd amounts for the girls. I wasn't sure what to do, so I just offered to help if she wanted me to. This time she accepted gratefully, and together we finished the two checks to her granddaughters and the remaining cards.

I didn't realize I was still holding the fifty-five dollar check in my hand. She saw it, took it, stared at the amount, and said, "Did I write this? What a strange amount. What was I thinking?"

I didn't know, but I certainly wanted to. Cautiously, I asked, "Would you like me to look through your checkbook? Maybe I could help straighten it out a little?"

Her previously stressed expression melted away as she smiled and looked up at me, almost with puppy-dog eyes, and said, "Yes. I would like that."

It was a disaster. There was no ledger. She had two check packets with checks missing out of sequence. Clearly she could not manage her banking anymore. With yet another brilliant idea from my husband, I took over all of the bills and the existing account. We opened a second one for her so she could preserve some financial autonomy. She wrote out only a smattering of checks to Saint Augustine's Church and a few other people, though, before more signs of trouble were apparent. The second account would not be open for long.

# CHAPTER 2
## *What's in a Name?*

### 1951 and 1952

"If it is a girl, I would like to name her Elaine." Mom said to my dad. She was meeting with the Catholic priest from their church in early January 1952. "I've been told that since there isn't a Saint Elaine, I might not be able to use it." It was a nun who had sharply informed my mom of this before Christmas.

Mom was polite as always but clearly disappointed that her first choice in girl baby names would have to be set aside in favor of something else. Mom was a devout Catholic, but she had her own ideas and, in many ways, she was a modern woman. Baby names probably would have fallen into her "you've got to be kidding" category of annoying Catholic nuances, along with the rhythm method of birth control. "I've had three kids on the rhythm method," she told me often. For a very long time, I was understandably clueless what she meant, but then one day, when I was older, I finally got it and laughed out loud at the thought of expecting any kind of birth-control success via the "rhythm method."

My mom was a closet advocate of birth control—real birth control, not the Catholic, Vatican-approved-but-does-not-work kind of birth control. Pope-approved or not, she might have seriously considered using it had she not needed a hysterectomy

10

several years after I was born. Again, although I nodded my head in understanding, I couldn't fully comprehend what she meant when she didn't seem very upset about having to have the surgery. "It's okay," she explained. "I really shouldn't have any more children, so this works out fine."

Was "I really shouldn't have" the same thing as "I really don't want?" The idea of a baby in the house wasn't very appealing to me. I was the baby in the family and liked my singular status.

My mom and dad had been through hell in the late summer of 1951. Their twenty-month-old son, David (my brother whom I never met, of course) had been killed in a car accident. They were T-boned by a young man who was driving too fast. My mom's jaw was broken and her front two teeth were knocked out, a head trauma that led to headaches. My dad suffered several broken ribs, and my older brother, Jerry, almost four years old at the time, had rolled off the backseat and onto the floor of the car on impact and sustained a bloody nose.

In addition to the physical injuries, their car had been totaled and medical bills from the hospitalizations were staggering. They had borrowed a considerable amount of money from my mom's father, Grandpa Oberle, to help them out, and my dad paid back every penny. I know my grandfather always respected my dad for his integrity. My mom's real injuries, however, were insidiously hidden and far more significant than some missing teeth. They would manifest themselves gradually but eventually with a vengeance in the years ahead. On top of everything else, she was about four months pregnant with me at the time of the accident. Mom often told me that her unborn child helped keep her focused and centered, although also worried, through the tragic loss of David and financial uncertainty. A parent should never have to bury her child. David was the first but not her last.

I could just imagine, after what they had been through, Mom's private thoughts when some nun told her she couldn't use the name she wanted for her baby girl. I had never been that fond of my name, although I liked that it was unique. I was in college before I met another girl named Elaine. My dad's given name was Francis Wayne. He hated the name Francis so much that he had his name legally changed to F. Wayne. I had considered doing the same thing when I went to college since my middle name was Colette, a name I liked. But E. Colette sounded too much like E coli, so I abandoned the idea and stuck with Elaine.

"I'll talk with Father at the church," Mom said to my dad. "Sister was very emphatic that we can't use that name because there isn't a Saint Elaine."

"Okay. Do you want me to go with you?" Dad asked.

"No. I think I can handle it, but thank you anyway. We might have to come up with another name."

"And, of course, it could be a boy," Dad reasoned.

"Yes, you're right," Mom laughed. "It could be, and then it won't matter."

I don't know if I ever knew their choices for a boy's name. My name, with such controversy swirling around it, made for a better story, especially because it was true.

Eventually Mom met with the parish priest. He told her that Elaine was an acceptable derivative of Saint Bernadette (seriously?), and so it was: Elaine Colette Ward was born February 2, 1952.

# Chapter 3
## Perfect Little Paws

1956

Late one fall afternoon, while the neighborhood kids were all out playing, I found a little baby bunny all alone without his mama. He was in the thick grass down the street from our house. It was near dusk, so I ran home to tell Mom.

"We have to save him!" I said, trying to appeal to her maternal instincts after detailing what I had uncovered.

"Why don't you show me," she said as she grabbed a soft towel and a flashlight. We walked hand in hand from our house to where the baby bunny was. She walked briskly, and my little legs ran to keep up. Carefully, she separated the long grass to reveal an adorable but very tiny bunny. "He's pretty little so I don't know how much we can do," she said, "but we'll try."

She draped the towel over her palm, gently scooped the bunny up, and folded the towel edges over him. She had me hold my hands together, palms up close to my chest, and she set the bunny in my hands. Very slowly we walked home together.

"Let's see if the little guy will take some milk," she suggested. She took the bunny from me and had me crawl up into a living room chair, and then she returned him to me. Mom rummaged through my green toy chest until she found a doll's baby bottle, poked a hole in the nipple, and then filled it with some milk she

13

had warmed on the stove. She talked me through how to hold the bunny and the bottle and repositioned it a few times. Through the eyes of a four-year-old, I was certain the bunny was drinking the precious liquid.

"Is he going to be okay?" I asked.

I'm sure my mom chose her words very carefully. "He's very, very young, Elaine. Baby bunnies, like babies of any kind, need their mothers for milk and warmth. We don't know how long he's been abandoned, but if he makes it, it will be because you found him and brought him safely home."

"What should we do?"

"In the morning, if he's still alive, we'll take him back to the long grass where you found him. We can only hope he is found by his mother."

"Do you think she's looking for him now while he's with us?" I asked.

"She might be."

"Should we take him back now?" I wanted him to survive, but I also didn't want to give him up so soon. Maybe he could sleep in the room I shared with Jerry.

"It's dark out now," Mom answered, "so let's just see how he does during the night and take him back tomorrow. Now it's time for bed, little lady." She often called me that.

Mom put the bunny in a small basket with his warm towel and placed it up high where the cat could not jump up and get him while I got ready for bed. I had lobbied only briefly to have the bunny sleep in our room until my mom impressed upon me the possibility that our cat could hunt him down as a snack. It took a while to get to sleep that night, but when I woke up in the morning, I ran to the living room to check on our furry friend. Mom was already up, peering into the bunny basket and smiling. She carefully brought the basket down to my anxiously awaiting hands. He was still alive! I was so excited. I "fed" him again, and, after we got dressed, we returned the baby bunny back to the tall grass.

"You need to leave the bunny alone so his mother will come back for him," Mom said. "If she sees you around too much, it makes it harder for her to get to him."

I sort of got that concept. I watched from a distance throughout the morning to see if the mama rabbit would come back. We were gone in the afternoon, but when we got back home, I ran down the street to see if the little guy was still there. I carefully separated the long blades of grass, but he was gone. I was so happy that his mother had obviously returned to get him but was also so sad. I ran back home and told my mom, but she could tell I was a little upset.

She beamed a smile, knelt down to meet me face-to-face, and said, "I'm sure his mother came back for him." So was I.

Of course, I know now that the bunny probably didn't live nor did the mother return for him. Any number of animals in the area could have gotten to him, but we had tried because my mom encouraged and supported me in my bunny-recovery efforts.

## 2009

"What's the dog's name?" Mom asked me again, for the fifth time possibly.

"Bailey," I answered.

Bailey was a beautiful but energetic golden retriever. At only two years old, he was still a puppy. But there was something about my mom's soft, lulling voice and mannerisms that he responded to very well, as if transfixed around her. Bailey didn't jump on Mom like he did everyone else. He moved more deliberately rather than bounding through the house. Bailey just sat there, leaning into her while she rubbed his ears.

Her next remark, however, was bizarre. "When he dies, I want his ears."

What? "I'm not sure what you mean, Mom?" I said, trying to tease out a little more information, but I had understood it clearly the first time.

"You know, when Bailey," she remembered his name this time, "dies, I would like to have his ears removed so I could rub them all the time. They're very soft." Was she kidding? I honestly wasn't sure. I was about to respond when it got worse. "I had dog's ears when I was younger, but they might not have been this soft."

Okay. Now I knew for sure she was goofy. What an odd and creepy thing to say. I couldn't imagine ever having dog's ears removed. What a disconcerting idea. I got chills and shook just at the thought of it. I couldn't fathom how scrambled her mind had become to have and express an idea like this.

"Well, Mom, Bailey is still rather young, so he could live a long time yet." How was that? I was getting better at diffusing strange remarks to avoid confrontations or disrespect her in any way. It worked this time, but I had no idea how often I would be put to the test in the upcoming months.

# CHAPTER 4

## *Horses, Trains, and Automobiles*

Circa 1957

When I was a kid, the trip to my mom's childhood home in Lafayette, Indiana, was a fun adventure. Sometimes we left very early on a Saturday morning and stopped at a picnic site nestled in the trees near a narrow stream about a third of the way from Kalamazoo to Lafayette. My mom had thoughtfully packed frosted, cinnamon bakery rolls, a rare breakfast treat that we never had at home. She had chilled milk in a small thermos for Jerry and me and hot coffee in my dad's tall, green thermos for them. I relished those mornings. They happened about twice a year, in the late spring and early fall.

The road to Lafayette was rural and winding and took us through Amish country. I was curious about why anyone would forgo the speed of the automobile for a slow horse and buggy rig. The ladies were dressed in what I perceived as long, dark costumes and funny, ruffled hats. The men looked scary dressed in dark clothes with long beards. I couldn't understand their choice of lifestyle until, on one of our trips to Lafayette, we came upon the remnants of a serious car accident between two vehicles.

One car, headed in the direction we were going, had careered off the road into a ditch and was teetering at a precarious angle. There was a second car stopped on the opposite side of the road with smoke billowing from the engine. My dad slowed down and started to pull onto the shoulder when we all noticed several Amish buggies at the scene. At least fifteen bearded men were gathered in a cluster talking, their hands waving and fingers pointing. It didn't appear to me that they were angry, just strategizing. A few of the Amish men were conversing with two other men dressed in modern clothing, probably the drivers of the two cars. Then, from a distance, we could hear a pounding, thundering sound that escalated quickly, getting louder and stronger. The ground started to shake, and gradually six huge horses came into view pulling a big, heavy, wooden cart.

I could feel my mouth unhinge in amazement. Even a little distance away from us, they were impressive. The road was not heavily traveled, so we were the only ones waiting and watching. While I was taking in the whole scene, my dad started to pull back onto the road. I was surprised until I realized that he was being waved ahead by an Amish man. I turned around and peered out the back window to watch. As we slowly pulled away, the horses were being directed to a spot in front of the teetering vehicle. I could see them walking backward, bringing the cart closer to the car. It was incredible to watch. The scene gradually went out of view as we drove away.

I was just about to ask my mom what was going to happen when she volunteered. "The horses will be directed into position until the cart can be hooked up to the car near the ditch and pulled out of trouble. Do you remember seeing the policeman directing traffic when I picked you up from school Friday and the stoplight was out?"

I nodded my head. I had seen the officer blowing his whistle, waving his hands to call cars forward, and then quickly holding up his palm to indicate when a car should stop. Especially because I couldn't hear anything, his hand and arm movements reminded me of a conductor summoning his orchestra, like the one I had seen at the youth symphony. Then, as if she could read my mind, Mom confirmed what I was thinking.

"It is a little humbling to think that the Amish who live their lives very simply, without cars, electricity, or telephones, are able to help out two drivers who have all of these modern comforts."

Even as a young child, I could appreciate the incredible irony of the situation—the presumably antiquated horse and buggy saving a modern day, multiton vehicle.

## August 2007

My mom and I were at the train station in Kalamazoo on a beautiful, sunny summer day. The remodeled station was simple, attractive and safe, with a huge, fenced-in parking lot for passenger cars and travel buses. I had seen the old station years before and couldn't help but wonder if it had looked that dingy when Mom and her college girlfriend, Margene, first arrived in 1945. I doubted it. I had driven over the night before and stayed at Friendship Village so Mom and I could take the almost nonstop Amtrak train to Chicago to see Aunt Dee, Mom's sister-in-law; my cousins; and our extended family. I was certain this would be my mom's last trip to Chicago, and, sadly, it was.

It was a fun, uneventful trip, most of which I slept through. The gentle rocking of the train was mesmerizing, and I thoroughly enjoyed the warmth of the sun through the windows and the repetitive white noise of the cars clicking over the tracks. I glanced in Mom's direction. She was looking at the pages of her *National Geographic* but never turned them, a telltale sign that she was reading without processing the words, just staring at the magazine's print. She camouflaged it well, though. I'm sure no one else noticed. I wondered how long this had been going on without my noticing either.

My aunt had arranged for Mom and me to share the guest room at her assisted-living facility in Lombard, Illinois. I had been concerned that my mom would become disoriented if I didn't stay in the room with her, but it turned out to not be a problem anyway. Even when Joe and I traveled with Mom to Alpharetta,

Georgia, to see my brother, Jerry, in June 2004, she had done a few strange things. I particularly remembered that, at the restaurant, she seemed completely indifferent to what she ordered. Typically my mom was very specific about her meal selections—no garlic, dressing on the side, decaf coffee, nothing spicy. But that evening, she told Jerry to order for her, saying she would just have what he did. There were a couple of other strange things, but since my dad had died just two months earlier, I had attributed her odd behavior to stress and adjustment. On our Atlanta trip, grief might have been a contributing factor, but, looking back, I know I missed many indicators of my mom's declining mental status.

We had a great visit with "the Chicago family," as I referred to them, although my mom recognized only Dee. I was very surprised that she didn't remember Maggie or Craig, Dee's daughter and son-in-law. They lived nearby in Lombard and always saw my mom and dad during my parents' regular trips to Chicago.

In contrast, our train trip home was a *real* adventure, but not because of Mom. My daughter Christie had just announced that she was pregnant with her first child, which would also be my first grandchild and my mom's first great-grandchild. Christie had wanted to tell her grandmother in person, so we had planned for all of us to meet in Kalamazoo on Sunday after Mom and I returned from Chicago. It was a great plan, but like many plans, it fell apart, this one when the train broke down. The train was literally stuck on the tracks in a field of tall grass in the middle of nowhere. We sat there for about fifteen minutes, and then the train started up and chugged along until it quit a second time, then a third and a fourth, and every time there was literally *nothing* around us but green.

We were well over an hour behind schedule, so I called Christie from my cell and had her postpone her departure to meet us. On the fifth stop, we were finally at a crossroads in a small town. I could see a Ford dealership, a gas station, and a diner. Then I noticed that some passengers were getting up, gathering their belongings, and exiting the train. I decided to do the same. My mom was a trouper and laughed as we schlepped our bags along the railroad tracks. The sight of a petite, eighty-three-year-old, white-haired woman dragging a wheeled suitcase had to have been hysterical, but we did it.

Of course, I thought we would grab a cab and pay whatever it cost to take us to Kalamazoo. It never crossed my mind that a town big enough to have a car dealership wouldn't have cab service. Oops! But some very nice ladies at the local gas station offered to take us closer to our destination along I-94, where Mom and I waited just under an hour at a fast-food restaurant before Christie met us there. Our plan took a few detours, but eventually Christie was able to tell her grandma in person that she was pregnant. I smiled as I watched my mother's face beam when she heard the news.

My mom talked about our great train escape for a while. "I will never forget that train ride," she would say. "That was really something." Ultimately, however, she did forget it, like virtually everything else.

# CHAPTER 5

## *Elizabeth and Margene*

### 1924

My mom, Elizabeth Ann Oberle, was born July 21, 1924, in Lafayette, Indiana. She was the fifth of six children born to Frank and Lillian Oberle. Betty, as she preferred to be called, was beautiful as both a young and an older woman. I once saw an amazing picture of her in a bathing suit on a beach, probably Lake Michigan, circa 1946. She was sitting in the white sand, her arms supporting her from behind, legs crossed at the ankles, smiling into the camera with a playful expression. Even as a child, I could recognize the warmth in her face, the comfort in her touch, and the depth of her soul.

My grandparents' home in Lafayette was a child's dream playhouse. It was a big, old house with real leaded-glass entry windows, high vaulted ceilings, oak window trim and baseboards, and heavy solid-wood doors. There were three consecutive rooms leading from the doorway: the foyer entrance, followed by a big living room with a piano, and then the dining room where the huge, oak, oval table was. Many big family gatherings were held around that dark wood, oval behemoth. If the table could talk, it would tell a rich history of family drama during the devastating era of the Great Depression and colorful stories laced with laughter and disappointment.

My only memory of my Grandma (Lillian) Oberle was seeing her stand up from the couch and leaning over to give me a big hug as I ran toward her. It was mid-March and I was six years old when our family went to visit her. Grandma was terminally ill from cancer and died on Sunday, March 16, 1958, while we were on the road driving back home to Kalamazoo.

The bathroom—with indoor plumbing, thanks to my grandfather, the plumber—had a huge ceiling. I remember the small, white tiles on the floor with a smattering of black ones in a random arrangement and a footed white tub. There were also huge, big-enough-to-crawl-inside-and-hide cupboards.

My brother and I, and sometimes a random cousin or two, slept in the long bedroom in the front of the house. We could look out the bay window and see the front porch swing and hear the coo of the doves, a soothing sound that I loved and that still reminds me of my childhood fun. My cousins and I played hide-and-seek constantly when we visited, and the big, spooky walk-in closet behind the bedroom door was my personal sanctuary. A downward-angled ceiling created a very small cove that none of my taller cousins could slip into. I'm not sure anyone else even knew it existed, but I did.

## Purdue University, 1943

Every girl needs a great girlfriend, or three. My mom had several with whom I remember her shopping, golfing, or playing bridge. But her trailblazing, close college girlfriend was Margene Fawbush (Fuller). They first met at the coffee shop in the Purdue University Union in early January 1943. Mom was having lunch with two other Purdue classmates. They were known as town girls since they commuted to campus and needed to arrange for lunch when they had long days of classes.

Mom told a delightful story of her almost unsuccessful efforts to attend Purdue. My grandfather protested his daughter's plan to pursue a degree in chemistry, but my mom had her own ideas on her life's pursuit. I can just imagine the intensity of the conversation between them. Grandpa Oberle was short and slender, but his presence filled a room. In vigorous discussions, he was animated and loud, his hands waving in the air as he punctuated his words. My mom made her points with a quieter voice; she never shouted. She was firm, poised, and organized. She had a lethal weapon of rational arguments that were hard to refute.

"Dad," she would have begun, "I did very well in high school and have the intelligence given to me by God to pursue a college degree. There are so many opportunities in medicine or science research to help others. Pursuing a degree in chemistry is what I want to do with my life."

Mom knew the buzzwords to use in a discussion with her dad. Where her ideas clashed with his, she stood firm if she perceived her position as meritorious. She certainly would have considered her desire to go to Purdue and pursue chemistry worth fighting for. She did, and she won. Mom had strong principles and backed them up with action. I inherited her drive and rational thinking; my voice was just much louder.

Margene shared some of her memories of my mom from that time:

> I was a first-semester freshman when I met Betty. She was having lunch one day with two other girls whom I knew who invited me to join them. Betty and I hit it off instantly and continued to see each other. We became better acquainted as winter melted into spring and the beginning of another semester. This was the middle of World War II, and everything was geared to the war effort.
>
> I learned Betty lived in Lafayette, only seven blocks from me, and rode the Lafayette city bus to Purdue, just as I did. I got on the bus first and watched hopefully that

Betty would appear at her stop too. We had to make a bus transfer in downtown Lafayette, so it was great to share the lengthy ride with a chatty girlfriend.

I invited Betty to have lunch with me at my house sometimes. She and my mom soon became a mutual admiration society. Mom admired Betty's ability to crochet. She, too, was accomplished with handcrafts, but her greatest love was tatting [making delicate lace by hand], and Betty asked my mom to teach her how to tat. Betty was my mom's prized pupil. Later, Betty introduced my mother and me to tatted stationery, a hobby I still enjoy, using Mom's little tatted pieces.

## Circa 1964

Finances must have been tight at various times growing up. Although I never felt concerned, I do remember the day Mom brought me some quality card stock on which she had glued tatted loops, arranged into beautiful, dainty flowers. I was impressed with her exquisite daisies and roses, but her hand-drawn leaves were pathetic. Mom may have had the tatting skill, a craft I never learned, but I was more the artist.

"I tatted these and then glued them on the stationery. I was thinking maybe you could draw better stems and leaves than I did. Then we could sell them, and I would share some of the money with you."

*A blind squirrel could draw better than that*, I was thinking, *but make money?* She had my attention.

"I have a few cards here that have the flowers on but aren't connected by leaves yet. Maybe you could see what you can do with them."

"Cool," I replied. "Yeah, I can do that." And I did. Her drawing touch was a little heavy, but mine was spot on. Periodically she would bring me a stack to finish and then must have networked to sell them as occasionally she would hand me some silver or a dollar as my share of the proceeds. I doubted she made much money, but it was fun and I was flattered to be included in this enterprise with her.

## 1943–1945

Margene shared another story about my mom:

> It was 1945, and Betty and I started thinking about our impending graduations from Purdue, job interviews, and where we might live next. Upjohn Company, a drug manufacturer located in Kalamazoo, Michigan, seemed like a good place to start. Betty became interested too, and we thought it would be fun to see if we could visit Upjohn's at the same time. We wrote our respective interview letters and were thrilled to both be invited for the same Saturday morning visit. The train left Lafayette at 6 p.m. for Chicago with a three-hour layover, which got us into Kalamazoo at two thirty in the morning. We made reservations at the Burdick Hotel, which was within walking distance from the train station. We were surprised at how noisy the traffic was outside our hotel window and decided we were indeed in the big city!
>
> Our Kalamazoo/Upjohn adventure was so fun that it motivated us to interview in other cities. Eventually we completed plans for New York. I went to Albany, and Betty interviewed at Eastman Kodak Company in Rochester. We traveled what we considered at the time to be first class, which was a Pullman coach. We saw the New York City sights and were not afraid

to ride the subway, go to Times Square, and attend a play.

All of our interviews produced job offers. We each made the decision, independent of one another, to accept the Upjohn Company positions and relocate to Kalamazoo. We were both happy and relieved to learn of the other's choice. Betty started in early September 1945, and I arrived a few weeks later. She lived briefly in the Burdick Hotel until she found a room for us to rent in a private home. Later we moved into a furnished apartment on West Dutton Street with a wringer washer and clotheslines both in the basement and outside—all this, and we could still walk to work!

Marines, sailors, and Air Force and Army personnel had been abundant in our classes at Purdue. As the holidays approached and we returned to Lafayette, the train trip from Kalamazoo was unforgettable. The trains were so packed with servicemen that we used our suitcases as seats.

We learned about the infamous Michigan winters immediately upon returning to work after the holidays. We experienced bone-chilling wind and blustery snow on our daily treks to work, but we were young and didn't mind. We tobogganed at Echo Valley, were invited to dinners at the homes of our individual bosses and other coworkers, and traveled by train or bus to other cities.

As the year unfolded, a coworker of Betty's wanted her to meet a young serviceman, F. Wayne Ward. As their relationship became more serious, they decided to marry. We all agreed that they would keep the apartment, but Wayne helped me find a place in Kalamazoo's beautiful historic neighborhood. Friends always, we were there for each other whenever needed. Wayne and Betty married August 10, 1946.

# CHAPTER 6

*House of Dreams*

1957–1958

Our new house on Olney Street was built in 1957. My parents worked very hard on our house, putting in long days of sweat equity, but I was oblivious to their efforts. Building, packing, and moving appeared seamless through my eyes as a child. In fact, it was fun. We would pack a picnic lunch, and Mom would let me pick out a special snack like potato chips or cookies. It was so hard to choose that sometimes I would sneak in two treats. She never seemed to mind that I had smuggled contraband goodies into the picnic basket. We brought an old but clean brown, quilted comforter, which was transformed into a tablecloth and laid out on the unfinished floor of what was to be our kitchen.

Our first house was a small ranch-style house, but I don't really remember it very well since I was too young. Most of what I recall is probably from the wondrous bedtime stories told to me by my mom as well as memories from a barrage of black-and-white photos and slides. I loved slide-show night. It was usually a Friday evening, so we could stay up late and sleep in the next day. My dad would set up the slide projector in the basement of our new house and then call us down when he was sure his photo journey was ready to be revealed. Mom would pop corn upstairs. To this day, the smell of popcorn triggers memories of those slide-show nights of long ago.

The projector was flawlessly placed at just the right height and distance from a white, collapsible screen. Dad orchestrated the evening like a symphony conductor. He inserted the first selected tray like he was cuing the violin section. Then he readied the second tray, the woodwinds. Next came the horns and trumpets followed by his big percussion finale. By the end of the night, we had seen ten or eleven trays of slides and I was very sleepy. My mom was the featured symphony soloist, a.k.a. the narrator. She described the pictures and retold the funny stories behind them. The stories were sometimes better than the slides. No one was a great photographer.

My favorite slide of Jerry showed him, at about eight years old, sleeping in bed with his left arm under his head and his right arm on top of the covers. Sleeping next to him, also under the covers, was Blackie, the cat, in the *exact* same pose, her head on her front left paw. It is an almost unbelievable photo. If either my mom or dad had been a better photographer, I would have suspected it was doctored. I was always disappointed that Blackie never sought me out like she did Jerry. Someday I would have an Elaine-only kitty. I also remember seeing a slide of me cradling the baby bunny, the one I rescued from the grass, feeding it with a doll bottle.

While the new house was under construction, it was strange but fun to roam about the vertical two-by-fours and try to figure it all out at five years old. There were big, open spaces where the living room, kitchen, and my parents' room would be. And then there were little studded boxes that would be the closets. Sometimes I would hold onto two studs not too far apart, rocking back and forth from one foot to the other. One time, teetering on my left foot, I was in my room; but on my right, I was in Jerry's.

I remember singing a made-up tune to accompany my antics: "My room is bigger" (poised on my left foot), "Jerry's room is smaller" (now on my right foot). This went on for a while until my mom came over, and I boasted my discovery. "My room will be bigger, and it has more windows."

She suppressed a big laugh, no doubt, and then very gently explained, "You are indeed in your room when you lean this way," she said, pointing to my left foot. "But when you are on your right foot, you are actually in Jerry's closet and not his bedroom."

I was so disappointed. "Really?"

"Yes. His actual bedroom is here, and he has two windows also." She fanned her hand in a sweeping motion to point me in the visual direction of his room. I took a deep sigh. I should have known that my big brother would certainly not get just a snippet of a studded box for his bedroom and let little me have the prized corner room, but it was a nice thought while it lasted.

Mom tried to explain the wood-stud house mystery to me a few different ways, but at five, it was just too confusing. Of course, I never sang the little song again, but I was still intrigued by room possibilities and made up all kinds of creative alternatives. In my fantasy, the living room was going to be an indoor ice-skating rink. Gradually, though, on each subsequent visit, my skating rink fantasy slowly melted away as the walls were attached to the studs and each room, closet, and door opening came to life.

Many wonderful events happened in that house—memories made and forgotten.

# CHAPTER 7
## Cooking Chemistry and Cauliflower

### 1950s–1960s

Mom was a great cook, at least when she made my favorites. She made some awesome and some awful dishes. My favorites included pork roast with lots of potatoes, chicken, and standing rib roast, usually served for birthday dinners. She also made soup (boring), stew (yuck), chili (yum), pea soup (double yuck), cookies (yum), and cinnamon sugar pie (yum! yum!).

I'm told Mom was an accomplished pie baker. Apparently her first ones were not edible, according to my dad as well as by her own admission, but she must have learned. I never really liked pie nor did I eat much of hers, but other pie aficionados sang her praises enough times that I was convinced of her baking skill. I remember her making several piecrusts at a time. She looked like a chemist, measuring, mixing, and timing her craft to perfection. I commented once that she needed a lab coat rather than an apron.

She laughed and replied, "Actually, there is a lot of chemistry in cooking and especially baking."

"Really?" I was sitting on a step stool in the kitchen while she kneaded the pie dough. She had small but strong hands, and the dough was quickly succumbing to her masterful control. The stool was usually out and ready to use when she baked. It was an integral part of Mom's meal preparation since, at four feet, eleven and a half inches, she frequently needed it so she could get something down from a higher shelf. "What kind of chemistry?" I was mystified by what she meant.

"There's an exact science to baking," she started to explain. "Breads are made from dough similar to piecrusts, but they have leavening agents that allow the dough to rise slowly so it is soft."

Leavening agents? She caught the "what are you talking about" look on my face. Her answers rarely left me with more questions, but this time I was stumped.

"Leavening agents include baking powder, baking soda, and yeast." She let me think about this for a few seconds. "We add baking powder or soda to Toll House cookies," I said. We never called them chocolate chip cookies; they were always Toll House. I was quickly grasping the idea and said, "So they can rise a little and are chewy, not flat and crunchy."

"That's right."

"And yeast we use in cinnamon rolls. It's used in bread too," I added.

"Yes. So bread starts out as a heavy dough, a little like the piecrust dough here, but it's allowed to rise slowly with the leavening agent—"

She didn't get to finish as I chimed in triumphantly: "Yeast!"

"Very good, Elaine. You figured it out all by yourself."

I smiled but then was silent for a moment or two before I asked hopefully, "Is there extra dough this time for a cinnamon pie for me?"

Mom was furiously rolling the dough out forward and back, right to left to right. Her pattern was perfectly synchronized, her arms moving smoothly and effortlessly but with great power. Her back was to me, but I could see the corners of her lips start to retract into a smile and then I heard, "Yes, there will be." She turned her head, and her smile met mine. I loved my personal cinnamon pies. She would roll out a small ball of extra dough, lather melted butter on it with a pastry brush, sprinkle it with cinnamon and sugar, and then jab it with a fork. She baked it until it was just cooked. I ate it warm and slightly raw. She would try to make it early enough in the day so I could eat it all up and not spoil my dinner. I would hang out in the kitchen and pull over the stool so I could stand on it in order to warm myself by the built-in oven door and peer through the tempered glass while awaiting my cinnamon sugar treat.

## 2009

It was Christmas morning 2009. After opening presents, I prompted my mom to join me in the kitchen so that together, we could begin dinner preparations. Company cauliflower was a long-standing holiday favorite. I had never actually made it, so I assigned it to her. Making it was a culinary task she enjoyed, along with anything else she could do to help. I got out the coveted, slightly food-stained recipe card and put it in the clip of the recipe holder that Mom had cross-stitched for me years before. As I started to mentally organize the multitude of remaining cooking projects, I noticed that she was staring at the recipe.

At first I didn't think anything of it since my recipe cards were not like hers. My mom's recipes are written in her beautiful handwriting and have very detailed, step-by-step instructions and a meticulous ingredient list. I, on the other hand, had writing that was sometimes illegible and a tendency to abbreviate cooking procedures to the frustration of anyone who might want to follow one of my recipes. I assumed that Mom was just stumped by the poor quality of my printing or was deciphering the information underneath a cheese-sauce stain. Surely, she would begin doing something in another minute or two. But as the seconds passed, she was still literally just standing there, staring.

Then it hit me: Mom couldn't process what the recipe instructions were telling her to do. I had not observed this disconnection before. It was like how her failure to print a packing checklist was a result of her not being able to read the e-mail and complete the suggested directions. There wasn't time to dwell on it then. I quietly got out the cauliflower, mushrooms, and the big skillet to help her get started.

I gently put my hand on her shoulder to get her attention and said softly, "If you cut the cauliflower into pieces, I'll start with the mushrooms." Immediately I detected a sense of relief from her as if she had been rescued from the strangle hold of confusion. Did she realize she was stuck but couldn't express it?

She smiled and said, "Okay."

We finished the rest of the cooking project together. I was becoming very conscious of the fact that she could not read and execute a direction any longer. It was mind numbing! This woman had taught high school calculus and now couldn't read a simple amount like "a half cup of milk" and know what to get out or how much to pour. Later I also noticed that she could follow only one verbal direction reliably. When it came time to set the table, she was fine if I only asked her to put out the plates or spoons. An encompassing direction like, "Could you set the table for me, Mom" was lost on her. However, the most telling drama to date was yet to reveal itself.

# CHAPTER 8
## Dragon Tales

Circa 1957

"Mom, look!" I yelled. "There's a dragon over there. They *are* real! And there's smoke coming from his nose!" I pointed in the direction of the monstrous dragon's steaming nostrils so my mom would not miss it. "And look, his feet have huge claws!" I was practically squealing to make sure she saw every detail.

Mom slowly leaned into me to get a better look and confirmed my discovery. "He looks so powerful!"

We fell silent for a while, staring at the majestic creature before us. His face and horns were sharply chiseled, his wings so wide they perfectly complemented his stature. I started to see the detail of the pointed spikes and the spade on his whipping tail. Despite his foreboding size, I was not scared. He projected a calm and dignified aura. He didn't move but stood perfectly still in his resplendence.

After a few minutes, as we slowly drove farther away, the dragon gradually started to diminish from view. I could barely make out his powerful tail any longer. His sharp claws now looked like toothpicks as the distance increased between us. We continued to watch as the dragon's form slowly dissolved into the cumulus clouds that had come together to project his majestic image. I felt a little disappointed as my dragon friend faded into the blue sky, but then my ever-perceptive and creative child eyes spotted something else. "Look, Mom! There's the new cartoon dog, Snoopy."

She laughed. I nuzzled my head into her lap, and she stroked my hair. We were riding in the backseat of the car on the way home from a weekend in Lafayette to see Mom's family. Dad was driving, and Jerry was riding shotgun. I continued to gaze out the passenger-side window, searching to find as many creatures as the cumulus clouds would reveal. Sometimes it rained on the trip home, but when the puffy white clouds were in the sky, I loved laying on my mom's lap and watching the parade of creatures pass by. As we traveled, the images slowly came into view as they took form and then gradually faded into some nondescript, boring, white cloud without imagination. I rarely made it home without succumbing to the gentle, hypnotizing motion of the car and usually woke up as we pulled onto our street. Sometimes Mom would tell me that she had seen a hippopotamus or a tiger. I didn't feel like I had really missed anything; I was just happy that she had been watching out for my cloud friends when I couldn't stay awake.

## January 2010

Seeing something that wasn't actually there was harmless when it was a cloud creation, a child's invisible friend, or a dancer brought to life by the light and shadows from a howling wind blowing the trees. Otherwise, it was cause for grave concern.

I had gone to visit my mom on a Saturday in early January 2010. It was a typical visit: I would sort through her financial statements, go out to lunch, and chat. She had been so meticulous and organized for as long as I could remember, but increasingly her things were disheveled and misplaced.

After my mom's bizarre Christmas checkbook fiasco in 2009, I wasn't completely surprised to get a call on Monday from Judy Savoy, the resident services director at Friendship

Village. I had not yet met her, but we had spoken on a few occasions. The first, as I recall, was the missing brown pants caper. This time, however, Judy called with very disconcerting news. Apparently my mom had pulled the emergency cord just after midnight on Saturday, alerting the security team. When they responded, Mom was up, wandering about in her room, agitated and pacing. Her hands were flailing randomly and they described her as manic-like. She told them, "Elaine left her baby here."

I stood in stunned silence for a moment with my cell phone plastered to my ear, having a difficult time really absorbing what Judy was telling me. My baby? I had just been there Saturday, I told Judy. I had shown my mom new pictures of the grandkids, so perhaps this explained the baby reference, but still—it was bizarre. Judy added that the security team had checked all of the closets and then helped her back to bed. Apparently she went to sleep without further incident, and when the nurses spoke with my mom the next morning, she didn't indicate any awareness of the previous night's events.

"This could be an isolated incident, like a bad dream, or indicative of a psychotic episode," Judy explained. "I've seen it before in some people as they age." I surmised that "some" meant people with dementia. Judy had a degree in social work.

"Psychotic episode." I repeated the words audibly.

Judy cautiously started laying the groundwork for making a case that my mom needed more supervision. She recommended that we visit Woodside, an assisted-living facility, and gave me the name and contact information for the director there. Woodside was physically connected to Friendship Village. It was a smaller unit with substantially more staff for better supervision, organized activities, and considerably more cuing. Not surprisingly, it was also considerably more expensive.

"At the rate she's progressing, I believe she will probably need Woodside by September," Judy concluded.

I could barely process what she was saying. Word phrases were whirling around in my head: "psychotic episode" and "Woodside by September."

How baffling that Mom had the presence of mind to pull the emergency call cord, and yet she honestly thought I had a baby and also left it there. I couldn't reconcile these conflicting events. They seemed so dichotomously opposite—lucid versus confused, responsible versus bizarre. This was my dilemma as, most of the time, Mom seemed more functional than dysfunctional to me. It wasn't denial as much as it was ignorance of incomprehensible experiences constantly at odds with events as I saw them. I needed to witness more of what others saw in order to get on board with moving her. And I would. It would be ominous. It would be ugly. It would be emotional. However, I would eventually witness the ugly truth.

As usual, Joe and I discussed Judy's call and recommendation at the kitchen island, over a carton of Ben and Jerry's chocolate fudge brownie ice cream. (It's better from the carton than a bowl). I didn't sleep very well that night. I couldn't wrap my head around the words of the day: "left her baby," "psychotic episode," and "Woodside by September." Usually my sleeping habits were predictable and consistent. I could literally feel the events of the day fade away as the evening advanced, especially in front of the "boob tube," as my mom called it. She had never watched TV much; that was more my dad's and my thing. At eleven o'clock or so, I would crawl under the covers, nestle in, snuggle with the cat, hug my honey, and then I'd be out.

That night, I was pretty wound up, and the day didn't simply fade away. I wondered if my mom had already experienced other "psychotic episodes" that no one knew about. The next morning, I called Woodside and made an appointment for a Saturday in mid-January so that Joe and I could see the facility.

---

I had my six-month appointment with my internist in January also and, when asked, mentioned my new and atypical sleeping difficulties. I explained the quandary revolving around my mom. He shared with me that his mother was at Hearthstone, an assisted-living center close by, and he volunteered that he was quite satisfied with her care. I made a mental note of Hearthstone—*nice name*, I thought. *I might need it.* I confided that I was struggling to balance the Village's assessment of Mom as needing more care with my perception of her resisting a move and often seeming amazingly intact.

He was always vigilant about my medical health but seemed to be particularly attentive to my newly deteriorating nighttime habits. They were more telling than I realized. He made several insightful recommendations and then added another casual remark that had a powerful message: "It has been my experience that the professionals in these places are very knowledgeable and usually very accurate with their observations."

Then even more phrases were haunting me. I was juggling the label "psychotic episode" and the "Woodside by September" prediction with "professionals are accurate...." No wonder I couldn't sleep.

# CHAPTER 9
## *Dining Magic and Disasters*

### 1960–1970

When I was growing up, going out to dinner was a very rare treat that I savored. We didn't go out to eat because it was convenient or because Mom was too busy to cook; it was always a special occasion. I was amazed that at the nice restaurants, the waiter often didn't even write down what we ordered. He just remembered it. I knew I couldn't do that. When we went out as a family, my mom did her hair up, and sometimes she did mine special too. She dressed up, and so did I. I wore my black, patent leather shoes for those wonderful evenings. My dad wore a suit, and my brother, when he was old enough, wore a sport coat. I didn't really understand why a jacket that didn't match the pants was called a sport coat, but that's what I was told.

There was a special restaurant a distance from our house where a young lady server carried around a deep bin of fresh-baked, warm rolls. A leather strap was attached to the sides and went around her neck to help support the bin's weight. I could smell the wonderful, addictive aroma of just-out-of-the-oven delights as she got closer to our table.

I remember staring at the waitress as she used her silver tongs to pick up and place each precious roll on a plate. Through the eyes of a budding teenager, a twelve-year-old wannabe grown-up, the server was beautiful. She had boobs, and I had buds. She was tall, and I would never be. Her eyes glistened as she walked around the restaurant, smiling at the customers. My eyes were hidden behind ugly, thick glasses. I admired her shiny, brown hair swept up in a stylish updo, her slender figure, and the perfect touch of makeup. Even my dad wouldn't have called her Raccoon Woman, as he referred to some ladies who tried to camouflage their years with too much rouge and glaring red lipstick.

Dad was rarely critical, but occasionally he would make an observation of someone, a rare glimpse into his complicated and otherwise private persona. "She looks like a raccoon," he said once, a clearly critical assessment of some poor woman's makeup mess. I hadn't seen this person, but I remember bursting out in laughter. I was equally amused by his sudden remark, the casualness of his delivery, as well as the picture in my mind of a Raccoon Woman with wide, dark rings encompassing eyes blackened by too much eye shadow and mascara.

## Circa 1960

Of all of my restaurant experiences, the one I remember best was a magical night in New York City. I was maybe eight or nine when we visited my mom's youngest sister, Miriam, and my uncle Jack in New York. Mom had arranged for us to see the long-running Broadway hit *My Fair Lady*. My dad had had limited cultural exposure growing up but supported Mom's efforts to expose the family to new and different experiences. Aunt Miriam had actually arranged to purchase the tickets for us—almost a year in advance, I was told—as long-distance interstate phone calls were expensive back then.

I dressed up for what would be one of the most wonderful, enchanting evenings ever. My mom had studied the subway maps and guided us from my aunt's apartment to a stop in downtown Manhattan near the theater for a Saturday matinee performance. It was a day of a lot of firsts, and not just for me. It was my first trip to New York and Jerry's too, but for the three of us, it was our first subway experience and our first Broadway performance. I had overheard my aunt go over the color-coded subway system map with my mom.

"This is the closest stop to our place," Miriam said while pointing to a crisp, neatly unfolded map with colored lines and grids that represented the routes. "You'll pick up this line, and then transfer to this one. The Broadway Street theater district stop is here." She firmly pointed with her index finger to different places on the map and drew her finger in one direction and then another to reinforce her subway instructions.

"Okay," Mom said. "Thanks, Mimi" (Mom had always called her that).

"It's a great show. You'll love it. Have fun. You can pick up a cab outside the theater to get to the restaurant. We'll meet you there tonight." They hugged good-bye, and we left on our incredible adventure to Manhattan.

As we walked to the subway entry point, Mom and Dad were explaining to me what to expect on the subway: deep sets of steps, lots of people in a hurry, the deafening sound of multiple trains, and the importance of staying together to be safe. I squeezed their hands a little firmer. I couldn't really understand what the subways were for or why New York had them and Kalamazoo did not.

Jerry was particularly chatty that day. He chimed in far too often. He hadn't been on a subway before either, even though he implied that he had. I knew he was a novice just like me because I had asked my mom. Jerry was starting to annoy me, as he often did with his encyclopedic knowledge. After we descended what seemed like hundreds of steps, we arrived at a congested, loud, cement-gray area like a lobby.

A gentleman in uniform took our money and gave my mom tokens. I saw Mom glide through the turnstile effortlessly as her token slipped into the slot, but I was nervous about stepping forward and hesitated too long. In the seconds I wasted in apprehension, the turnstile locked and I was stuck behind it. Jerry, however, was an impatient show-off and took his token to the adjacent turnstile, where he tried to impress us with his masterful knowledge of subways.

I was scared and confused until the gentleman in the uniform calmly stepped out of his booth to override the gate and let me through. Jerry was already leaning against a support pillar, gloating.

"I told you to push through the turnstile quickly after putting your token in, but you just stood there and it locked," he boasted.

*What a know-it-all*, I thought, and I may have mumbled it under my breath, knowing me. I didn't say anything to him, but I sensed that my mom might have given Jerry her evil eye—her "that's enough" look—as he piped down pretty quickly after that.

"Let's stay together," was the only thing she said.

"We'll head down this next flight of stairs to a platform where we'll pick up the train," Dad added.

The subway was both impressive and intimidating, a tribute to amazing underground engineering. It was impossible to visualize digging out tons of dirt from underneath existing roads to build this monster. I stayed close to my dad and squeezed his hand tight. Jerry had been corralled between my mom in front and my dad, with me in the rear. I snickered to myself that Jerry was in a little bit of trouble for his show-off behavior. I wasn't like that—yet. I could hear the muffled but still very loud crescendo of approaching trains arriving at other platforms in other terminals, followed by brief moments of relative quiet before they took off for their next stop.

"The train will arrive soon," Mom said. "When it does and the doors open, lots of people will be getting off. We need to stay together and get on quickly but safely." I followed Mom's instructions exactly and noticed Jerry wasn't quite so cocky.

The subway train roared down the tunnel to a precise stop

at our platform, and soon we were inside. I had wanted to peer down the tunnel to watch our train arrive, but I was too scared and hid behind my dad. The dark tunnel seemed eerie when the train exited the well-lit platform area, but I enjoyed the ride's gentle rocking as we made our way to the theater district. When we got off, I was relieved to find moving-stair escalators, like the new ones at Gilmore's in Kalamazoo, so we didn't have to schlep up all of those steps. The daylight outside invited us to the street at the top.

The city of New York was astonishing! I had never seen such incredible tall buildings, cars, congestion, and crowds. We would be returning to another part of the city to see the Empire State Building, but for the moment, the scene was completely overwhelming. It was a slightly cool, overcast summer afternoon in June. I could see beautiful people in nice clothes arriving in cabs, hustling quickly from parking garages possibly blocks away, but most impressive were the limousines, something else I had never seen.

The long, sleek vehicles edged gradually closer to the curb on 51st Street in front of the theater's open doors. A crisply dressed chauffeur with white gloves hustled out of the driver's seat and scampered around the limo to open the passenger-side door. If a lady exited first, the chauffeur would hold out his white-gloved hand to assist her in exiting. The ladies were "dressed to the nines," as my mom said about glitzy, outfitted people. I was absolutely mesmerized, and we hadn't even gone inside yet.

Mom had explained the story of the play to all of us, although I was more enthralled with the entire experience than the play itself. The theater left me breathless. The grand foyer was indeed grand, with its domed ceiling heavily adorned with painted murals. Personally I found the frescoes a little gaudy, but the overall effect of such a magnificent theater was captivating.

"Close your mouth," Mom whispered in my ear. I didn't even realize it was open.

My dad handed an usher our four tickets once we got inside, and he escorted us to our seats as he handed us our programs.

I never opened mine that afternoon, but I did bring it home as a souvenir of our absolutely incredible day. I remember the orchestra playing the overture, segments of the award-winning musical, as the heavy curtain gradually rose with seamless precision. I very clearly recall Stanley Holloway's character Doolittle belting out "Get Me to the Church on Time." I even heard my dad laugh out loud during the song. Everyone was laughing, but to hear my dad chuckle, to get another rare snippet of Dad's usually subdued personality, reinforced my memory of the event. To this day, although I don't hear it very often, "Get Me to the Church on Time" brings back nostalgic memories of that wonderful play and my family, now long gone.

We laughed and talked about the play in the cab, another first, all the way to the restaurant. I can't remember the name of it, how long we rode to get there, or when I realized that Aunt Mimi and Uncle Jack had joined us, but I do remember our waiter, the magician.

I first became aware of his antics when, while he was placing a napkin in my lap, a quarter appeared behind my ear. I was completely stunned. He certainly had my attention. Throughout the entire evening, he dazzled Jerry and me with his sleight of hand, producing coins from behind our ears, chocolate mints from under the napkin in his hand, and marbles that mysteriously appeared among the ice cubes in our water glasses.

With his magic wand, he made my boring white milk turn into delicious chocolate right before my eyes. And for his grand finale, he made an adorable, snow-white, baby bunny materialize from the sugar bowl when he pulled the lid off. He handed me the bunny to nuzzle for a while. I held her in my small hands for several minutes. She was so soft and pure white. I laughed and fixated on the waiter's every move. He was actually working too, taking orders, serving food, and pouring drinks. He served other tables, which I saw because I never let him out of my sight unless he disappeared into the kitchen, but he was only *my* magician.

What a day it had been for this little girl. I nodded off in the car as Uncle Jack drove home, but I couldn't get back to sleep once we arrived at their house. I lay awake that night, smiling and dreaming about the incredible theater experience, the mesmerizing magician—the entire day, in fact. Not much could top this day for me. I only vaguely remember the rest of the trip, including the Empire State Building and a day at the beach, actually by the Atlantic Ocean, with my aunt and my mom.

## Early 1960s

Sadly, some of my dining experiences were abysmal and nowhere near as wonderful as that magical night in New York. I could be difficult, often wanted what wasn't on the menu, didn't want what was, and expected the food to be prepared like Mom made it. I liked tomato soup made with water, no mayonnaise on anything, popcorn drizzled with lots of butter, and breakfast rolls without nuts. I was the nut police. I could spot a nut in any roll, brownie, cookie, or casserole anywhere. Unfortunately, I also spotted nuts where there weren't any.

Jerry and I were having breakfast one morning. Mom was in the kitchen, and we were sitting at the table, eating quietly. I had a doughnut. It was supposed to be plain, but as I was eating it I spotted little nuts.

"There are nuts in here," I whined.

"There aren't any nuts, Elaine. I made sure when I bought them," Mom replied, defending herself.

"Yes, there are. Look!" My emphatic response brought Jerry over for a peek. He started laughing, which made me mad. "You're mean!" I said as I threw a pout in his direction, like that would leverage my position. "Those are nuts!" I was poking at miniscule pieces in the doughnut.

By then my mom had come over to referee the impending

verbal battle that was on the verge of eruption between Jerry and me.

"Show me the nuts," she said calmly.

I took my fork and twisted it in the dough to show her my discovery. "See? Nuts." I poked at a few more places just to make sure she saw all of those nasty things ruining my doughnut.

"Those are not nuts, Elaine." She reached forward and pinched the incredibly small, brownish bits that I was twirling with my fork.

"Yes, they are!" I insisted again.

She had picked the substance from the pastry and was squeezing it flat into a tiny dough pancake and showed it to me.

"It is just dough, a little darker than the rest for some reason, but it's not a nut," she said.

I was sure Jerry was thinking that *I* was a nut. I crossed my arms in front of me in a pout and refused to eat the doughnut. When I saw Mom's eyes roll, I knew her patience had run out. "Six of one, a half dozen of the other," she mumbled quickly in exasperation. *What does that mean, anyway?* It didn't make any sense to me even though I heard her say it over and over.

And it didn't end there. At Thanksgiving dinner one year, when I was eating my turkey doused with Mom's yummy chicken gravy, she asked me how I liked it.

"It's great," I said. "It's chicken, right?" I didn't like turkey gravy.

She was about to muster a creative response that wouldn't catch her in a lie, like "I just wanted to know if you liked it or not," when my loud-mouth brother came back with, "No. It's turkey gravy, not chicken."

Within a millisecond, Mom had kicked him under the table and not very discreetly either since I was able to easily determine that her foot was swinging in his direction and felt the table shake.

"It is turkey gravy," she confessed. "You've had turkey gravy before and never said a word, so I thought I would try it again on Thanksgiving." She wasn't apologetic, just honest.

I was caught, but probably because Jerry was in trouble for "letting the cat out of the bag," as my mom would say, I just added with a smirk on my face, "Well, the gravy is fine even if it isn't chicken."

The last dining disaster I can recall occurred at a restaurant one afternoon. I was unhappy about something. Either I didn't like the food or was done and wanted to go, or possibly both. First I started entertaining myself with the toothpicks in those little sleeves, pushing each point through the paper at one end, until my dad told me to stop. I was going to doodle on the napkin, but it was not the throw-away paper kind. It was real cloth, so I thought better of that idea.

Then the waitress refilled my water glass and some ice cubes spilled in. If I pushed down on them, they popped up—cool! That was fun for a little while, but then my creative genius went into high gear. I picked up my spoon, placed an ice cube on it, and worked very carefully to balance the spoon across the rim of the glass. And then, as if the devil himself was sitting on my shoulder giving me bad advice, I mischievously hit the spoon's handle, launching it and the ice cube into the air. Both came crashing down on the floor near the adjacent table.

Instantly I felt my dad's firm grasp on my arm. "Go pick that up, young lady," he said with a controlled but very firm voice. I slithered out of the chair to comply. I couldn't look at him or my mom or the people at the table near where it landed. We left immediately after that. The ride home was very quiet.

October 2010

My normally weight-conscious mom lost her internal discipline filters for making healthy food choices. In the past, she would forgo dessert to have a brownie later or avoid second-rate, store-bought snacks in favor of warm, fresh-baked Toll House cookies or a slice of one of her wonderful pies. Frankly, I couldn't care less if she ate her way through every Snickers bar in Michigan, considering her age and condition. I brought her cookies, brownies, M&Ms, and especially Snickers bars, both minis and snack size. I could tell her clothes were getting a little tighter and that it wasn't just age-related loss of muscle tone. Mom had a bigger tummy and needed to have her pants let out. She owned many tasteful, timeless outfits, so where possible, I had them altered, let out the darts, moved a button over, or inserted a coordinating fabric band to widen the waist. It was cute to watch my mom sneak a goody or two from her beautiful, Waterford crystal candy bowl. Her smile and obvious savoring of her clandestine treats was a treat to me amid so many less happy events. I savored it like she savored her coveted Snickers. "It's decadent," she often said. I always thought she also meant "forbidden."

# CHAPTER 10
## *Fickle, Fat Feline*

### 1960

I am a cat person. I like most dogs and have two big ones, but I like all cats, except maybe Jerry's hissy-fit feline Harriet. Like many little girls, I was in the Brownies in kindergarten and then the Girl Scouts. I had a calendar with the cutest picture of a little girl in her standard green Girl Scout uniform holding the most adorable tabby kitten ever. I was mesmerized by the kitty's face staring at me from the calendar's cover. I wanted a kitten *so* badly that I started negotiating (or whining, to an eight-year-old) with my mom to get a kitten. I dreamed about that kitty, his cute little face just drawing me in. I pulled the calendar out nearly every night to nudge and guilt my mom into getting me one.

We had had cats in the past, but I was very young and only remember them through the stories my mom told about Tabby and Blackie, both run over by cars in the days when cats were as much outdoor as indoor pets. I learned that my dad had accidentally killed Tabby. Apparently the kitty had crawled up into the wheel well to get warm and curled up there to sleep. Not knowing, my dad started the car and backed up, causing the cat to fall off and get crushed under the tire. My dad was a wreck. I only vaguely remember my mom embracing me to tell me that Tabby was gone.

I don't think I processed that Dad had been "responsible," but if I had, she would have told me tenderly and I know my dad felt genuinely awful.

After we moved to the new house on Olney Street, I was a cat-deprived little girl for years, longing for that kitty on the cover of the calendar. It reminded me of the song "How Much Is That Doggy in the Window?" only about a kitty, of course. I had played it over and over on my little 45 RPM record player, along with "Teddy Bear's Picnic" and a song about a goblin: "Control tower to goblin, your broomstick is wobblin'/You better make a landing right away."

One day my mom and I were in the car together, running some errands or coming home after a dance class, when we pulled into the driveway of a stranger's house. She told me that she had to pick up something from a friend. An older, slightly heavyset woman with a smiling but unfamiliar face greeted us at the door. The lady offered me cookies, and while I ate them, the women chatted for a little while. Then, after several minutes, the lady left the living room and promptly brought out her big, gray, fluffy cat named Snooky.

My mom said, "Mrs. (So-and-so)'s kitty needs a new home. Would you like to have Snooky and take her home with us?"

I was really surprised. It was early spring, and I had all but given up on ever having the Tabby on the Girl Scout calendar. Of course, I said yes, but deep inside I was a little disappointed. I didn't want to decline and possibly forever miss my chance to own a cat, but I didn't really want somebody else's overweight, older cat named Snooky. I wanted a small, cuddly, cute, mewing kitten that I could name myself, but I exuded delight anyway and Snooky came home with us.

The first evening Snooky was there, my dad was reading the paper after dinner. While my mom and I completed our after-dinner kitchen cleaning ritual together, Snooky was acclimating nicely to her new home. I couldn't wait to finish drying the dishes so I could play with my new feline friend. Snooky had other ideas, however, and had already staked out my dad. Just as I excitedly walked into the living room, she jumped up into his lap, pushing Dad's newspaper out the way with her determined, gray furry body and curled up, purring audibly. I was crushed.

I went complaining to my mom. "Why is Snooky on Dad's lap?" I whined. "She's my kitty." This was like Blackie all over again, a cat that only went to Jerry and never to me.

My mom knelt down to meet me face-to-face, a respectful habit of hers that I emulated when I became a mom, and gently explained, "Cats like to choose their people. If you sit very still and don't try to go after her, Snooky might jump into your lap too."

So I plopped onto the rich hunter green velour couch near my dad's chair and waited and waited. After what seemed like forever, my dad finally got up, forcing Snooky onto the floor. Maybe the now lapless cat would come, I figured. I called her name softly over and over. Gradually she sauntered closer to the couch, and I held my breath, hoping that she would dole out her affections to me. I sat very still with my legs crossed, creating the perfect cat lap, and beckoned her, "Here, kitty, kitty, kitty." Snooky was getting closer. I waited some more and called to her again. Finally she stood at the bottom of the couch and gracefully launched herself up and into my lap!

For maybe a half hour, she made my dreams come true. Perhaps the heavy-duty feline would work out after all. Snooky got on my lap that first night but never again after that. She was forever my dad's cat. He ignored her, tolerated her, and was basically indifferent to her, and she loved him for it. So my fantasy of snuggling my very own tabby kitten every night imploded in crushing disappointment. It would be years before I would finally have the lap kitty of my dreams. But on some young child level, I knew my mom had worked very hard to acquire that cat for me, and I was still happy that she had, albeit for the wrong feline.

Mother's Day 2010

"What is that?" my mom asked, looking in the direction of our cat.

"That's Snoopy, Mom." I was certain Mom had misspoken. She didn't mean "What is that?" but "What is his name?" Or was I wrong?

"Snoopy? What is Snoopy?"

Did she mean, "What *kind of animal* is Snoopy?" I would be genuinely surprised if that's what she meant. I honestly couldn't imagine her not recognizing that Snoopy was a cat, but her actions and remarks were getting more and more unpredictable and goofy. Was it possible that she just couldn't retrieve the word *cat*? But even so, she wasn't forming her question correctly. I decided to preempt her and give her all the facts.

"This is our cat, Snoopy. You've seen him before."

"I have?" After a short pause, she smiled reassuringly. "Oh."

"Do you remember Snoopy?" I asked.

"Of course." She was quite emphatic, but I was getting savvier to her responses.

Questions that elicited a yes/no response, including an assortment of similar replies such as "of course," "sure," "okay," and "maybe" weren't reliable. Sometimes she was right on topic and her responses were plausible, but in the absence of supplemental dialogue that could confirm she was on the same page, short answers were a toss-up when it came to reliability. Probing questions such as "What did you do today?" were equally unreliable in revealing any dependable information. It was a communication quandary, so I muddled through polite head bobbles, sometimes exhausting redirection, smiling until my face hurt, and steering practically any topic she would latch onto into a reciprocal exchange.

# Chapter 11
## *Shopping Sleuths*

### 1960s

June was always a great month. Every kid's dream of summer vacation began in June, with warm weather, sunny days, family trips, parks and picnics, and strawberry season. My mom and I, and sometimes Jerry, went to pick-your-own strawberry farms. We carried baskets into the orchards and climbed over slightly prickly strawberry vines to search for the rows with the biggest, reddest, and sweetest strawberries. Like many events with my mom, it was a tradition, one that I replicated with my daughters.

We went to open-air markets together too. I would stretch up on my tiptoes to peer at the tops of the flat tables with the plethora of vegetable choices. Mom would let me pick out my favorites, corn on the cob or green beans, and put them in the paper market bags by myself. We ran errands to the grocery store, where she let me push the cart, or the bakery, where the smell of fresh-baked bread, rolls, and cookies bombarded the olfactory sense. Of course, Mom always let me pick out something special to be my treat. And then, there was clothes shopping. For that we usually went downtown, and one time we even went shopping at Jacobsen's just for me. It was a day I would not forget.

My mom was especially proud of the outdoor pedestrian mall

in downtown Kalamazoo, completed in 1959. She was a visionary and recognized the commercial strength and unique appeal that the Kalamazoo Mall provided. She liked "spending my money there," she would say. Shopping there was her way via one small but financially powerful voice to acknowledge the city's efforts at revival.

One special Saturday afternoon, Mom and I went downtown, where she often went shoe shopping. Mom had a very small foot, "a five and a half with a quad A heel," she would tell the salesman when he asked her size. Stores rarely carried them, but sometimes they could be ordered. This time, however, we went to Mom's favorite upscale store, Jacobsen's. There must have been a special event coming up because she said something about getting me a new dress.

The little girl's department was downstairs, and we walked together down the wide steps to the lower level. The steps were too deep for me to handle alternately, so I used the railing to guide me and took one step at a time. As I reached the bottom, I slowly turned to the left. There it was. Off to the side, I saw a girl mannequin, a little taller than me, wearing an unusually light olive-green, A-line dress with two pleated inserts in the skirt in a subtle, muted fabric. I stood and stared, but my mom never missed a beat.

She noticed me noticing the dress. "Would you like to try it on if they have it in your size?"

"Yes," I said, beaming. I remember holding my breath while the saleslady went "in the back" to look for the coveted olive dress for me. It seemed like forever before she strolled out from behind a door. At first it looked like she was empty handed, but then I saw in her left hand, which was almost behind her, the dress. When I tried it on, it fit perfectly. I stood at the mirror, smiling. When I twirled around in circles, the skirt's pleats flared out. It was so cool.

Then my mom knelt down in front of me to make direct eye contact. "Do you like the dress, Elaine?"

"Yes, of course. It's very pretty." I was a little confused by the question. Wasn't it obvious that I liked the dress? Could my sparkling brown eyes be any brighter as I twirled around and around, watching the pleats flare out until I became dizzy? Quickly, though, I understood.

"If you really like the dress and will wear it, then we'll get it," Mom said. "It is a little more than I usually spend."

Even as an eight- or nine-year-old, I understood that this was an expensive dress. I reassured her that her purchase would not be wasted on me. I felt so special that she would trust me, at a young age, to keep a promise and wear the dress, and I did not let her down. I loved going places, seeing things, and hanging out with her.

## Spring 2008

My first communication with Judy Savoy at Friendship Village, was by phone in the spring of 2008. She introduced herself and explained that she wanted me to know that she was with my mom in Mom's apartment. Judy said she was trying to help my mom "look for two pair of brown pants" that Mom had reported missing. *How strange*, I thought, but I couldn't help much as I didn't know exactly what was in my mom's wardrobe.

Judy confirmed that there was one pair of brown slacks hanging in her closet but that Mom was adamant that two other pairs were missing. I had bought her a pair of brown pants the previous Christmas, I told Judy. I thought Mom had told me she didn't have any brown ones but that she had been looking for some. I just couldn't be sure. This conversation, however, was not just about mysteriously missing pants. It was a prelude to future issues. I realize now that I never heard Judy's couched warnings that my mom was acting paranoid and insistent to the point of being hostile.

At the end of the phone call, I promised to contact Judy after I had been to Kalamazoo and looked into the matter further. Two weeks later I was rifling through Mom's closet on a search-and-rescue mission for missing brown pants. I felt it was ludicrous to repeat Judy's fruitless efforts, but there I was checking anyway. It's not like they would have evaporated only to mysteriously reappear in two weeks. Of course I did find the one pair, pulled them out, and set them aside. After I checked the tag, I was almost positive that these were the ones I had purchased for my mom.

"I think the cleaning ladies took them," Mom insisted.

*You've got to be kidding, Mom,* I thought. Why would anybody take size-four petite pants? I shook my head repeatedly as I simultaneously visualized either of the very tall or the short, overweight cleaning women swiping brown slacks and inconspicuously stuffing them into their carts. It was hard not to laugh at the visualization.

"Mom, why would anyone take your pants? Hardly anyone can wear petites."

"They take them for their kids." she snarled. "I have nice things, and they want them." Her voice took on a sinister tone, punctuated with a slight hiss. I remember being so stunned by Mom's stern voice that I stepped back a bit.

What a ridiculous accusation, I wanted to say, but I settled on, "I really doubt it, Mom."

We rehashed the issue for a while, but I couldn't convince her of the absurdity that anyone could or would steal pants. It was so futile that I gave up. Logic wasn't working, and I was just getting frustrated at what I perceived was her obstinate attitude. This was not *her* usually but was becoming *her* more frequently. It was time to switch tactics.

"Well, Mom, I don't know what happened to them," I said, "but let's go shopping sometime for new ones."

"Okay, I guess," she agreed, but we never did. I offered on subsequent visits to take her, but she always declined and eventually moved on to other mysteriously missing items.

Judy had witnessed disconcerting behaviors and emotional outbursts in my mom that clued her in on "Betty's fragile memory, likely dementia." She said that Mom repeated herself, was suspicious that people were stealing things, and exhibited flashes of hostility. Logic and reasoning were helpless interventions against her flawed, deteriorating mind. Mom marched down to Judy's office or the front desk repeatedly to make her case about some perceived injustice and demanded that it be resolved.

There were no satisfactory long-term solutions for people suffering with memory deficits. Their minds were warped from disease. Their truth was distorted, and their reality was invisible to everyone else. Mom's dementia would take its course as it saw fit. Everything was right there in front of me, hidden in plain sight. I saw and experienced everything Judy and others did, albeit less often, but I did not allow myself to interpret Mom's behaviors as Alzheimer's disease.

On subsequent visits over a period of a year, there were increasingly more reports of missing things. Mom accused someone of taking her stamps. "Seven dollars' worth of stamps," she said. "I just bought them and now they're stolen." They were "found and returned," she wrote in an e-mail several weeks later. Then Dad's wooden stamp holder was supposedly taken until it reappeared in the back of her desk drawer. "They snuck it in here while I was out" was her warped explanation. "They" were often different people—the cleaning ladies, someone with a key, and so on. "Anybody can get in here," she said.

Then my mom complained that her mother's nail file had been taken. "It's very good," she said. "That was my mother's, and they had no right to take it."

"That's true, Mom," I replied. "No one should take anything that doesn't belong to them." I was doing better about diffusing potential flashes of anger by validating her remarks, when on point. Who would steal a nail file? She had tens of thousands of dollars in diamond, gemstone, and gold jewelry—some of it 18 carat—in her dresser drawer, and "they" stole a nail file or stamps?

It made absolutely no sense. As usual, however, I didn't connect the proverbial dots that her paranoia and accusatory, irrational behaviors were red-flag indicators suggestive of underlying dementia.

I was never the one who found the missing items except when her black pair of Rockports were apparently taken. "I have two pair of black ones, and they stole one," she complained one day. "I asked the other residents, but no one has things stolen except me."

*Maybe that's because you misplace things,* I was thinking, *rather than the work of an invisible lock-picker stealthily roaming your room, stealing nail files and stamps.* I glanced down at Mom's feet; she was wearing black shoes. I casually scanned the room. On the floor right next to her bed were another pair of black Rockports.

"Are these the ones you're looking for?" I asked as I scooped them up and dangled them from my fingertips with a hint of sarcasm. Finally I had caught her in a mistruth, and sadly that's how I felt. I figured maybe I could bring closure to at least one of the reportedly stolen items.

"Oh, yeah. Those are mine," Mom answered nonchalantly.

*Say what?* "Mom, you just told me these were stolen, but they are right here," I said. My voice escalated a little in exasperation.

"Yeah," she replied. "I have two pair of black." And that was it. By the time the shoe fairy incident occurred, it was winter 2010, and not much she did or said could shock me anymore—or so I thought.

# CHAPTER 12
## *Trinkets and Trash*

### 1950s and 1960s

Many people in my mother's age group lived through the Great Depression, which began with the catastrophic stock market crash in October 1929; my mom was five years old at the time. I remember stories about how my grandfather bartered his plumbing skills for food from the local butcher or fixed the doctor's broken sink in order to receive medical care for the family in return.

Mom's experiences growing up in uncertain financial times significantly affected her. She saved and reused everything of value. An old sheet became extra fabric to try out a new dress pattern before cutting into the expensive stuff. Buttons and zippers were confiscated from donated clothing to adorn other garments. She used a hand-crank grinder secured to the kitchen stool, the same one I often sat on to watch her work her hand magic with the pie dough, hoping for my cinnamon one. Using the hand grinder, she would propel her shoulder forward, down, and around like a Ferris wheel to shred meat scraps to be used later for meat loaf or stew.

The funniest recollection I have of her saving things, though, was what I perceived as her obsession with reusing aluminum foil. I vividly remember her gingerly washing, flattening, and refolding the silver beast so as not to tear it. My sister-in-law

Wendie and I teased my mom unmercifully at times—and, I might add, unfairly—about saving aluminum foil.

Wendie once sent me a copy of one Sunday's episode of the newspaper cartoon strip Cathy in which, frame by frame, Cathy attempted to salvage a piece of foil. Cartoon Cathy's impatient approach, however, resulted in failed efforts to save it as the foil tore apart with every stroke. In the end, Cathy wadded the silver fragments into a solid ball and threw it in the garbage. I shared the cartoon strip with my mom one day, but she didn't find it very funny. Mom became a little defensive, in fact, about her saving efforts and snapped a short, "Humph." (Recently, I started reusing aluminum foil and smile as I think of my mom and all of the times she did the same.)

Conservation and recycling efforts were initiated in our house well before they became the popular social endeavors they are today. There were three baskets—actually, a wastepaper basket, a metal bin, and a paper bag—in which items were to be disposed of, sorted into garbage, trash, and waste. Honestly, though, I always had trouble understanding the specific differences. *Webster's Dictionary* defined *garbage* as "wasted or spoiled food," and *waste*, on the other hand, was defined as "material that is not wanted." They both referred to unwanted materials.

I got the distinctions among paper, glass, and recyclable plastic, but my mom's system would have stymied even Webster. Paper didn't actually go into the wastepaper basket; it went in the paper bag. Used Kleenexes, for example, went into the wastepaper basket, but scrap paper didn't. Food scraps such as banana peels and apple cores went into the garbage bin, but since it was outside, they went into a basket inside first. It was confusing, but global warming is not my mom's fault.

## Circa 1962

"Mom!" I called loudly as I stomped out of the half bath to find her and register my complaint.

"What's the matter?" she asked. She looked concerned, probably because of the sound of my screech.

"Jerry didn't flush the toilet again! It has pee in it. That's disgusting!"

She started to respond as she headed toward the bathroom to flush the toilet—something I could have done myself, of course—but then she paused. I noticed her eyes well up with tears.

Now it was my turn. "What's the matter, Mom?" I remember being so surprised by her unexpected reaction that her tears melted my frustration away. When I first heard the Rob Thomas song "Her Diamonds" (2009), I immediately thought of that moment that occurred more than forty-five years ago: "Her tears like diamonds on the floor/And her diamonds bring me down, 'cause I can't help her now." My mom forced a reassuring smile, but I pressed her to answer me.

"*I* didn't flush the toilet, Elaine. It wasn't Jerry's fault. Flushing uses water, and water costs money. I was trying to save a little money by not flushing it. I'm sorry." If she said anything else, I didn't hear it. My dad was changing jobs. He had been home more than usual, but it was years later before I realized that he had taken a severance package and was actually unemployed for a short time.

*Water costs money?* I really didn't know that water cost money. My dad would mumble remarks about not leaving the lights on because electricity cost money. In fact, he threatened to charge us a nickel if we left the lights on in our bedrooms, but no one had ever said anything about water. Rain falls from the sky so—I don't know. I never thought about it. She was still a little teary eyed but was hiding it pretty well. I will never forget wrapping my arms around her, giving her a big hug.

My brother and I learned financial management probably because our parents lived through the very real hardship of the Great Depression. As my mother used to say, "Waste not; want not."

# CHAPTER 13
## *Money Laundering*

### 1960s

I love Fridays. Even as a kid, I quickly learned the special magic of Fridays. It was the end of the school week so I could sleep in on Saturday mornings, and I got my allowance. Sometimes Fridays were extra special when we visited Grandma and Grandpa Ward. I remember playing dominoes endlessly with Grandma Ward. Actually, we made a domino rally, and I was so excited when we were about to tap the first domino to start the assault. We ate popcorn with butter and drank little Coca-Colas in six-ounce glass bottles. I miss Coke from a glass bottle. It tastes better than from a plastic bottle or a metal can.

I was pretty good with money, saving and spending. My mom taught me the basics of money management, the importance of saving, how to decide if something you wanted was worth the cost, and more. I learned gradually, but as a kid it was the simple stuff that I cared about: what kind of bank or jar to keep the money in and how to count it.

I never had a real *piggy* bank, but I did have one shaped like a bunny, a white ceramic rabbit with pink-tinted ears. He stood tall with his front paws tipped downward and one ear bent over. The coin slot was in his back, and underneath it was a cork that kept the coins inside. Sadly, it was a very tight-fitting cork and difficult to get out.

That's how I broke the bunny bank. I was trying to pull the cork out to count my change when the bunny slipped out of my hands and fell to the hardwood floor, smashing into hundreds of pieces. Tears were welling up in my eyes when Mom came into my room, having heard the crash. Her primary concern was that I hadn't gotten cut by the ceramic shards, but once the immediate crisis was handled, she gave me a big hug and promised me another bank.

I remember her long laugh when I said, "But if I use the money *from* my bank to *buy* a bank, then I won't have any money to put *in* the bank." It didn't seem that funny to me, but my mom must have thought it was hilarious. It seemed like she laughed for a long time. Looking back, I think it was both funny and a rather astute observation for a young child.

I started saving a year in advance for our 1965 trip to the World's Fair in New York. I was very excited and worked hard to save up a hundred dollars for the trip. (With inflation, that's about seven hundred dollars in 2011 currency.) Mom had taught me well. My parents were surprised to learn that I had saved so much, although I did get into a little trouble with one of my saving strategies.

We lived about two miles from St. Augustine's School on the western edge of downtown Kalamazoo. My dad dropped me off on his way to work, but I usually took the city bus home. Mom gave me bus money for the upcoming week on Sunday nights, thus I quickly saw an enterprising opportunity to save money: walk home and pocket the dough.

It was a steady, uphill, two-mile trek from the school to our house, but on a nice day, it really was pretty. Big beautiful trees shaded most of the uphill walk. A bunch of us started out together, but gradually the others would trail off en route to their own homes. I didn't walk home every day after school. Sometimes I had too much homework or the weather wasn't very nice. But when I did, I successfully pocketed the bus money that I didn't use and added it to my World's Fair fund—until I got caught.

My mom had gone back to college to get her teaching certificate and had started subbing, so I usually got home before anyone else. One Sunday evening, though, when she gave me the bus money for the upcoming week, she said, "You told me you walked home last Friday, so you should have that money left over." She handed me only four days' worth of bus money.

"Oh," I responded, clearly baffled. I had never thought about the money not really being mine, although I should have.

"You still have the money, don't you?"

I sensed that she was a little annoyed. "Yes. I kept it, but I have it."

"Have you been walking home regularly?" she asked.

"Maybe once a week, I guess."

"What have you been doing with the bus money I gave you?"

"Keeping it for our trip to the World's Fair," I answered honestly.

She acted stern, but I think she was suppressing a little smile. "Well, the money isn't yours to keep. You get an allowance for that. The bus money is supposed to be used for riding the bus." There was a short pause before she added, "I tell you what. If you walk home every day in the same week, you can keep one day's worth of bus money," and she left.

I remember thinking, *How would she know if I walked home since I got home before her?* but I nodded my head in acknowledgment of her instructions. Although I didn't admit to *every* time I walked home, I made my goal of a hundred dollars, and mostly by legitimate means.

### Late Fall 2009

"Look at this, Joe," I said. "What was she thinking?" I was aghast. I had printed out Mom's checking account statement for October. "What a mess. It's almost unbelievable." The statement clearly showed that my mom had written five consecutive checks to her car insurance company.

"She really wrote all those, huh?" Joe said. He just shook his head. "I'm sorry she's going through all of this. Such a great mind slipping away."

---

"I decided to stop driving," Mom announced while Joe and I were at her place.

We had driven over the first Saturday in October to visit and take Mom out to dinner at Great Lakes Shipping, our restaurant of choice. It had been one of my dad's favorites, as well as Joe's, and I liked the endless choices of draft beer.

"I got lost going to the dentist office recently, and I felt a little anxious getting back here. I think it's time I stopped driving."

"Okay, Mom," I replied. "Whatever you want."

"You and Joe can take the car back with you," she said.

Joe shot me a puzzled glance and a subtle head shake. We were almost positive my mom would change her mind, so we were stalling about taking the car to our house only to possibly have to return it in a few weeks.

My mom had been waffling for months about continuing to drive or not but always ended the conversation with, "I like driving to church."

"Well, we won't take the car with us tonight, but we will get back here to get it." I offered.

Mom valued her independence, and I appreciated her spirit. She contradicted herself more than a few times that Saturday about continuing to drive or stop. I had checked her proof of insurance certificate and saw that she was insured through October 30.

"I bet she keeps driving," Joe said to me later with a chuckle in his voice. "What a spunky woman. Gotta love her."

Joe and I laughed about Mom's idiosyncrasies on our ride home and, as predicted, she e-mailed me later to say that she was keeping the car. I reminded her, also via e-mail, that she needed to renew her car insurance by October 30. (My mom was completely deaf without her aides and since phone conversation was difficult for her, we corresponded exclusively by email.) She wrote back that she hadn't received a bill yet but would pay it as soon as it came. I found this puzzling as it was approaching mid-October. My car insurance company sends out renewal notices almost six weeks ahead.

I should have been connecting the dots. It never occurred to me that the statement had indeed come and was tucked away in some bizarre place. In my determined efforts not to demean her by asking probing questions, I was inadvertently contributing to my own naïve misconception of her situation. When she told me that the bill hadn't come, I presumed her information was factual. I didn't appreciate that her short-term memory had deteriorated so significantly that she didn't remember getting it and then misplacing it, a very different scenario from what she reported.

I hadn't planned a return trip to Kalamazoo before her insurance would expire, so I wrote her that she absolutely couldn't drive until I could get over there and get everything straightened out. Then, on Halloween morning, she e-mailed me that she had received the bill and paid the car insurance. *Strange*, I thought, but okay.

By the time I arrived for an early November visit, her apartment literally looked like a windstorm had strewn papers everywhere. My mom's impeccable organizational skills were nearly kaput, one of her favorite adjectives.

"I paid the car insurance," she said proudly as she walked in.

"Yeah, Mom, you wrote me," I said. "That's good."

Armed with a strong cup of coffee, I rummaged through unfolded newspapers and scattered bank statements. In the paper ruble, I uncovered her original car insurance bill from Citizen's, still in the unopened envelope. I assumed she had received a duplicate bill and paid it. The confusion had mounted, however, when Mom wrote a second check in response to the second notice, forgetting she had already written one. She did the same to a third notice. She never mentioned to me until the last day of October that *any* checks had been written, let alone five! And none were recorded in her checkbook ledger.

"Did you get your proof of insurance certificate yet?" I asked.

"I don't think so?"

"Really? It should be here by now."

"I don't know." Now *that* was an understatement.

"I'll call them next week and check on it." I just took the previously unopened bill with me.

I contacted Citizen's Insurance on Monday and learned that she had written several car insurance checks, but the amounts weren't always correct or even the same and none of them had the account number written on them. Sandy, at the local office in Kalamazoo, was very helpful. She knew my mom and dad from their many years with Citizen's.

"Actually, Elaine," she said, "your mom has written nine checks."

"Nine! Nine? Really! She wrote nine checks? Oh, my goodness." I was stunned. Her bank statement had shown only five, but she had literally written nine checks over a two-week period, totaling an overpayment of nearly $2,400. Five of the checks were written on consecutive days.

"A few of them were sent to this office, and I can return or shred them, but the ones she mailed to the New York office have to be processed and then refunded."

I was still baffled about how my mom could have written nine checks to the insurance company. I responded, "If you could, please just give me the check numbers, then you can shred them. What a mess."

"Yes. Your mom is such a nice person," Sandy replied. "I'm sorry she's having some trouble."

*Some trouble? More like an avalanche of trouble,* I thought.

"Thanks, Sandy," I said.

I logged on to the bank's website to confirm that five checks had already cleared. Altogether, nine checks had been written: one was applied to the actual premium, five were to be refunded by the New York office, and Sandy shredded three. What could have possibly possessed her to write nine checks, five with consecutive dates? Was she standing by the mailbox every night? How did she get nine envelopes addressed correctly? *That* was a mystery too. I couldn't fathom what she had been thinking. Instead of recognizing her actions as a clear indication of a mind riddled by memory-cell-devouring Pac-Men, I wallowed selfishly in personal frustration.

To the trained eye, obviously not mine, these were alarming and very telling warning signs that Judy, the resident services director who was keeping close tabs on my mom's tragic missteps, could perceive clearly as indicators of impending decline. It would only be a month before Judy would share some stunning projections as to my mom's situation, and, despite my skepticism, she would be remarkably accurate. How did she know? Why didn't I?

Judy confirmed a few weeks later that Mom had gotten lost going to her dentist's office, which was only one mile west of her apartment. She had wandered perhaps twenty miles in the opposite direction. She wrote nine checks to her car insurance company because she couldn't remember writing even one. These were not just quirky, odd behaviors but bells and whistles signs indicative of my mom's very real, very serious underlying dementia. I was finally starting to really see, hear, and step up to handle the problems.

# CHAPTER 14
## *Wicked Weight and Wigs*

### 1963

My mom's hair was always short, although she might have worn it longer when she was a child. It was light brown and naturally curly. One day, when I was maybe thirteen, she called me into her bedroom when my dad wasn't home and showed me the custom wig she had ordered. Before I could even form an opinion, she said proudly, "I've worn it a few times already, and your dad hasn't even noticed." He wasn't the only one. I hadn't noticed either.

My mom was "tickled," a word she used often, in addition to a multitude of other idioms, that she had pulled off this incredible charade on my dad. She confided in me that she always had to look nice for work, and she did, but that it took too long some mornings to wash and style her hair. She decided to have a wig made so she could just slip it on and go. It seemed ridiculous to me in a way and impressive in another. She was so cute, standing there gloating about her very well-kept little secret.

"Six and a half, a dozen of the other," I quoted her, giggling.

"Do you realize that you say that wrong?" she asked casually.

"Say what wrong?"

"The expression. It's 'Six of one, a half dozen of the other.'"

"Oh." I was genuinely pondering the phrase and realized that when Mom said it, she ran it together so fast that I had heard it wrong. No wonder it had never made any sense. For the first time, I really understood it.

My mom described herself as being four feet, eleven and a half inches tall. I always found that amusing: "eleven and a half." Anyone would grace her the extra half-inch to make it an even five feet. I know I would. Mom was always slender from my perspective, and I was oblivious to any weight gain. I do remember once that she was working on a gorgeous, soft pink, crepe coatdress with satin trim. She was an accomplished seamstress and taught me her craft well, although I never mastered the fine touches she had with delicate, invisible hems. The dress was almost done except for her finishing touches when I saw her ripping the seams apart.

"What are you doing, Mom?"

"I've lost those nasty extra pounds I put on over the winter, so I'm remaking the dress for my trimmer figure," she answered.

"Isn't that a lot of work, taking the dress apart only to resew it?" I asked.

"Oh, yes, definitely. But in order to be a good seamstress, you have to be willing to rip the mistakes apart."

And so she did, and when she wore the finished dress one evening, it looked beautiful and was perfectly fitted to her. I remember smiling proudly when I saw her looking so stunning in it. Pink was an especially flattering color on her. Later on, however, her "pink period" would reveal significant telltale signs of her advancing dementia.

In striking contrast to the attire she selected for an evening gala, she put on worn pants and an old shirt to trim the bushes, paint the window trim on our house, unroll muddy sod in our spacious backyard, paint the laundry room's concrete-block walls, and more. My dad was no slouch either, but I don't recall my friends' moms or the neighbor ladies undertaking such physically demanding tasks with her effervescence. She cooked, baked, cleaned, sewed my Halloween costumes and some of my clothes, as well as hers, went back to college to get her master's in education, and taught high school math at Kalamazoo Central.

She was our chauffeur to ball games, golf lessons, dance classes, parties, friend visits, overnights, and school concerts. She did it all patiently, selflessly, and always graciously. I don't ever remember her complaining about or being unwilling or unable to carry out all of her maternal jobs. She was a great mom, and I was blessed to have had her as mine.

---

We wore ugly uniforms to school. They were hideous and I hated them. In elementary and junior high, they were blue-and-green plaid skirts, a white blouse and an optional navy sweater. In high school, the skirt was brown-and-green plaid, and a funky, Peter Pan collared, white blouse. We needed an *Extreme Makeover: Uniform Edition* intervention. Although Mom enforced the uniform policy, I knew she privately thought it was stupid.

When I was in the seventh grade, I was still two inches shorter than my mom but ten pounds heavier. She made occasional remarks about what I ate, trying to nudge me into making better food choices, eating less goodies, and so on, but she was never demeaning. One day, after I walked home from school in my ugly blue-and-green-plaid uniform, I complained to my mom that my inner thighs hurt. They rubbed together, leaving circular, red abrasions on the skin.

She suggested, very carefully I'm sure, that I might be a little heavier than I should be. We dragged out the scales. They would soon become both my fiercest enemy and my best friend, forever. She got on and recorded her weight, and then I did the same. Hmm. I certainly could tell that she was still taller than I was, but, despite her warnings about eating fewer snacks, I had apparently eaten my way to being chubby.

"Do my legs rub together because I'm too fat?" I asked. "Do I have thunder thighs?" I wasn't *exactly* sure what thunder thighs were, but they sounded awful.

"Elaine, you're not fat," she answered, "but you are a little heavier than you should be. If you want to trim down, I can help you with that."

I knew absolutely nothing about calories, fat grams, or sugars. I just knew my legs hurt. "Okay," I agreed.

Mom was a great role model for weight management, teaching me what I needed to know, how to make substitutions, and how to avoid dangerous starvation habits that could lead to bulimia or anorexia. I don't recall how long it took, maybe several months, but I was a very motivated and quick learner, and I started to "see" myself differently. As I lost the weight, my legs quit rubbing together under those ridiculously ugly uniform skirts, and in the years ahead I surpassed my mom's height, which wasn't that hard, of course. I never made it past five feet, one inch, but even that was an improvement over my mom's.

## March 2011

Kim, the medical technician, called me from Hunter Place and said, "Some of your mom's pajamas are a little tight, especially the ones from LL Bean, the ones marked 'petite extra small.'" I had to contain my snickering on the other end of the phone, but I thanked Kim for the heads up. I had scoured online shopping sites for petite pajamas for my mom before Christmas, and now they were too small? Strange, and yet I wasn't that surprised. I had noticed that she didn't have her regular slacks buttoned sometimes and she was wobbly when she stood to zip them.

She had walked miles every day at Friendship Village but now was sleeping more and doing less. I had an alteration seamstress let out every pair of pants she could. Mom no longer had the endurance or mental capacity to go shopping, plus she had a considerable wardrobe of beautifully tailored clothes. I bought her new pajamas and a few pair of pants with elastic waistbands, without zippers and fasteners, for her to try. She loved them. My mom, who had been so meticulous for so long about her weight—eating right, shopping appropriately for her age and trim figure—did none of this anymore. She had aged so much in such a short time and cared so little about anything.

I remembered her saying many times in the past, "I wouldn't be caught dead in elastic-waist pants," and "When there's nothing I want, it's time for me to go." I was struck by the reality that my mom had deteriorated so much that the casual but prophetic remarks she made years ago had come true. I gently shook my head. Maybe Mom didn't want anything, but I needed more Kleenex, a dozen chewy, Toll House cookies and a tall glass of chilled milk.

# CHAPTER 15
## *Teacher's Pet*

Circa 1965

I was playing at my cousin Jan's during Christmas vacation. She was two years older than me, but her sister, my other cousin Margaret—nicknamed Maggie—was six years younger than Jan. With the age difference, Jan was not prone to include her little sister in our grown-up adventures. Since Jan had more privileges anyway, she was the cool one to be with back then. Their mom, my aunt Dee, called for me from the kitchen.

"Your mom is on the phone for you, sweetie." She always called me sweetie. She still does.

*How strange,* I thought, but I wasn't worried because Aunt Dee didn't look worried.

"Hi, Mom."

"Are you having fun?" she asked. She sounded fine to me.

"Yeah. We're just hangin' out."

"I got a call from the principal at the school I have been subbing at," she began.

Okay. *Boring. So what?* I was thinking, but fortunately I kept my often-in-trouble mouth shut.

"The teacher I have been covering for has decided not to return to work after the Christmas vacation. They want to know if I would like to take his position until the end of the school year.

We had not planned on me working full time for so long, so I just called to find out if you were okay with it. I won't take it if you don't want me to."

"Sure. That's fine," I replied casually. It really was fine with me, and so she finished out the year as a permanent sub at the junior high "across town," as she referred to the location of her school.

I never really thought about her having asked me for permission to stay on longer. Her sub position was supposed to have expired at the semester break in January. I would be a big high school student the next fall anyway, so it didn't really matter to me if she was working full time and wasn't there when I got home after school.

Despite my cavalier attitude, however, I was always touched by the respect she had shown me. She considered my feelings and my opinion significant. I had forgotten that phone call until many years later. I don't know what triggered me to remember that day, but I reflected on it and realized that it was very cool of her to consult with me. It made me feel important in a special way that I had not felt before. It would take years and some major, life-altering drama to make me really understand the validation and consideration she had shown me via a simple phone call.

After her subbing stint, she landed a permanent job at Kalamazoo Central High School. When she first started there, it was an old, gray, two-story building in a poorer section of downtown Kalamazoo. Eventually the district built a new high school, where she taught until she retired.

When I was older, I had the opportunity to meet some of her students and got a sense from them that she really was a great teacher. She certainly was a great teacher for me, when I was listening. I could envision Grandpa Oberle, Mom's dad, smiling down from heaven as he watched his spunky daughter raise her even spunkier daughter. He would have been as proud of her as she was of herself for acquiring her degrees.

# CHAPTER 16

## *The Ménière's Monster*

### Summer 1977

The house my first husband and I bought in Garden City was a cute bungalow with a huge country kitchen that I loved. We lived on a corner lot with big, full silver maples in the front yard, vibrant red maples in the side yard, and a cove of dense pine trees at the corner. It was under the red maple that I finally had the opportunity to tell my mom I was pregnant.

It was a great house for raising a family. The girls were born on January 14, 1978. The following summer, when they were toddlers, we girls had picnics on the front lawn and enjoyed the shaded canopy created by the beautiful silver maples. When Christie and Angie were four or five years old, the pine tree cove became a great hiding place or a young child's creative expedition site for hunting.

I had graduated from Wayne State University with a bachelor's in occupational therapy in 1974 and was working in special education in a local district. My mom had retired from teaching around that time, in part due to her deteriorating hearing from Ménière's disease. Initially I had been an idiot about really understanding and validating my mom's comprehensive difficulties from Ménière's, but after earning my OT degree, I really started to put the medical pieces together.

Ménière's is a condition of the inner ear in which excess fluid builds up, affecting hearing and balance. It is characterized by episodes of vertigo, ringing in the ears referred to as tinnitus, and progressive hearing loss. No specific causes are known, but it is widely held that the excess fluid might occur secondarily to head trauma, among other possibilities, and be exacerbated by stress. Also, women experience it more than men. Bingo! My mother had the Ménière's disease trifecta: first, the 1951 car accident with probable head trauma; second, years of postaccident stress, not the least of which was brought on by David's death and the threat of financial ruin, and third, being female. Too bad she didn't bet on horse races.

I had only witnessed her vertigo once in the summer of 1977, although I know it happened in frequent clusters and was insidious and brutal. I had just found out I was pregnant and drove over to tell my mom in person as well as spend the day shopping with her. My dad was home that morning when Mom's vertigo started. He had tried to call me to cancel our social plans, but I was already on the road. (Cell phones have been one of the very best technological achievements of all time, right after color television and dishwashers.)

I walked in through the back door and called to her. She didn't answer, and I had a disgusted, so-what-else-is-new attitude. It was becoming more obvious that her hearing had declined, but no matter how many times she explained it to me, I couldn't understand why she just didn't get hearing aids. I was crazy excited to tell her I was pregnant.

I made a quick circuit of the house that landed me in her bedroom. The instant I saw her, I knew something was terribly wrong. The body in her bed barely looked alive and certainly didn't look like her. Mom was semiupright, leaning over to one side with her hand perched haphazardly on The Bucket. It was the designated barf bucket. I knew it well; that was the *only* thing it was used for, regardless of how often and how well it had been thoroughly disinfected with bleach.

Mom looked like death, and as horrible as she felt, she might have welcomed a quick end to her misery. Her face was completely devoid of color, and her eyes were barely open. I rushed over to her. She recognized me and tried to muster a smile. I started to sit down on the bed, but she grimaced. With a weak wave of her hand, she warned me to stop, and I did.

For several seconds she looked paralyzed, as if afraid to move. In fact, as I learned later, that was exactly what was going on. Even miniscule movement nauseated her more, causing indescribable and uncontrollable waves of vertigo. It was a while before she turned her head ever so slowly in my direction. Watching her was sheer agony. I felt impossibly helpless to do anything, and in fact I was. There was literally nothing I could do to stop, alleviate, or improve the whirlwind in her head.

"I'm okay," she managed to say.

*No, you're not,* I thought. "Can I do anything, Mom?"

"No. It's the vertigo. It's dry heaves now, but when I try to throw up, I can't tell which way is up. I don't know where the floor is." Those were her *exact* words. They are branded in my mind. "You can go—"

I interrupted her immediately. "I'm not going anywhere until Dad gets home from work. I'll be in the den or the kitchen and will check in on you regularly. Sleep if you can."

I called my dad and let him know that I was there and would stay until he got home. He thanked me. *No need to thank me, Dad,* I thought. *I should have been more aware and less cavalier.*

Mom did not move for some time. I poked my head in every few minutes initially until, at least an hour later, I found her lying back on several propped-up pillows with her eyes closed, but she was breathing. The bucket was still on the bed but had fallen over on its side; it was empty. She looked completely drained: her face was still ghost white, her wrists were flexed downward, and her fingers were bent in a creepy pose. I shuddered. It was a horrific scene, and it had happened many times before.

My dad left work a little early and came home in the late

afternoon. I had a gazillion questions, things I should have already known and had probably been told before. He explained about the inefficiency of hearing aids for Ménière's patients. Basically the "hardware" inside her ear—specifically, the sensory hair cells and the nerve from the ear to the brain (the vestibulocochlear nerve)— were shot. Amplifying sound, as hearing aids were designed to do, would not help her because she didn't have a functioning nerve to carry the sound to the brain, where it is converted into meaningful words or environmental noises like the phone ringing.

However, it was the vertigo more than the hearing loss that defined the Ménière's for my mom. By textbook definition, she had one of the worse cases of debilitating vertigo possible (the sensation of spinning when no movement is occurring). Where had I been that I didn't know that? She retired not only because of her hearing loss but also because of the unpredictable and horrific vertigo.

"I'm sorry, Dad," I said. "I really feel stupid that all this was playing out and I missed it."

"To be honest with you, Elaine, she masks it very well. She doesn't really want you to know how bad it is."

I could understand that, actually—a mother wanting to protect her child. Mom's disease was choking her functional abilities and progressively getting worse. She had no treatment options, and no hearing device would help. It would take several years, but a fortuitous opportunity came up at a professional conference that I attended, and it would change her life. Although *she* did all of the work, I was forever grateful to have been the catalyst in Mom's return to the hearing world. In the many years since that vertigo attack, Mom's hearing continued to slowly spiral downward and her tinnitus escalated upward, but the vertigo decreased from occasional to sporadic.

## Circa 1990

"Please welcome our next speaker, Dr. John L. Kemink, Director of Neurotology at the University of Michigan, Ann Arbor. He's on the cutting edge of cochlear implants for deaf children."

The conference was an eclectic symposium on intervention strategies for special needs children of varying disabilities. I was working as an occupational therapist for Taylor Schools. The area of hearing impairments was not my specialty, but it was applicable to my good friend and speech therapist coworker, Pat, who was sitting next to me.

It wasn't long before Dr. Kemink's concisely presented overview of conductive hearing loss had me captivated. He had me at "sensorineural loss," the buzzwords that applied to my mom's situation. I listened intently, took notes, and then nudged my way through the crowd to meet him face-to-face after his presentation.

"Excuse me, Dr. Kemink," I said as I approached him, "but my mother is nearly completely deaf now from Ménière's disease, as well as severe accompanying vertigo and tinnitus. Could she be a candidate for a cochlear implant?" I didn't even take a breath as I spoke. Suddenly there were a lot of eggs in that basket, and he just had to say yes. He just had to.

"Yes, she might be," he answered. I could feel a hopeful smile come over me. "Have her call the office and set up an appointment. I look forward to meeting her." He gave me his card.

I finally took a breath. I called my dad that night with the information. He and Mom made the appointment, and on April 22, 1991, Mom had the cochlear implant surgery. Someone told me she was the first Ménière's patient in the United States to have an implant.

Mom was religious about practicing sound retraining. I remember her telling the story about trying to figure out a noise she described as "click, click," a tinny, unfamiliar sound, which she finally was able to identify as the doorbell. Mechanical noises sounded particularly different to her than they did to others, but the human voice was more predictable.

Her original cochlear device had a cord connected to a cassette-size processor, which she kept in her pocket, but advancements in micro technology led to the development of an enclosed receiver/processor housing that hooked behind her ear. The device was a battery hog, but other than that, it was perfect because she had sound. In a small-group setting without extraneous background noise, for the first time in literally decades, my mom could hear flawlessly. The vertigo gradually diminished as she approached the end of the disease cycle, a "burned out Ménière's," as she called it.

## Circa 2005

"Would you have to relearn new maps if you need a new processor?" I asked Mom. I was reading the letter she had received from the Ann Arbor Audiology Department.

"Dear Elizabeth Ward," it began, and it went on to inform her that her current processor, the Esprit, was being discontinued. She would be eligible for a new processor, covered by insurance, if or when her current device malfunctioned or needed a part.

"No, not specifically," she replied. "The processor would be sent to me after it had the maps loaded onto it already."

Mapping was the process by which her original cochlear device was programmed to her specific hearing needs. My dad and she had driven over to Ann Arbor in the early 1990s many times after her surgery to have it programmed and to get the next series of homework assignments. She was a stellar student and practiced regularly. Fifteen years later, I dreaded the idea of driving her back to Ann Arbor for appointments, but gratefully I didn't have to.

Suddenly I remembered another aspect of her Ménière's. "Mom, do you still have the tinnitus?" I asked.

"The ringing? Yes, but I've had it for so many decades now that I'm not really aware of it. Ménière's is a terrible disease. It robs you of your hearing and balance and leaves vertigo in its wake."

"And it robbed Dr. Kemink of his life," I added, reflecting on Dr. Kemink's murder in his own office. The pioneer of cochlear implants was shot and killed on June 25, 1992, by a disgruntled patient, who, I had heard, was reportedly suffering from untreatable and disabling tinnitus.

"That's right," Mom said. "I remember reading about his tragic death. That was terrible, but I can identify with the debilitating, never-ending ringing."

I suddenly recalled the time when my mom had checked out a record from the Kalamazoo Public Library years before, probably in the mid-1980s. The record played loud, whooshing, underwater sounds, like your head was in a fish bowl. It was designed to duplicate the tinnitus that Ménière's patients endured twenty-four seven, bombarding and drowning out their already legitimately reduced hearing capabilities. Mom had taken it out to help my dad and others understand what the ringing sounded like to her.

Judy's first meeting with my mom in 2005 was no doubt memorable. As Judy recalled in an e-mail to me, "I noticed Betty had on a cochlear implant. It was tucked in neatly under her white, short, cropped hair. It became clear that this had been a lifelong struggle for Betty, advocating for those with hearing impairments." I would find out later from Judy, however, that over time, my mom took her singular mission to correct all the sloppy talkers of the world to new and ridiculous heights as Mom's strategies conflicted with reasonableness.

# Chapter 17

## *Hidden in Plain Sight*

Wednesday, May 12, 2010

My cell phone rang at 8:30 a.m. I recognized the Kalamazoo area code, 269. *This can't be good*, I thought. It never was.

"Hi, Elaine. This is Marilyn, one of the nurses at Friendship Village. Your mom can't find her processor. She can't remember when or where she might have lost it, but we think she had it at least two days ago. We've thoroughly searched her apartment and let the staff and other residents know to watch for it, but so far it has not turned up."

"Oh, my God!" I answered. "Why am I not surprised? I'll see about ordering a replacement. Thanks for your call." Joe had driven my mom back on Monday, May 10, after she had been with us for Mother's Day, so we knew she had it then.

Mom had lost parts of it before, but in the past, she knew immediately when her hearing was gone and was instantly alerted to a problem. In the past year, however, her awareness of audio cause and effect had declined. Cochlear of Americas in Colorado had replaced essential parts of the device before at a moderate cost, but an entire processor? Although partially covered by insurance, her original cochlear device was nearly eight thousand dollars. I cringed.

I called Cochlear and was informed that they had a one-time,

85

full-replacement policy for loss. I was stunned but very relieved. I juggled phone calls to Cochlear and the audiology department in Ann Arbor, sent and received faxes, drove to the bank to have documents notarized, made copies, and took copious notes as usual, and by the end of the day everything was in place. Her literally precious processor would be picked up Friday morning in Colorado by FedEx and then sent overnight for a Saturday morning delivery to Mom, or so I thought.

On Saturday morning, May 15, I waited until noon before calling Friendship Village to see if FedEx had delivered it, but the receptionist Irene told me that FedEx had not been there. I was getting worried. On a whim, I called Cochlear at 12:50 p.m., assuming they would be closed on a Saturday, but gratefully they were open. Maureen confirmed that the processor had been picked up by FedEx and then she gave me the horrendously long tracking number. I was just about to hang up after thanking her when I heard, "Oh, no!"

"What?" I asked.

"The box requesting FedEx overnight delivery is *not* checked as it was supposed to be," Maureen answered. "They picked it up Friday but probably won't deliver it until Monday. It might not even get to Michigan today. I'm so sorry. I see you paid extra for the special delivery. We'll refund the charges."

I didn't care about the charges. I just wanted my mom to have sound. I kept it together enough to ask her for FedEx's phone number. I felt overwhelming frustration, but I had to persevere.

At 1:10 p.m. I called FedEx, punched in the tracking number, and then waited for the prompt that eventually connected me to a real live person. He was able to confirm that the package (an eight-thousand-dollar processor is *not* just a package) was in Portage, fifteen miles from Kalamazoo. The bad news was that no FedEx driver, not for any amount of money—and believe me, I offered—could deliver it to her on Saturday. It was so close and yet so far away. I absolutely refused to give up, but the hoops to jump through were not insignificant, and timing was everything.

First, it was 1:40 and the Portage office was open only until 3:00. Second, the "package" required my mom's signature. I called Irene back to see if she could arrange for a cab. That was my husband's suggestion; at least he was thinking clearly. Irene said she would try to make cab arrangements and call me back.

At 2:00 p.m. I called FedEx, desperately lobbying for any compassionate option. The face on the wall clock started to take on a demonic look. Maybe I was having a psychotic episode. I certainly felt possessed. Finally a different FedEx representative came on the line. My voice definitely started to crack as I succinctly explained a complex situation and practically begged for help. She put me on hold briefly and, when she returned, told me the Portage employee could stay until 3:30 if that would help. It *would* help and I thanked her, sniveling.

It was 2:20. I made another call to Friendship Village and was told a cab was en route and at 2:30 p.m. Irene called me back. "Betty just got picked up." Irene said. I recontacted FedEx and confirmed that my mom was on her way via cab and that the Portage office would *definitely* remain open for her. I waited impatiently until after 3:00 p.m. I kept watching the second hand on the wall clock—tick, tick, tick. I stared at my cell and my watch. No matter which one I looked at, the time kept advancing and I waited. Then 3:25 went by. I was going crazy or was already crazed and then 3:40, 3:55, and 4:10 all came and went.

Finally at 4:25, I couldn't stand it any longer and called Friendship Village *again*. The receptionist's office had closed at 3:00 p.m. on Saturdays, so my call was routed to the nurse's desk. "Yes," they said, my mom was back, and yes, she had her processor. An employee had helped Mom make out the check to the cab company and loaded the batteries into the compartment for her. Mom had sound again, and the drama was finally over.

Then I literally collapsed on the floor, a hysterical, emotional blob. My husband cradled me in his arms, rocking me gently as he tried to stop my body from shaking. We sat on the floor for several minutes before I looked at the clock again. It was 4:45, only fifteen minutes until pub time.

My formerly unstoppable mom was no longer capable of problem solving on her own behalf. That job fell to me. I have no doubt that she was just as strong and proactive for me when I was little as I was then for her. Because one person had failed to check a stupid box, I had spent hours moving a mountain that shouldn't have been in my way in the first place. But as I regained composure, an unexpected feeling of tranquility surfaced. The experience, albeit exhausting, had been a genuine honor for me. I had been able to give back to my mom after she had given so much to me. And there would be ample additional opportunities in the near future to give back some more. By the time I processed all of these thoughts it really was five o'clock!

### Early June 2010

The rain was coming down hard as I scurried into the building. I was back in Kalamazoo for the day. Mom was resting on her bed when I opened her door. Her naps were brief but becoming more frequent. In the past, she rarely took a nap and couldn't understand why anyone would since, when she did, she woke up feeling foggy, not rested.

Her place was a train wreck of paper, as usual, and I started my new ritual of sorting into recycle, pitch, and shred piles when I heard her stir. She greeted me with a big smile and said, "Oh, Elaine, it's so good to see you."

Her memory and e-mail correspondence were erratic, so I didn't expect her to remember that I was coming, but her smile was validating enough. We were standing in the small area just outside her bedroom chatting. She had mirrored bifold doors on her two closets. One set was open, and something caught my eye on the carpet. It was her processor. *Oh, my God, Mom! How careless can you be?* I thought. *Insurance won't replace this again!*

I leaned over and swiped it up off the floor, shaking my head in frustration.

"Mom, what is your processor—" I stopped midsentence as I turned toward her and realized she was wearing her device. We were talking, and she was hearing me. I was holding the missing one.

"Mom, what is this doing on the floor?" I started again. "This is your original processor. It couldn't have been here all this time." I was looking right at her, palming this innocuous looking, beige, C-curved, incredibly valuable and literally irreplaceable piece of equipment. I knew she couldn't absorb all of the information and questions I was spewing at her, but I was replaying in my head the phenomenal emotional drama that I and others had gone through just getting a replacement device to her.

"Oh, yeah. That's my processor," she said. *Okay, Mom, this much I know already.*

I broke the questions down one by one. "This is your original processor. Do you remember a cab coming to pick you up last month so you could go get the replacement?" She shook her head, clearly baffled. "Do you remember being without sound for a week after your processor was lost?"

She still had that bewildered look on her face. She really couldn't fill in any of the blanks for me.

"I think so," she finally said. *Yeah, you're bluffing,* I thought.

She was just savvy enough sometimes to dodge probing questions with vague responses. I wasn't going to be able to gather any more factual information. Where had this little thing been for a month because surely it had not just been lying there on the floor. If only it could tell me. Mom had a small floor safe in her bedroom closet, and I decided that this puppy was going to be crated in there, except I didn't know the combination. It was in my mom's notebook, which I had left in my car because it was raining so hard.

"Mom, let's put this extra processor in your safe. By any chance, do you know the combination?"

"Sure." She beamed proudly. *Yeah, right,* I thought, *another bluff.* "Don't you?"

The proverbial shoe was on the other foot. Now I was the one staring at her with a somewhat blank look. "I have it written down, but I don't have it memorized," I replied truthfully. Could she retrieve it? I so wanted her to be able to recall the combination but was extremely suspicious of that possibility.

"It's your birthdate: 2-2-52," she replied with a triumphant smile.

I went into her bedroom, got down on the floor inside her closet, pushed aside the low-hanging clothes to access the safe, and pressed 2252 on the keypad. *Voilà,* as Mom would say. It opened. I tucked the processor inside, shut the door, and made sure the safe was relocked. I breathed a deep sigh of relief knowing that we had a backup processor for her after all this drama. And we would need it.

# CHAPTER 18

## Car Crazies and Other Crap

### 1969

*Crap! What just happened!* I didn't actually say anything out loud, but all the expletives I knew were flying around in my head. I had just pummeled the neighbor's car, which was parked in front of their house but across from our driveway. The sound of crunching metal on metal was unmistakable, and our neighbors came out the front door of their place. We had a very long driveway, plus our street was very wide. I had taken advantage of every foot to floor the car in reverse in order to get out of the house as quickly as possible. Now I would have to go crawling back inside with my tail between my legs.

I shifted out of reverse and inched back up our driveway. My dad was already halfway down, walking briskly to the crash site. Mom was right behind him. I averted my gaze, slumping down a little in the front seat and staring at the steering wheel. I couldn't even bear to look back and see who else might have run outside to investigate the disaster. The dinner table chatter and phone gossip would resonate throughout the neighborhood for some time to come.

I stopped the car on the cement apron before the garage. By then my dad had wandered down our hundred-foot-plus driveway and crossed the street to assess the obvious damage to

Mr. Gridley's daughter's car. I shot a cautious glance down what then seemed like a dark, foreboding driveway tunnel of despair to see my dad shake hands with Mr. Gridley.

I slithered into the house, went straight to my bedroom, and shut the door to sulk. From there I could watch the scene unfold because my bedroom faced the street where the carnage had just occurred. I stared out my front window, carefully standing far enough back so as not to be spotted. I didn't want them looking at me looking at them. I could make out hand gestures in the direction of the driver's side rear door, or what was left of it. My mom was trying to see into the car. She cupped her hands around her eyes and leaned forward toward the side window to peer in. "What is she looking for?" I muttered to myself.

"It's not my fault that you're so mean!" The underlying reason for my emotional wrath was starting to push through to the surface of my mind. "You're so unfair!" I was replaying the bitter exchange of verbal ping-pong between my mom and me just before I ran out of the house. "Everybody else can stay until midnight. Why can't I? Why do I have to be home by eleven?"

"We are leaving very early tomorrow morning for Chicago, and eleven is late enough." My mom was calm but firm in her position on curfew.

"Well, I'm not going!" And for added effect, I stomped my foot.

"You always like our trips to Chicago."

She was right. I did like going to Chicago, and since I was seventeen, there would be so many cool places to go and things to do with my older cousin Jan and her friends. Chicago was an awesome city, I thought, and Kalamazoo was so dull.

"No, I don't." Lie!

"Eleven is late enough, and besides, you don't know that everyone has permission to be out until twelve."

"Yes, they do," I replied, like I had polled everyone for his curfew. "It's stupid that I have to be home so early."

"Eleven is late enough," she said again.

I was getting nowhere, and Mom was not budging. Usually I could negotiate a little fissure and then bulldoze my way through it to get what I wanted, but this time she was standing firm—calm but firm.

"More coffee, Wayne?" she asked my dad.

Now I felt ignored. I was not winning this battle with her, and the loss of power was frustrating. I upped my game. Big mistake.

"You're not listening to me!" My voice started to escalate a notch or two. "And Dad can get his own coffee. Why are you so mean? Why can't I stay out later? It's summer." I rattled off my new, heightened negotiation strategy in one long, verbal assault. By spewing out all of the ploys together, I hoped I could disarm her resolve.

If I had just glanced in my dad's direction, I would have caught his own parental resolve starting to build. Dad rarely entered into the mother/daughter battle of wills, so I felt I had my own verbal license for maternal disrespect. Unbeknownst to me, however, he was rapidly reeling in that long, fatherly rope he usually allowed me to have. In just a few more sentences, I would be hanging from it. But even if I had recognized the changes in his posture and telltale facial grimaces, I was already out of control and way too far past the point of no return.

Mom made one more attempt to calm me down, but it was hopeless. "Would you like anything, Elaine? Coffee? I know strawberry rhubarb pie isn't your favorite, but we also have sherbet."

Coffee? Pie? Sherbet? Heck, no! I just wanted to win.

"No! I don't want any stupid pie," I replied. "I just want a mom that's not so mean! You're so unfair!"

"That's enough, young lady," my dad finally said. I was headed into serious trouble and had no way out. "Your curfew is eleven, and if you continue, you're grounded. Now apologize to your mother."

My dad had all the rope, with the noose around my neck, and

it was getting tight fast. He rarely played the "young lady" card so I knew I was in deep trouble, but I didn't feel apologetic and couldn't get the words out.

I stood there in silence. I couldn't speak. I couldn't say anything, let alone mutter an apology to my mom that I didn't mean. Impasse! Now what do I do? I was rapidly forming an exit strategy. I had already been given permission to use the car earlier in the evening when I was calm and polite. Since my dad had not revoked his decision—yet—my plan took form. I picked up my purse, palmed the keys to the car, and stormed out of the kitchen through the back screen door, which slammed behind me, possibly with a little help just for effect. I got into our big, tan Oldsmobile and floored it in reverse, gaining speed down the long driveway and slamming just seconds later into our neighbor's car door.

I was a mess. The neighbor's car was a mess. I hadn't even looked at the rear end of our car to see how much damage I had done to it. Great! I was still staring out my front bedroom window when the crowd around the car started to break up. Dad shook Mr. Gridley's hand for a second time, and my parents headed back up our driveway. Mr. Gridley and his daughter, who was older than me, maybe twenty-five, returned to their house.

I took a deep breath, and then the tears came flooding down my cheeks. I slumped to the floor, buried my head in my hands with my arms resting on my knees, and cried. It wouldn't be long before I would have to face up to the disastrous consequences of my undisciplined mouth and poor judgment. Soon either my mom or my dad, or, God forbid, both, would come in to talk to me. I don't know how long I huddled on the floor. It seemed like forever before I heard a couple of gentle taps on my door and my mom's soft footsteps on the wood floor of my room.

"Elaine?" I didn't answer or look up. "Kathy called to make sure you were still coming to pick her up. I told her you were running a little late but would be on your way in a few minutes." There was a pause after she finished, but I knew she was still near my bed. I waited for the inevitable lecture or punishment or eviction notice, but all she said next was, "So you need to get going," and she walked out of my room.

I had completely forgotten I was supposed to pick up my friend Kathy. That's where I was headed first when I stormed out of the house, to pick her up before the party. She had a ten thirty curfew and a crazy dad, so lobbying for a later curfew for myself made no sense anymore. What a fiasco. I stood up, cleaned up, and walked into the kitchen, still wobbly inside from the emotional train wreck I'd been through.

My dad handed me the keys, which I had left in the ignition, and said, "If you're okay to drive, here are the keys. Have a good time." That was it? No punishment? No lecture? I doubted it would be that simple. I knew that while I was gone, they would be plotting my demise.

It was not the first time, nor would it be the last, that my mouth had created problems. I didn't dare inspect the car until I got to Kathy's house, just a few blocks away. There was barely even a scratch on it compared to Mr. Gridley's daughter's accordion-pleated door panel. I showed Kathy the scrape when she came out of her house and told her the whole story.

"You're lucky," she replied. "My dad would have killed me and certainly wouldn't have still given me the car after all that."

She was right, and somewhere deep down inside I knew it. I *was* lucky, and her dad might have literally killed her. I don't remember the party, but I know I was home before eleven.

A few weeks later, when the owner/daughter drove up in front of her parents' home, I noticed that her car door was fixed. I overheard bits and pieces of conversation between my parents about insurance claims and deductibles. We never did talk about that disastrous night. I wasn't grounded. I wasn't made to pay the deductibles. Strangely, no punishment seemed worse than actually getting one. I always felt the weight of my transgression held over me like a blackmail card. If I screwed up again, I figured, then they would lower the boom on me.

I had a few other driving debacles. There must have been something about cars and speed. I loved the feel of the wheel and the power of the engine under my command. I got my driver's permit the year I turned fifteen.

Kalamazoo and the surrounding areas were often hit hard with long, snowy, icy winters due to the meteorological effects of Lake Michigan. I vividly recall the "Great Midwest Blizzard," when twenty-eight inches of snow fell over two days at the end of January 1967, closing schools for a week over my fifteenth birthday. My dad, like many others, was stranded at work overnight. There was snow up and over the window ledges outside, a sight I had never seen. My friends and I had a ball romping in the white stuff, but it was a very deadly storm that knocked out power lines, caused treacherously icy driving conditions, and stranded motorists for days. The colloquialism was, If you learned to drive in Kalamazoo's wintry conditions, you could drive anywhere.

The large, beige Oldsmobile that I would later use to crush the neighbor's car was the same vehicle I was driving in late March. We were returning from church one Sunday morning. I was driving, and my dad was riding mandatory shotgun in the front seat. The roads were slick in spots, covered with a light dusting of new, white, fluffy snow. I was nervous, especially negotiating West Michigan Avenue, the uphill and winding but beautifully treed street I traversed when I walked home.

I had been doing okay, but I was anxious and just wanted to get home when I turned from Olney Street onto our driveway. The entire length of our long, black-topped approach was bordered with arborvitae shrubs. As I turned the wheel of the monstrous vehicle, it started to spin out of control. Although not going very fast, I got scared and overcorrected, careering the car into the shrubs, taking out one and crushing another. I was shaking and refused to back the car up to correct my mistake. The driver's side door wouldn't open as it was engulfed in shrub fronds, so I put the car in park, crawled over the front seat and into the back, and exited out the passenger door. Then I ran into the house crying.

I could vaguely make out my dad calling to me from the front seat of the car, trying to be reassuring and telling me it was okay, that "these things happen all of the time."

It was at least a half hour before my mom came in. I was still trembling from fear and embarrassment. She sat down next to me, put her arm around my waist, and pulled me toward her. When I finally stopped sniveling, I could hear that she was part of the way through telling me the story of her first driving disaster, something about avoiding a scampering squirrel only to hit a tree. I started laughing aloud at the visual image of her debacle.

Then there was the time my cousin Jan and I, ages six and four, respectively, were playing in my dad's green Oldsmobile, definitely something we shouldn't have been doing, while it was parked in the driveway of our old house. Somehow we put the car in neutral, and it started to slide down toward the end of the drive, picking up speed as it advanced into the street. Genuine blood-curdling screams of two terrified little girls filled the air instantly.

Either my uncle Ken or probably my dad somehow managed to get inside the car, shift it into park, and stop it. Then I ran out of the car toward the house, still screaming, shaking, and hysterical. Inside the house, my mom had heard the commotion and was moving briskly toward the front door as I plowed inside, crashing into her. I remember her enveloping me with her arms and cradling me securely for a very long time. She tried to ask me what had happened, but I couldn't talk. Even at four and a half, I knew I shouldn't have been inside the car at all, but despite my definitely mischievous misbehavior, I felt mom's compassionate forgiveness and comforting caress. She was my rock. Someday I would be hers.

### 1965–1970

Of course, the car disaster wasn't the only teenage-rebellion debacle, just the best. During my teenage years, I also tried to guilt my mom into putting my clean clothes away instead of just leaving them on my bed. She gave me a choice: (1) stop complaining, or (2) do my own laundry. I chose door number one.

I whined constantly about doing the dishes. Several of my friends had dishwashers, and I wanted one too. When we finally did get a dishwasher, then I started whining about unloading it. My dad threatened to return it, and I stopped complaining.

But the coup de grâce of my teenage years was a terrible exchange between my mom and me. I vividly remember her standing at the bottom of the basement steps, looking right at me as the tears streamed down her cheeks. "We used to be so close," she spewed. "Now you won't even talk to me."

I rolled my eyes and pushed past her to get up the stairs and away from the hysterical woman. *What a bitch*, only it wasn't her. But I knew deep down inside, on a level I wasn't mature enough to reach or understand, that we were fine. It would take several years; two teenage daughters of my own; and endless drama, worry, tears, hope, faith, and friends, but eventually I would realize what a great mom I really had. We would be close. We would talk. We would shop, laugh, and share, and then I would lose her. Life's a bitch too, sometimes.

## 1991

When my twin daughters turned thirteen, thus launching me into the unpredictable world of being a mother of teenagers, my mom sent me a condolence card. Oh, did I get it! What I put my mom and dad through was ridiculous.

My don't-take-no-for-an-answer personality, although clearly abrasive and difficult for others to tiptoe around, did have a plus side. With experience and maturity, I learned how to control my impulsive and undisciplined attitude and develop it into a persuasive and articulate demeanor. I learned to pick and choose the battles really worth fighting. I learned how to see more than just my perspective and, when the time came and I needed to lobby powerfully on behalf of my mom, I was a piranha. After all the years of smart remarks and lip I gave my mom, she would finally benefit from the strength of character she had modeled for me. I was just a slow learner.

# CHAPTER 19
## *Hard-Boiled Eggs*

January 1972

I was hard-boiling eggs recently, something I have done numerous times before, and with my mom ever present on my mind, my simple cooking endeavor reminded me of when she had hard-cooked eggs for me years before. It was January 1972, and I was a sophomore at Michigan State University. My boyfriend and I were traveling late one wintry evening in January headed to Bay City, Michigan. We had plans to meet up with his friend, who was a radio DJ working the late-night shift. His friend got off work at one in the morning, as I recall, so we had left East Lansing around eleven o'clock. It was very cold, but the roads were mostly clear.

We were riding in an older car. I don't believe it had seat belts, but even if it did, no one really used them back then. Late at night, traffic was virtually nonexistent, and we owned the road. It was a completely benign, quiet trip until, without warning, the car spun out of control as we hit what was possibly the only patch of ice anywhere on the road. Suddenly I was like a Raggedy Ann doll being violently tossed around in a metal coffin. One moment I was hurling forward into the dashboard as the vehicle spun, and the next I was thrown forcefully back into the seat. (I know how my lettuce feels when I plunge the salad spinner down with a vengeance. I hate wet romaine.) Then the car came to a stop in the ditch near the road.

A few seconds passed, and then I started to assess the damages. There was a space in my mouth where a tooth used to be, and my back and arms hurt. Then I saw blood dripping from my chin onto my coat. I pulled the dangling rearview mirror toward me, which reflected the ugly, bloody mess that use to be my chin. There was a jagged, open wound across my lower jaw where my face had smashed with astonishing force into the dashboard.

I'm not sure how long we waited in the cold car, but eventually another vehicle stopped, a small truck I think. Thank God. Given the very few vehicles on the road that night and having no cell phones then, we were very fortunate. I was helped out of the car, but with every movement I could feel excruciating pain in my lower back. Although that area hurt the most, it was my face that concerned me. It wasn't vanity, exactly, but the mirror's reflection had been very confirming and not very comforting.

The man drove us to the nearest hospital in Owosso. The details after that are a blur. I don't remember the man's name, and I don't remember arriving at the hospital or the initial triage experience. What I do remember is the ER physician. He was a jerk. I was scared, and he was impersonal. I was hurt, and he was indifferent. I was bleeding from my chin, and he stitched me up as if I were just an old shoe. He did such a terrible job, in fact, overlapping the jagged tissue rather than trying to abut the edges, that it would take three additional plastic surgeries and over fifteen years of natural absorption before people wouldn't notice my chin before they noticed me.

Someone called my parents—not a call anyone wants to get. I can imagine the fear, worry, heartache, and sheer terror my mom and dad must have felt. They had already lost their infant son, David, also in a car accident twenty years earlier. They were reliving the anguish a second time for me.

Somewhere in the emotional fog of the traumatic night, I overheard the obnoxious ER doc with no finesse callously tell someone that I had a "broken back." What exactly was a broken back? I remember wiggling my toes, reassured that they were all still there and still working. Strange what an apparently simple act like wiggling one's toes could reveal. I drifted off to sleep from the combination of stress, shock, trauma and probably some really good drugs.

The next thing I remember is seeing my mom's smiling but clearly stressed face leaning over me and saying, "Hi. Are you all right?"

She was wearing one of my favorite suits, a smart olive knit with contrasting trim. (After forty years, I still remember that suit.) She squeezed my hand, and I felt her reassuring warmth radiate through me and knew everything would be okay. "Yes," I managed to say, speaking for the first time in a while. It hurt to talk or, as I would soon discover, smile, laugh, or chew. I couldn't purse my lips to kiss her or wrap them around a straw. I remember thinking that my favorite food vice, chocolate, was out of the question, even in liquid form. Bummer!

My mom carefully detailed my injuries to me. The missing tooth and rearranged face I had already figured out. Then she explained "the broken back."

"The doctor has met with us," she began—I learned later it was not the jerky doctor—"and explained that you have a compression fracture of your lower back. It happens when the vertebrae fold rapidly on top of one another, when the accident impact occurred. You'll miss some school and have therapy for a while, but you'll be fine. It's swollen at the injury site, which explains your lower back pain."

I nodded in understanding. I trusted her. She would not lie to me, plus I had wiggly toes. I had a cousin in Lafayette who had been rendered a quadriplegic after a tragic diving accident, but it had been years earlier and I was very young. All I could recall was the tail end of a sentence: "… and he can't wiggle his toes either."

I was going to be taken via ambulance to Borgess Hospital

in Kalamazoo, where my dad was financial controller—how convenient. Ironically, a former high school classmate and friend of mine, Dennis, was on the medical transport team that picked me up and rode with me to Borgess. I was rapidly feeling better and couldn't wait to get home and then back to Michigan State University. Their cafeteria made the best frosted chocolate-fudge brownies. Until I could actually open my mouth without pain, however, I would have to settle for soft foods.

The hospital food was awful: Jell-O (boring), pureed green beans (ugh), or tuna. To this day, I think tuna is cat food and am still baffled why anyone who can actually smell it would still eat it anyway. I vividly remember my mom bringing hard-boiled eggs to me at the hospital. They were perfect: soft, not too cold, and with a dash of salt and pepper. I hadn't particularly favored hard-cooked eggs before that night, but those were the best. Even a college student needs her mom sometimes.

I spent a day or two at Borgess Hospital under my dad's watchful eye and then was discharged to home before returning to Michigan State. For the predischarge physical therapy assessment, the therapist had me do several leg and back movement patterns and then reviewed the home exercises and a few precautions. Just as he was turning to leave, he said, "You know, you are very lucky to be walking."

*Really?* I thought. *Why?* I could hear the words but, despite my cousin's experience, could not fully process their medical meaning. My toes wiggled, and my cousin's had not. It would be later, almost on the one-year anniversary of the car accident, that all of the pieces would fall into place for me in one revealing, nauseating moment of medical discovery.

## January 1973

Over the summer, I transferred from Michigan State to Wayne State University in Detroit to pursue a degree in occupational therapy. One morning early in the winter semester, I was sitting in my neurology class along with forty other occupational and physical therapy students. We often had guest lecturers who explained their specific medical disciplines in depth. That morning's speaker was detailing the distinction between the central and the peripheral nervous system.

"As future therapists," he said, "you need to understand the significant difference between patients who have brain versus limb and back injuries. Patients with brain involvement would include stroke, Parkinson's, and more. Your approach to their treatment would be different than someone with a peripheral nerve injury, which usually occurs in a crush or a car accident."

Car accident! I had been paying attention and furiously taking notes in my own college-created shorthand, but now I was leaning forward in my chair.

"One type of peripheral nerve injury causing weakness of the lower extremities is referred to as 'seat belt syndrome,' in which an occupant is thrown forward and back so fast, either unrestrained or with only a lap belt, their vertebrae are compressed or crushed together. In extreme cases, the spinal cord can be permanently severed, resulting in partial or complete paralysis …" I didn't hear another word.

In that instant, I finally absorbed the reality of what "broken back" meant—the life-changing, one-way, permanent path to a wheelchair. I had miraculously escaped seat belt syndrome paralysis only a year before. The memories of the car accident, my mother's fear-ridden face, my ragged chin, and the pain in my lower back came flooding back to me like a tsunami. As I sat in the lecture room finally processing the neurological consequences of vertebral fractures, I felt nauseated and light-headed.

My physical therapist's comment about how "lucky" I was reverberated in my ears. I ran out of the classroom and down the hall and threw up in the lady's bathroom. My legs felt weak. My mom had understood, but I hadn't. Tears rolled down my face as I thought of how she must have felt. I called her that night just to chat. I didn't specifically recount my day to her—once was enough—but I called her just the same.

## July 2005

My lipstick-red Crossfire sports car was a blast to drive. I loved cars, a trait I shared with my dad. Not being a car person, my mom just shook her head every time she got into it.

"Your dad was into cars, not me. But it's cute," she said.

We were sitting in the Crossfire but were still in the garage. I helped Mom with the seat belt as she always had trouble securing the latch. Then I adjusted the seat so she could sit up and see out of the front window.

"Yeah, I know, Mom," I replied. "Remember when Dad gave me such a hard time when I got that red Bonneville and then later you guys ordered the red Olds?"

I remembered that series of conversations vividly. Around 1990, I had a new red Pontiac Bonneville. The girls and I had driven over to Kalamazoo in it for the first time. My dad, a man who rarely expressed an opinion about anything even if you asked him, remarked several times about my red car.

"Why did you pick red?" he asked.

I'm not even sure what his objection was, except that maybe it was such a bold color.

"It suits me," I said. "I like red." I especially liked deep, rich, lipstick red, not wimpy, cherry-orange red.

My mom had been right there in the kitchen, actively participating throughout the entire conversation but mostly laughing at the ridiculousness of discussing car colors. A few years later, when they spent a weekend at our house, my dad drove up in a brand, new red Oldsmobile. I teased him unmercifully about his red car after all the flack he'd given me. It was all very good-natured bantering.

"I don't remember that," Mom said. She had been smiling

through my animated retelling of the events, so I was surprised by her remark.

"Really?" I asked, like some doubtful plea from me was going to trigger an *aha* moment, but I tried anyway.

"Well, I know your dad always bought Oldsmobiles," she said. *Where is this thought coming from?* I wondered. We weren't really talking about what model of cars Dad bought. There was an odd pause like she was searching through her memory archives for some snippet of detail. "And I know my car is red." Hidden under the dark tint of my sunglasses, I rolled my eyes in frustration.

Then I heard a subdued but distinct laugh. I knew that laugh. It was her signature, telltale sign that she was pretending to understand a conversation when in fact she had either not heard it or not understood it. Clearly she didn't remember any of these events.

We were together in my little red sports car, headed to the local Catholic church for the Saturday afternoon mass. Actually, she was going to church, and I was going to run a few errands. I was tooling along and enjoying the open sunroof, revealing a beautiful, warm, Michigan summer day. Mom had been quiet for a few moments after the red car exchange, so I was curious what she was thinking. Was she still trying to research her memory for that series of conversations, or had her attention drifted elsewhere?

The silence was broken with, "What kind of car is this?"

"It's a red (I had to get that in) Chrysler Crossfire." I leaned over slightly and tapped the wide plate of raised letters directly above the glove box at her eye level.

I wasn't trying to be flippant when I pointed to the car's name. It was very difficult for my mom to hear while riding in or driving a car, and not just because of the extraneous road noise. Mom supplemented her hearing by observing the speaker's nonverbal cues like facial expressions and lip movements or, in this case, tapping a plaque. She had taken lip-reading classes years before she got her implant and continued to enhance her comprehension by viewing the speaker's face and the subtle clues it revealed as his or her lips moved. While I was driving, I had limited safe opportunities to turn and look at her as we talked. The same was true when she drove.

"What kind of car is this?" she asked a minute later.

"A Chrysler Crossfire," I replied. Maybe she hadn't heard me the first time.

Another minute or two passed, and she asked again. I answered and tapped the logo again so she could refer to it. "It's written here too, Mom." I was starting to feel a little frustrated.

And then the fourth time: "What kind of car is this?"

*What the heck, Mom?* I thought. If she had legitimately not heard me, she would have said something by then. We were approaching a light, and stopping provided more communication options. I turned to look right at her and gently touched her left shoulder to get her attention. She turned to look at me. Very distinctly, I said, "My car is a Chrysler Crossfire. The words are also written here," and I simultaneously tapped the plate. "You have asked me a few times already. Did you hear me?"

"I did?" she said with a laugh. There it was again—the giveaway sign.

Never before had this verbal recycling occurred with me. She asked me one more time before we arrived at the church, by which time I was seriously reevaluating my plan to just drop her off. Mom had attended this church many times before, so it was familiar to her. Still, I had decided to scrap the inconsequential errands and accompany her to church when her brain fog cleared.

"Just pick me up in about an hour," she said. "I'll be looking for your red Crossfire."

*Crossfire!* How strange. Had it really taken five times before it registered? And then suddenly she had the magic words. Had reading the car sign triggered her short-term memory? It's not that she couldn't remember the name of the car so much as she didn't remember asking the same question over and over, five times in ten minutes. I was definitely concerned and made a mental note to contact Friendship Village to explore it further with their nursing staff. I drove away slowly, watching to make absolutely certain she entered the church.

I ran my silly errands and returned to pick Mom up. I was expecting that she might be waiting outside for me as she had mentioned she might "duck out after communion." The car was barely in park when a church usher approached me. I powered the window down as he quickly glanced at a note in his hand.

"Are you Elaine?" He didn't really wait for an answer before he added, "Your mom passed out during the service. No one nearby knew her, nor could we be sure she hadn't hit her head, so we felt we had to call an ambulance. She was coherent, however, by the time the paramedics arrived and gave us your name. She said you had a cute car." He glanced at his cheat sheet again. "The ambulance left a few minutes ago for Southshore Hospital."

Reassured, I smiled a little at her description of my car as cute and thanked him. I called my husband to update him and drove to the hospital. I knew Mom had passed out a few times before. After my dad died, she had accidentally overdosed on her blood-pressure medication. One of the menial jobs my dad could do every week was organize their pills, so she had not handled them for several years. Mom admitted to having difficulty keeping her meds organized and had inadvertently doubled up on blood-pressure medication, causing hypotensive blackouts. The Assistance in Living staff at Friendship Village had eventually uncovered the mystery and offered to manage her medications.

I was a little surprised that Mom gleefully accepted their offer and willingly relinquished that aspect of her independence. She was thrilled, saying, "They just bring me my pills." Mom also admitted that sometimes she forgot to eat breakfast, "felt woozy, and had to sit down." I strongly suspected that her description translated into passing out episodes also.

En route to Southshore, I reflected on the day's events. For ten consecutive minutes she had asked the same question over and over five times and couldn't hold onto the answer. Then, miraculously, she had it, and just as mysteriously, it faded away into oblivion. I shook my head in confused disbelief as I parked my little red sports car.

I found Mom in the ER and waited throughout the evening with her until the multitude of tests was completed and she was transferred to a room. When they finally brought her dinner about seven thirty, a hard-boiled egg was on the tray. Instantly it brought back memories of my car accident years ago, and a smile came over me. She noticed, but I avoided any more discussions with a wave of my hand. I was exhausted, and we both had been through enough wistful nostalgia, even if she didn't recall most of it.

The tests revealed that Mom had pulmonary emboli. Possibly her incidents of passing out in the past were symptomatic of the emboli rather than medication confusion or forgetting to eat, or they could have been related to all of the above.

"It's not a bad way to go," she said after getting the diagnosis and as we were discussing the implications. "I'm not ready yet, but it's a quick and relatively painless end. It's better than losing your mind."

She threw out those one-liners, idioms, and intuitive remarks like that from time to time. After all she'd been through—burying an infant son, watching her husband die by inches, and then losing her daughter-in-law and other son—I did not rebuff her comments. I tried to validate them and really listen.

"Well, I'm not ready for you to go yet either, Mom."

"You know what I mean." She looked me straight in the eye with a very emphatic expression that left absolutely no doubt about her message.

"Yes. I do." And I did. Mom was very transparent about her end-of-life care wishes. As difficult as it was sometimes to listen to her discuss death and dying issues, I appreciated her transparency. I would rely on every fragment of insight to help guide me through the murky dilemmas ahead and gradually became her voice.

After five days in the hospital, she was discharged on Coumadin. The emboli-busting wonder drug, however, would not remain so wonderful for her. I followed up with the nursing staff at Friendship Village and alerted them to Mom's future need for Coumadin blood level draws, as well as to her short-term memory blips. They would handle both and contact her physician, the wonderful Dr. Bradtke, for prescriptions for Aricept and Coumadin. Namenda was added to the cocktail later to help stall the progression of her dementia. I couldn't imagine what my mom might have looked like *without* these meds.

# CHAPTER 20

## *Not a Stroke of Genius*

### 1995

It's somewhat of a blur, looking back, but I remember the night Mom called to tell me that Dad had been hospitalized with stroke symptoms. She and I normally talked occasionally by phone, but with her hearing loss, it was infrequent and frustrating.

For when we had to communicate by phone, Mom had given me a transcription device on which I could type what I wanted to say and she could read it on her end, like reading a ticker tape. It certainly was helpful, especially for communicating dates and times or answering specific questions, but it was painfully slow. She would talk to me, but I typed my responses, which showed up eventually on her device. Then she could read what I was saying. It took some prearranging too, as my device was upstairs. My parents' house was a ranch-style home, and her phone gadget was more accessible in the den.

Their den had been Jerry's bedroom, the room I had danced through when the walls were just studs. It had been converted into a multipurpose guest/TV/craft room. It was the only one with parquet wood floors, an intentional design in their long-term plan to convert it after Jerry moved out permanently. The room was warm, with inviting grass cloth walls, textured tan drapes, tasteful lighting, and a comfy couch and throws. I found my dad there often, asleep on the couch and wrapped up in the comforter with the TV on. I recalled that visual image as I listened to Mom on the phone and smiled.

Dad had been hospitalized since Thursday, so on Saturday, I drove over to Borgess Hospital to see him. I could tell immediately that he hadn't just experienced stroke symptoms; he had had a stroke. He slumped over to one side, a drop of drool suspended from the corner of his mouth. He was pale and disheveled, his foot slid off the wheelchair footrest, and his fingers were already tight, the unmistakable, classic stroke pattern.

How awful. As a therapist I could quickly assess his compromised future and what impact it would have on him, as well as on my mom. He opened his eyes, righted his head, and smiled. "Hi, Elaine," he said. I grabbed a tissue and blotted the drool from the side of his crooked mouth and smiled back. We talked a little. His speech was soft and mumbled, but I got most of it.

Mom arrived later. She had stopped at the cafeteria downstairs and brought us salads so we could join Dad at lunchtime when he got his tray. He peered into Styrofoam boxes of colorful greens and said to mom, "Betty, where did you get that salad, from the florist?" We laughed so hard that it hurt. He looked different and had a lot of therapy ahead, but he was still in there. Dad probably had experienced multiple ministrokes over the previous year; his hearing on one side had just quit in the fall. And in the summer he had lost his footing walking up the gentle slope of the tee box on the golf course and tipped over, almost in slow motion.

Dad received occupational, physical, and speech therapy services at Borgess, then in-home care, and finally outpatient therapy. It was an exhausting time for both of them but especially for my mom since everything fell on her shoulders. Besides what was already on her plate, she had Dad's endless care plus considerable additional responsibilities. Dad had filled the bird feeders every morning, and since he couldn't, he wanted her to do them. He wanted the paper every day, so she walked down the long driveway to fetch it. Dad needed railings installed at the entry doors, so she made those arrangements and so much more.

It was a very long couple of years poststroke. Jerry came up from Atlanta every few months and helped with repairs like a fallen drapery rod and a lengthy list of other guy chores. I drove over to help also, alternating my trips with Jerry's visits, but my daughters were seniors in high school and had constant sports and social events, so my travel time was limited. I savored all of their senior year, and my mom understood.

When Dad's poststroke recovery leveled off, he could dress himself with extra time and used a quad cane when he walked. He needed railings or physical assistance for steps, a wheelchair for distances, and help with small things like cuff buttons and some containers. It was Dad's judgment and impulsivity that put him at risk. If he saw a piece of fuzz on the floor, his meticulous nature compelled him to lean over and attempt to pick it up. He fell several times and suffered two closed-head injuries and intracranial bleeds as a result. When I saw him after one of his numerous falls, he looked like a mummy with his head turbaned in white gauze.

Mom dutifully drove over on the holidays and other weekends for visits, but whatever help she gained by having Joe and me around was outweighed by the exhaustive pre- and posttravel arrangements. Dad always fell at least once every visit at our house, and I didn't sleep very well, always keeping one ear out for any possible signs of trouble during the night.

### Early October 1999

A few years after the stroke, my parents started investigating alternative living situations and eventually decided on Friendship Village. I had concerns about my mom giving up her flower gardens and the house she had seen her kids grow up in.

"Mom," I asked her with genuine interest, "if Dad died a week after you sold the house and moved, how would you feel?"

"I would be fine, Elaine," she replied. "I'm ready. Houses are a lot of upkeep, and it is very difficult for me to handle things by phone." With those words, I was on board too. She added that although Dad did make most of the phone calls for repairs or service issues, she tried to listen in as he often transposed numbers and made day, date, and time errors. She told me more than once about how she worried that Dad would make an easy victim for solicitors and scam artists. Apparently a few absurd purchases slipped through the cracks, but fortunately they were nothing too expensive.

Their house sold within a week. Large, unneeded items like their second car, treadmill, pool table, dad's workbench, extra furniture, and golf clubs were sold or donated. Jerry flew up on a few weekends to dismantle hardware, sort and pitch, take stuff home with him, or sell things. I was there the weekend of the actual move to pack and buffer. My mom was overextended and overwhelmed, and Dad was an emotional train wreck, crying and yelling. The stroke had robbed him of the ability to adapt to change and of the filters necessary to regulate and suppress emotional outbursts. He was frustrated, rude, and profane. It was an ugly scene.

It took several more months, but eventually they settled in very nicely. Dad got a power scooter, which gave him in-house mobility, and Mom met new people since she was no longer constrained by the limitations of phone communications. She was grateful they had moved to Friendship Village, where she didn't have to cook, clean, or handle yard work and snow removal. There was emergency help available with the pull of a cord should Dad fall and need help getting up, which had started to occur more often. After a year of grumpy complaining, Dad acquiesced as well and loved it there. It had been a genuinely painful transition, but I give Mom kudos for really nudging it along.

# CHAPTER 21
## Blind to the Signs

### 1964

My brother Jerry was a genius, literally. His IQ fell somewhere in the 140s or 150s I was told—and not by him but by my dad, who did not embellish. In 1964, he graduated as the valedictorian from Monsignor Hackett High School and started at the University of Michigan, where he later received his bachelor's in chemical engineering. He went on to earn his PhD from the California Institute of Technology, where he also met his future wife, Wendie. Such a deal!

In Michigan, the biggest college rivalry is between Michigan State, in East Lansing, and the University of Michigan, in Ann Arbor. Amid the vibrant fall colors, State's green and white battled the maize and blue of Michigan for prestigious wins on the football field and other venues. Local news stations promoted the good-natured competition with photo arrays of babies decked out in competing collegiate colors and the best tailgate party goodies. Sharply dressed bands moving with precise synchrony, energetic cheerleaders, and face-painted fans surrounded the time-honored traditional battle between MSU and the U of M. Flags and streamers adorned homes, showing allegiance to college favorites and, in some cases, both teams, like our house.

My daughters Angie and Christie followed in their uncle's

and their mom's footsteps by graduating as covaledictorians from Riverview High School in 1996. Jerry had attended Michigan, but I was the green-and-white girl. MSU and UM collided again when it came to my daughters' choices of colleges: Christie to Michigan State and Angie to Michigan.

For their high school graduation presents, in addition to their party, I bought them collegiate approved, licensed T-shirts with the Michigan or State logos on them. For my MSU girl, Christie, I had printed on the back: "My twin sister goes to the University of Michigan." Of course, the back of Angie's Michigan shirt read, "My twin sister goes to Michigan State." They were great gifts, I thought. They were pleasantly surprised, and they wore them on their first day of college.

---

My daughters spent quality time with their grandparents in Kalamazoo: Easter, Christmas, birthday celebrations, and miscellaneous weekends. When the girls were little and for many years after, my mom would take them for a week or a long weekend in the summer. Mom refurbished the little metal table and chair set I had used constantly as a kid for reuse by her granddaughters. My dad helped her take the old, worn, red vinyl, which was long discolored, marked on, and cut up, off the top of the table and backs and sides of the chairs and replaced it with clean, new yellow vinyl. She repainted the banged up and scratched white table legs and chair frames in brown.

My mom taught them how to cross-stitch, emphasizing that the backside had to look nearly as good as the project's front. Her cross-stitch skills were impeccable, as was her work with pulled thread, silk embroidery, black work, and Hardanger. My girls learned how to take stitches out and anchor the embroidery ends securely but attractively without knots. And in turn, they taught me.

She also taught the girls her luscious pie-baking craft, a skill I still don't have probably because I liked only her signature cinnamon-sugar delight that she made just for me with the leftover pie dough.

## 2006–2009

My mother's Purdue University girlfriend, Margene, and she started getting together for lunches in March 2005. Because both ladies had hearing difficulties that were exacerbated by crowd noise, Margene suggested meeting at her house on the third Thursday of every month. It was great fun until January 2006, when Margene started noticing glimpses of odd behaviors. Mom was a half hour late one time, and when she finally arrived, she pulled into the driveway of the house next to Margene's. Mom admitted she had gotten lost, thus explaining the delay.

The ladies alternated driving dates—Mom one month, Margene the next. When it was Margene's turn, she drove over to Friendship Village to pick my mother up, but Mom wouldn't always be waiting at the door as prearranged. On those days, my mom had completely forgotten about their get-together and Margene had to search for her.

When it was Mom's turn to drive, she had increasing difficulty with reliably finding Margene's house. Once, Margene even stood in the driveway and watched helplessly as my mom "sailed past and pulled into a driveway four doors down on the opposite side of the street." Mom got out of her car, knocked on the door, and waited. When no one answered, she got back in the car, but it was another ten minutes before she got to Margene's.

Mom admitted to Margene that she was having difficulty identifying her house. Mom asked Margene to put a red cloth on the light post on the Thursdays of their lunches at Margene's house. That strategy failed, though, as my mom forgot to look on that side of the street and was oblivious to the red shirt waving in the yard. Another time, on a Tuesday—not their agreed-to Thursday—Margene arrived at her home to find a note that my mother had been there for their Thursday lunch and wondered why Margene wasn't there.

As the frequency of the incidents increased, Margene suggested that she could pick Mom up, but my mother refused to give up her "turn to drive." As Margene put it, "If there is a fun part of dementia, I guess this is it—everything was forgettable except what really meant the most to Betty: her turn to drive."

In October 2009, the monthly lunches ceased when Mom stopped driving. Mom e-mailed me that she and her college friend weren't getting together for lunch anymore, but she never explained why. It would be a few more years before I would learn the whole truth.

## Summer 2001

My daughter Angie had a long-standing dream to travel to Australia after graduating from the University of Michigan. After considerable networking and planning, it came to fruition in August 2001 when she landed a work opportunity in Brisbane and made additional plans to travel the magnificent country after finishing her work assignment. Angie made a point to visit her grandparents before embarking on her sixteen-month trek in Australia. The three of them had a great visit, but there were issues that troubled Angie, specifically about her grandma's memory. Concerned, she called to discuss them with me.

"Mom," she started, "Grandma gave me articles about the Sydney Olympics, but they were last summer in 2000. She wished me a great time there and hoped I would get to see lots of different Olympic events. What's going on with her?"

Angie added that she told her grandmother the Olympics in Australia had already happened, but when confronted, Grandma's face reflected confusion and her responses became evasive. Angie tried again to clarify the facts for her grandmother in case she literally had not heard Angie, but apparently my mom just started talking about something else.

Angie pleaded her case with me. "Grandma should have known this or at least understood me when I clarified it for her." Looking back, the first, obvious misstep in Mom's thinking occurred as far back as 2001 during Angie's visit. As I had not *yet* witnessed a single element of poor judgment or confusion up to that point, I dismissed Angie's concerns. I responded casually with, "Grandma does an awful lot for Grandpa without complaint or much help. Maybe she was especially tired or thinking about something else. I'll keep an eye out for other signs, though."

It was a puzzling incident, however. My mom was abreast with current events and politics via the *Kalamazoo Gazette, National Geographic,* closed-captioned CNN, and local television news. I really did not validate Angie's warnings back then to the extent I should have. In time, though, this incident, combined with so many other goofy behaviors and disconnected remarks, would gradually reveal her underlying condition.

I had ignored the first real, genuine evidence of my mom's dementia, possibly to her detriment.

# CHAPTER 22

*Death by Inches*

Circa 1971

I vividly remember meeting my future sister-in-law, Wendie, for the first time. Jerry had been dating her for a while and was finally ready for us to meet her and vice versa. They had met in Pasadena when Jerry was in California working on his PhD at Caltech.

Wendie and I were hanging out with my mom in the kitchen as Mom was preparing dinner. I could hear Jerry jabbering away to my dad in the living room. I had a question about something and had just started to walk in there to ask either of them for an answer when Wendie called out, "Jerry, in twenty-five words or less, what can you tell us about ..."

I stopped dead in my tracks in stunned disbelief. Did I really just hear Wendie put limits on my brother's mouth? I did. It was great! I thought I would fall over. Jerry talked incessantly. You had to be certain you didn't need to pee before beginning a conversation with him.

"Good job, Wendie," I managed to get out between giggles. Jerry had met his match, and she was a good one. They married in June 1973. Over the years, I noticed that Wendie might allow him fifty words to answer a question or she would fan her fingers and count the words as he rambled along. She would raise her hand, palm up and outward, imitating a stop sign when Jerry had exceeded his limit, and Jerry always laughed.

Wendie and I are very different women, with different goals, priorities, and ideas. We would not have been girlfriends had we not been brought together through my brother, but I came to respect and admire her. She was always great to and for Jerry. My brother was brilliant but socially awkward. Through my mom's unwavering guidance and Wendie's unconditional support, Jerry matured into a successful engineer and, above all, a caring, personable man of integrity, albeit a chatterbox.

## 1993

My brother and sister-in-law had a wonderful relationship that I didn't really notice or fully appreciate until after the divorce from my girls' father. I hosted Christmas in 1993 amid numbing emotional pain. I operated under the motto "Just get through it." I couldn't wait until the new year and hoped it would be a better one. I found that I had underestimated Jerry and Wendie's capacity for empathy. They made the long journey from Ohio just to help me make the difficult transition to the holidays' "other side."

My girls and I had established a tradition at Christmas, or actually between Black Friday and Christmas Eve. Our tradition was to complete a puzzle, usually five hundred or a thousand pieces. We started it just after Thanksgiving, and it had to be finished before Christmas so the table could be cleared for all of the festive holiday meals. Jerry and Wendie arrived Christmas Eve morning. Our Rodney Reindeer puzzle was well underway but not close enough to being done. Wendie loved puzzles and jumped right in. Jerry alternated between hunting for an annoying, difficult-to-find but crucial puzzle piece and getting things for me.

That Christmas, I saw them as a real, connected couple in ways I never had before. They acknowledged each other frequently but subtly. If Wendie walked past Jerry, she would touch his arm.

Later he might put his hand on her shoulder. *How wonderful*, I thought. *If I ever marry again, I want that.* And, lucky for me, I got it when I met Joe in 1994. We were married in 1998.

## New Year's Day 2001

Wendie was diagnosed with terminal glioblastoma on New Year's Day 2001. She and Jerry had been at our house for Christmas just the previous week. Stunned disbelief didn't even begin to capture how I felt when I learned of Wendie's diagnosis. Absolutely nothing, not a neurological misstep, a hiccup in her speech prosody, or a personality quirk of any kind alerted me to any medical concerns. My observation skills as a therapist were always honed and functioning. I never turned them off, not that I could anyway.

My brother related the events leading to her diagnosis. He and Wendie were shopping at a store, looking for containers or something. Suddenly she couldn't speak. She knew what things were and what she wanted to say, but she could not get the words out. Knowing Wendie, she would have been reluctant to go to the hospital, but, knowing Jerry, he would have insisted.

I remember thinking as Jerry detailed her symptoms that it sounded like a stroke. Tragically, however, she had glioblastoma with two tumor sites. One tumor was operable, but the surgery left her severely physically compromised, and the other was embedded in the base of the brain and could not be excised. She declined chemo and radiation, which would only have prolonged her life in an already debilitated, postsurgical condition. Wendie died a month later on January 31, 2001, with Jerry at her side. It was devastating.

## Saturday, April 7, 2001

There were three memorial services for Wendie: one in Atlanta where they had lived since the early 1990s, one in California where her family was, and the last at Friendship Village for Jerry's family. I tried to read a poem in her memory, but the sight of my dad sitting in his wheelchair sobbing (poststroke) was a painful distraction that was impossible to overlook. I bombed. Sadly I would have more opportunities to hone my eulogy skills.

"He's really upset about Wendie's death," one of the Chicago cousins said to me, referring to my dad, as we gathered around after the memorial.

"I'm sure he is," I responded. "We all are, but he cries openly because he doesn't have filters anymore."

Of course, I didn't mean furnace or coffee filters. As social beings, our brains learn to regulate what we say and how we act to blend appropriately in society. My dad was always emotionally level. He didn't have the all-over-the-map reactions that Mom and I did. He rarely shared his private thoughts, never made snide remarks, didn't raise his voice, and didn't swear or offer his opinions. Even when I specifically asked his viewpoint on something, his responses were neutral, which annoyed me. Who didn't have an opinion about something? I know I did; just ask me. I might tell you even if you didn't ask.

In brain injuries, like those related to strokes, the regulatory system that filters what we say or do can become compromised. My dad's personality had gradually but clearly changed after the stroke. He was definitely different. He laughed long, loud, and inappropriately. He cried often, although medication helped modulate it some, another common characteristic of strokes. The worst behavioral change, however, was his swearing, yelling, flailing his arms, and screaming at my mom, "No, over there!" or "I want it now!"

It angered and hurt me to see him be so brutal to her. I tried to rationalize it as "the stroke," but she was still "my mom" and deserved better. There were a few occasions when I did yell back at Dad in defense of my mom, but she was right: if she remained calm, Dad decelerated more quickly and the confrontational tone was diffused. This behavioral strategy would also prove itself effective with my mom one day.

Quickly, though, I realized that I needed to explain to my cousin what I meant by *filters*. After I did briefly, I added, "My dad would have traded places with Wendie if he could. He would have preferred to die when he had the stroke than to live this way." I extended my open palm in his direction. He was slumped in his wheelchair with a coffee stain on his crisp, white dress shirt and a spot of drool at the corner of his mouth. By then there were a few relatives around me. I let the words hang in the air for effect.

Although Dad couldn't stop the speeding train of derogatory words tumbling from his mouth, he almost always realized afterward that he lacked regulatory controls. He despised himself for the things he said, felt embarrassed and humbled. As time went on and he expressed wishing he were dead, I responded more appropriately by validating his frustrations and acknowledging his limitations, conceding his dependency on Mom. Then I reminded him how lucky he was to have her. He always smiled and answered, "Yes. I know."

## Wayne's (Dad's) Death, Monday, April 12, 2004

I was shopping when Jerry called me Monday afternoon. He told me that our mom had called him on Easter Sunday, the day before, to tell him that Dad had been taken to the hospital. Jerry wondered if I knew anything more.

"I didn't even know that much, Jerry," I answered, "but I'm driving over there tomorrow anyway since I have this week off. She didn't call me, and I didn't get an e-mail either."

"Okay. Well, let me know after you go tomorrow," he said.

I was very curious why Mom would call Jerry first and not me. She often said the low tones were the most difficult sound ranges for her to hear, like most men's voices. Although hearing via the phone was difficult anyway, she did better with me than many others, she said. But she also admonished me to slow down, enunciate my words, be specific, and don't laugh. I took a chance and called Mom from my cell while I was driving home. She answered. Once she knew it was me, I mainly listened. I did tell her that Jerry had already called me.

"So you already know Dad was taken to the hospital yesterday?" she asked.

"Yes. Yes." As a strategy, she had asked me to repeat the word as it helped her determine that she was definitely hearing an affirmative and not a different response.

Mom went on to tell me that she and Dad had enjoyed a "lovely Easter dinner Sunday," but shortly after they returned to their apartment, Dad became very pale, slumped over in his chair, and just looked "out of it." She used the emergency pull cord. The nurse came up and, after assessing his unresponsiveness, arranged for an EMS transport. Mom followed in her car. She spent the evening and into the early morning at the hospital. Finally, the physician informed her that Dad had suffered another brain bleed. They could do surgery, but afterward, he probably would be more physically compromised than he already was.

I knew Mom was on the cusp of making a very difficult decision to move my dad to the nursing home wing. She and I had talked about it at length during my March visit. It was becoming nearly physically impossible for her to transfer him without help. He was mostly incontinent, and she had noticed that he was having considerably more difficulties with memory and speech. I couldn't imagine her transferring him alone, especially for showers. I was taller than she was, a trained therapist, and I wasn't confident that I could do it alone.

Dad required increasingly more physical assistance with dressing, grooming, and bathing. Despite all of the obvious facts, however, I suspected that my mom would not be emotionally able to let go of his care and agree to the nursing home setting. My dad's protests that he didn't want to go would also play on Mom's emotions. But my dad also wasn't capable of logical thinking any longer. My prestroke dad would have hurled himself in front of a bus for my mom or, in this case, packed his things for the nursing home to save her from the physical and emotional burden of caring for him. The poststroke dad, however, was quite different: self-centered, explosive, and difficult. I knew my mom could not endure his wrath, his pitiful whining, his protests to stay, or his tears for very long. One or the other of them was going to be dead by the end of the year, I had predicted—either my dad from another stroke or my mom from exhaustion.

Thoughtfully, Mom declined the surgery and, in a matter of a few short hours, Dad was gone. He died very early in the morning on Monday, April 12, 2004.

"Okay, Mom. I'll be at your place at ten tomorrow morning." I waited to see if she had heard everything I had said. She would summarize and repeat the important information if she did.

"That would be great. You can help me with the funeral arrangements. Langeland is coming at eleven."

I called Jerry when I got home. He was as surprised as I was that Mom had not called either of us after Dad's passing. I would keep him updated on the funeral details after I got to Kalamazoo on Tuesday. I met my husband in the driveway when he got home. Joe could tell immediately that something was wrong from the strained expression on my face. I finally started to cry as I said the words: "My dad died yesterday." He hugged me tightly. I called Angie in Colorado and Christie later. She and her husband, Chris, were in Seoul, Korea, at the time, teaching for the Department of Defense.

Tuesday, April 13, 2004

I expressed my sorrow to Mom and hugged her as I entered her apartment Tuesday morning, but we knew it was for the best. Dad wouldn't have minded exiting the world years before rather than "die by inches." Mom and I visited for a short time, and then she handed me the Langeland folder for funeral arrangements, told me to meet with "the guy," and collapsed on her bed from exhaustion. I did my best to answer the more specific questions for the gentleman from Langeland, but Mom had actually scared me and I was preoccupied.

"I've never seen her like this," I said to "the guy," but he reassured me that he had seen others in a similar state. "It is not uncommon for the primary caregiver to be completely spent after experiencing such a loss." *Okay*, I thought. *I hope she pulls out of it.*

The funeral service was held on Saturday at St. Augustine's. Jerry flew in from Atlanta, Angie came from Denver, the Chicago family drove over, and friends from the Village and my parents' old neighborhood came also. I only remember watching my mom like a hawk for signs of disorientation or uncharacteristic behavior and giving the eulogy, which I had practiced in advance. The rest is blank. Mom wasn't the only one out of it; apparently, so was I. My mom did rally over the subsequent months, but just around the corner lurked another catastrophe.

A few months later, when I asked her how she was doing, she replied, "I have no regrets," referring to how well she had cared for her husband.

"Nor should you, Mom," I said.

I was proud of her for acknowledging that fact and giving herself the credit she deserved. My dad recognized that his compromised physical status was difficult, frustrating, and a "burden to your mother," he said often. When the "stroke emotions" were under control, Dad verbally expressed his deep admiration, respect, and love for his wife. It was rare and beautiful.

# CHAPTER 23

## From Vice to Valedictorian

Thirteen months after my parents were married, Gerald Wayne Ward was born on September 10, 1947. My mom wasn't in jeopardy with the Catholic church baby-name police since there *was* a Saint Gerald. David was next, and then I came.

One afternoon after school, I pranced through the living room where Mom was helping Jerry study. He may have been a genius in math and science, but he stunk at spelling and language arts—the typical left-brain-versus-right-brain scenario.

Mom was sitting in one of the matching upholstered chairs and Jerry was in the other. She was drilling him on his spelling words. I was maybe six at the time, so Jerry would have been ten. I had overheard him struggling with words like *smother* and *brother*. He paused after saying each letter, apparently thinking about which one came next. My mom was patient and dutifully waited for Jerry to sound it out for himself. Typically she put a small, almost indecipherable pencil check next to the words he had repeated difficulty with so he could practice them. Later they would meet back in the homework chairs, as I referred to them, for a recheck.

I had heard his painful rendition of brother: "B (pause) - R (pause) - O - T - H - E - R." I was out of sight in the kitchen, snickering and rolling my eyes. How pathetic. As soon as Jerry finished, I mouthed, *That's right* at exactly the same time my mom said it to him, mimicking her typical praise-word combo. His next word was *mother*. I was still munching on my after-school snack—no food allowed in the living room. "M (pause, repeat) - M (pause)—" Jerry's voice sounded strained. *I can help.* I bounded into the living room and said as I skipped past them, "M - O - T - H - E - R, mother. It's just like *brother* but with an *M*." I continued my prance, circling back into the kitchen and leaving behind a puzzled brother and a very miffed mom. I was never a great speller, but that was ridiculous. Jerry was four grades ahead of me.

We were a typical brother and sister pair growing up. He was older, had more privileges, and never seemed to be in time-out. I, on the other hand, was the rebel. Mom had her hands full with me.

## Circa 1960

Even though I was too young to really know what was going on at the time, I remember having inklings that something was amiss at our house involving Jerry. He was in junior high, making me seven or eight. One night Mom told me that she had made arrangements for me to go to Kathy's house straight after school the next day instead of home. She and Dad had something to take care of. I didn't think much of it, really. Kathy and I would have a great time.

It wasn't until Mom came to pick me up that I realized they were all in the car together. Dad was driving, and Jerry was in the backseat. I could tell from the unusual quiet and Jerry's and Dad's facial expressions that this had not been a fun outing. The human face is endowed with more than forty muscles, some of which are very minute and intricate, crossing over and near one another. It is extraordinarily difficult to prevent underlying emotions from leaching to the surface and revealing themselves on the face. Successful poker faces are the result of practice.

"Where have you been?" I asked. The strange mood in the car made me nervous.

Mom's words may have been comforting, but her tone of voice and the look on her face revealed the telltale signs of trouble. "Oh, we just had to go somewhere. It's nothing. What did you do in school today?" The atmosphere in the car on our way home was foreboding, and I remained quiet too.

Over the next few weeks, there were other times that Mom and Jerry came home together after school, but Dad was not with them. I went to a friend's house or a neighbor's. Eventually I became aware that everyone's routine seemed to be back to normal, perhaps two or three months later. It was many, many years before Mom confided in me about those secret sessions.

## Mid 1990s

Jerry's adult life took a different direction from mine. Jerry went to Caltech and met Wendie. They were married in 1973 in California and eventually moved to New Jersey, where they rebuilt the *Money Pit* house. We visited them in mid-August 1977, the summer I was pregnant with the girls. I vividly remember Jerry standing in line for hours to get tickets to the original *Star Wars* movie for all of us.

I traversed the wonderful road of motherhood, but Jerry and Wendie were DINKS (dual income, no kids). From New Jersey, they moved to Ohio and finally to their stunning home in Norcross, Georgia. We were never crazy close but always kept in touch. It wasn't until the Christmas of 1993 that I finally saw him and Wendie through emotionally opened eyes as I navigated through the last months of my own personal hell.

One day, in the mid 1990s, my mom and I were just talking like we often did, about everything and nothing. I ventured a question: "I know Wendie didn't really want children, but do you think Jerry would have had kids if he had married someone who did?"

Immediately I sensed that Mom hesitated and was carefully

choosing her words. "I think Jerry would have made a great dad if he had married a woman who both really wanted children and had the patience to guide Jerry through fatherhood."

Wow! Well, if *that* wasn't a loaded answer. Mom was not going to get away with just dropping an inflammatory remark like that and expect me to not press her further.

"What do you mean, Mom?" I asked, my tone very serious. "There's something you're not telling me. I can feel it."

It was the perfect opportunity to really talk. It was just Mom and me, with no expectations of husbands or kids suddenly interrupting us. She began, and I listened. "Sometime back, when Jerry was in junior high, I got a call from the police that he had been caught shoplifting some things from a local store." The shocked look on my face was obvious, but I said nothing. "Yes, I was shocked too, in a way. Jerry hadn't been doing that well in school. He did okay but not what he was capable of, and I knew it. Immediately I drove over to the store. The police officer showed me that Jerry had attempted to steal girlie magazines."

Inside I felt a tremendous sense of relief that he hadn't stolen a gun. I actually thought it was hilarious that it was just harmless girlie magazines. Discreetly, I slid my hand over my face to conceal any hint of laughter.

"I don't know why," Mom continued, "but the policeman suggested counseling. Something gnawed at him, having talked to Jerry for a while before I arrived. On the drive home, Jerry denied actually wanting the magazines, but I couldn't get him to tell me anything more. When I told Wayne about it, your dad was humiliated and initially refused to go to counseling, not wanting to discuss 'such things' with a stranger, but I was able to convince him to attend at least the first session. Jerry's actions were a cry for help and not about girlie magazines."

That much I had already figured out.

"I got Jerry in at the Guidance Center. He and I went for a few sessions together and then Jerry by himself after a while. They were his lifelines. Basically it came out that somehow Jerry had been made to feel that he would never amount to anything."

My eyebrows rose up at that remark. My brother, the genius, wouldn't amount to anything? This was the same guy with a PhD in chemical engineering.

"He suffered from low self-esteem. This incredibly brilliant young man wasn't able to handle his genius in social situations. Stealing the magazines was just a desperate cry for help. The counselor saw this instantly. She boosted Jerry's self-confidence, encouraged and supported him like no stranger had ever done before."

By then tears were gently streaming down my face. Poor Jerry. I had teased him mercilessly about his nonstop jabber. *Shame on me*, I thought, although it could be annoying.

"His grades improved, and you pretty much know the rest."

"Enough to be valedictorian," I chimed in. Mom smiled.

"He made real friendships in high school and college, and then he met Wendie, who has been wonderful for Jerry. Maybe having children just wasn't meant to be."

"Maybe not, but it really doesn't matter. I was just curious." I didn't tell Mom that I had vague memories of that time period. It wasn't necessary that I remind her unless she asked, and she didn't.

### December 2002–2003

Jerry put up a good front, but I believe he never recovered from his beloved Wendie's death in 2001. Mom and I talked often about Jerry's pain. "I would rather die with Wayne," Mom said to me a few times, "than to live alone, grieving without him. I think that's how Jerry might feel."

I could understand that. I wondered if Jerry felt that way despite his claiming otherwise. On the surface, Jerry never presented with depression or wallowed in despair. He made plans, traveled, and engaged socially. He talked about meeting new ladies and hoping to remarry one day. It was *way* too premature, so I just chalked it up to his therapeutic approach. He said positive, hopeful things to help him stay positive and hopeful.

My all-time favorite picture of Jerry and me as adults was from Christmas 2002, laughing as he leaned over my shoulder after I "stole" his bottle of favorite red wine.

"You'll get it back," I teased. "I don't even drink red wine."

"Yeah, but I do," Angie piped in, laughing. She and Jerry were wine connoisseurs, a.k.a. wine snobs. We were at our mom's in Kalamazoo. My dad was still hospitalized after his unexpectedly slow recovery following surgery for a throat tissue repair that year, but the rest of us were there.

Mostly Jerry and I corresponded by e-mail. I will never forget the one he sent me in early April 2003. He was up to something; I could tell by the vague references alluding to it in previous e-mails. I pressed one day for more information, and he wrote back, "I'll call you tonight with the news." I love mysteries except when I can't figure them out. And then, like a truck, it hit me: he was getting married.

"That stinker," I said to Joe. "He's either already married or he is getting remarried."

If so, I would not miss this one. When Wendie and Jerry married in California in 1973, I couldn't afford to attend. I was a full-time student at Wayne State. My parents' philosophy was that you were on your own financially once you were married, thus no offers of help with airfare or hotel expenses were forthcoming. That was perhaps the only decision they ever made that was flat-out wrong from my point of view. In retrospect, I came to realize that Mom was punishing me for having married so young.

"Already?" Joe asked. It had been just a little over two years since Wendie had died.

"I don't know," I replied. "They didn't have children. He's a mature adult. I've heard good marriages beget wanting to try again. We'll just have to wait and see."

I thought about calling or e-mailing my mom to see if she

had any scoop, but chances were that she would not be the first to know; I would. I couldn't wait for his call that night. I was so geeky and happy for him, but also a little miffed. When he called, I grabbed the phone and was ready to pounce on him for keeping a secret from me.

"So what's up?" I asked quickly when I saw his name on the caller ID. Jerry could ramble on forever. I was very curious about his news and hoped he would fast-forward to the punch line. He did.

"I saw my doctor today," he said. "I have stage four esophageal cancer with perhaps a year ..." I never heard the rest. I had gone from being ecstatic, elated, so happy for him, to complete devastation in the three seconds it had taken him to tell me. Despite my notable, endless repertoire of words, I had none. I was stunned. Shocked. Horrified. In utter disbelief. Nothing, none of them, could describe what I was really feeling.

And my poor brother! To have suffered Wendie's loss and now his own impending demise was simply not fathomable. Then I thought about my mom. She had already buried one child, and now she would have to bury another. I managed to say something consoling to Jerry, and he told me about the treatment plan ahead. However bleak his prognosis was, he would fight to the bitter end. Of course he would. When I finally hung up the phone, I was on the floor with my head in my hands, crying inconsolably. I genuinely could not even begin to process his news. My thoughts ran wild in my head. They tumbled back and forth with lightning speed—Jerry's deadly diagnosis; his long, painful sessions of chemotherapy and radiation yet to come with no reasonable chance of recovery.

Then my mind flashed to my mom. She had held her infant son David in her arms before he died. Without any muscle control, his little head hung downward over her forearm, his brain stem completely obliterated on impact in the car accident. His body no longer had temperature control, so his had spiked to ridiculous highs before he died a few days after their accident. What incredible devastation my mom and dad had already endured? And then there was my dad's stroke and Mom's unwavering commitment to his care and support. She had suffered enough for one lifetime. At some point I became aware that I was still crying hysterically and in emotional pain—only it wasn't for me. It really was for my mom. Just the thought of her eventually being told of Jerry's terminal diagnosis threw me into a tailspin of emotions. I was seething with anger and rage and crushed with sadness and heartache. This day really sucked!

## Mother's Day 2003

Jerry made plans to fly into Detroit from Atlanta on the Saturday morning of Mother's Day weekend. Joe, Jerry, and I would all drive over together to the Village and spend Mother's Day weekend with them as well as celebrate my dad's eighty-fourth birthday. Jerry would tell them his medical diagnosis that weekend. What an unbearable Mother's Day this would be for her.

"My flight into Detroit is canceled," Jerry said when he called early Saturday morning. "It looks like I can get a flight into Lansing with an afternoon arrival as my best option."

*Bummer.* I thought. I was anxious enough about this weekend, and now it was getting worse. We made a new plan. Joe and I would go over anyway. Christie and Chris, already in the Lansing area visiting with friends, would hang back, pick Jerry up, and then drive over. There were other hiccups in the arrangements, but by late afternoon Saturday, we were finally all together in Kalamazoo.

Christie called. "We're in the lobby downstairs. Uncle Jerry is with us, and we'll be up shortly." Her voice conveyed a distinct tone of concern. She didn't hide emotions very well, and this time I was grateful.

"Does he look different?" I asked, considering the possibility.

"Yes, Mom, he does." I knew from the punctuation in her voice that it must be bad.

I thought it would be best if I met Jerry before we went into our parents' apartment. I stepped out briefly to meet the group as they exited the elevator. My head was turned away momentarily as I heard the elevator doors open and my brother's unmistakable voice jabbering nonstop as usual.

As I turned to greet them, I froze. I couldn't speak for a second. I couldn't move forward to hug him. I just stood still, in shocked disbelief. Jerry looked absolutely horrible. He was gaunt, bald, and pale. If I hadn't heard his distinct voice first, I wouldn't have even recognized this person as my brother. His stomach was already distended. I had seen him just four months earlier at Christmas and he had looked great, but now his cheeks were hollow; his thinning, dark hair was completely gone; his chest was sunken; and his stomach was bloated. *Crap,* I thought. How would Mom react when she saw her son? My dad most likely would be oblivious, but not Mom. I dreaded the next few minutes.

It was nearly five o'clock and we still needed to go out to dinner, so Jerry said, "I'll just tell them tomorrow" as we walked down to their apartment together.

*As soon as Mom sees you, she'll freak out,* I thought, but strangely I was wrong. We went in and exchanged hugs and greetings. I was glued to Mom's face, watching and waiting for the inevitable tearful fallout and questions like, "Jerry, are you okay? Your face is so pale. How come your tummy is so enlarged?" She said nothing. She conveyed nothing. Her face showed no signs of concern or bewilderment. I was eternally grateful not to have to deal with this right then, or ever, but how could she not notice? I hadn't even recognized him, and Christie certainly felt the same way.

We went to Great Lake's Shipping, my dad's favorite restaurant, and had a nice dinner and visit. I sat next to Jerry. I felt like a coward because I didn't want to sit across from my own brother, but it was still difficult for me to look at him. Christie and Chris were seated at my end of the table. They were headed somewhere that evening, so I mostly visited with them.

Jerry's flight home was out of the Kalamazoo airport on Sunday, so Joe and I planned to drop him off en route to our house in the early afternoon. We gathered in my parents' apartment. Jerry sat down opposite my mom so that she would hear him. I don't even remember exactly what he said to them that Mother's Day morning. I watched their faces. As expected, Dad was clueless, but as I saw Mom tear up, I knew.

She bowed her head, and I'm sure she said a quick prayer before looking back up at her only living son. I felt such incredible emotional pain for her. My heart was breaking for my mom and for Jerry. No parent should ever have to bury a child, and she had already lost one. I had had the foresight to bring a card of comfort and support for her, and I left it on her dresser that infamous Sunday. It had taken me forever to find the perfect card with the perfect verse as the tears constantly filled my eyes and clouded my vision. This was the worst, crappiest, saddest Mother's Day ever.

Jerry fought hard for twenty months, through energy-sapping, nauseating chemotherapy and radiation. There were setbacks when his platelets were too low and his treatments were suspended. And there were encouraging months when he enjoyed lengthy plateaus, able to keep the cantankerous cancer cells at bay. The next time we saw Jerry was in June for Christie and Chris's wedding in Ann Arbor, Michigan. At least he didn't look any worse.

Jerry updated me on his progress and setbacks regularly via phone or e-mail. He took predictable, proactive steps to sell his gorgeous house in Norcross, liquidate furniture, and generally streamline his physical possessions. He even found a home for his snooty cat, Harriet, probably the only kitty I didn't like. Our cousin Mike flew out from Sedona to help Jerry also.

At Dad's funeral in April 2004, Jerry met with Joe and me away from my mom. His previous plateaus and progress had stalled, and although he was moving forward with scheduled treatments, his future was bleak. I don't remember if he said anything else, but I could tell he was scared. It had been a long day already, and my emotions and attentions were split between my mom and my brother.

After working for Ford Motor Company and then Gorno Ford, my husband retired in June 2004. We took advantage of his first summer off and my break from school to take my mom to Atlanta to visit Jerry. He had already honored me with his request that I serve as his executrix. He capitalized on my being physically in Atlanta to escort me to his bank, show me his safe, and give me the combination. He showed me where his financial files were and gave me his lawyer's name and other contact information. When he spoke in his foreign financial jargon, I couldn't even begin to keep up with him, but I took notes furiously everywhere we went and tried to jot down everything he said. I would need and use it all.

# CHAPTER 24

## *Angel Antics*

Christmas 2004

I hadn't heard from Jerry in a few weeks, and when my call to his apartment on Sunday evening (December 19) went unanswered, I knew something was wrong.

"I bet he's in the hospital," I said to Joe.

"If he doesn't call back soon, do you have numbers for the condo office or his friends?" Joe asked.

"I have a few. I'll find the rest."

"That's my honey." Joe backed me up, knowing I was quite resourceful and would find a way to reach Jerry through any means necessary.

Jerry called me Monday. I was right; he was in the hospital. He was still hopeful that he would feel well enough to fly to our house for Christmas on Saturday. I could hear the cautious *but* in his voice. Although unspoken, we both knew his end was near.

I glanced at our calendar. Angie was flying in on the twenty-third, and Mom was driving over on Christmas Eve morning. I ran an idea past Joe and then called Jerry back at the hospital. "Would you like some company?" I asked, fully expecting him to decline with some false bravado like, "Thanks, but I'm okay." When he enthusiastically accepted our invitation, it confirmed my suspicions that my big brother was indeed a very ill boy.

Joe and I booked our outbound flight for Tuesday morning with a late Wednesday return. I don't like hospital environments but trudged through it anyway for my brother. He tried to look chipper but told us honestly that his oncologist had been in earlier that morning and confirmed that there was nothing more to be done, except palliative care—translation: hospice. Jerry said he would be transferred to an in-house hospice facility on Thursday and obviously wouldn't make it north for Christmas. He had prepared a list of things for us to take care of, and Joe and I were grateful for the opportunity to really help and do something productive. We moved his car, called some people, and made arrangements for the other things he listed.

Before our departure Wednesday, fighting back the tears, I asked him, "What else can we do for you, big brother, except to be here?"

"Enjoy Mom's and Angie's visits, and your sons too, Joe. If I'm still here after Christmas, maybe you can come back, but—" and he was emphatic, "I do not want you to do a bedside vigil."

"Hang in there," Joe said as he shook Jerry's hand. I hugged and kissed him good-bye. I *promised* we would be back.

---

"How's Uncle Jerry?" Angie asked almost immediately when I picked her up at the airport on Thursday. I filled her in. "I'd really like to get down there to see him, Mom. This might be my only opportunity."

I was touched and added, "I also have to find a way to get Grandma to Atlanta too sometime."

"What about Christmas Day?" Angie asked. "It's usually a good day to travel because it's not as busy."

I will never forget her great idea. I'm not sure I would have thought of it, but it was perfect. I ran it by Joe, because obviously I would miss Christmas Day with him and his sons, but not surprisingly Joe was very understanding. He would have done exactly the same thing if it were his mom and brother. I knew that. Good man!

My mom was so grateful for the opportunity when we told her our idea. When I awoke on Christmas morning, it was an exquisite scene outside as a soft dusting of snow had fallen overnight. It defined every branch on the trees, and they glistened in the morning's sunlight. It evoked a sense of tranquility amid mind-numbing emotional pain. Joe dropped us off at the airport and gave us all big hugs and goodwill wishes to Jerry.

My girlfriends, especially Val, had offered their help and asked what they could do. My reply was always the same: "Pray the outbound flight is on time." I didn't care if we were stranded in the Atlanta airport or our return flight was diverted to the North Pole, but it was crucial that my mom could see her dying son one last time. Wendie, however, had other, even better plans.

Angie realized at check-in that she had left her purse at our house. She had no ID, no cell, and no money. That was *so* not Angie. She was thorough, organized, and way too young for memory lapses.

"Here's money for the cab," I said. "I'll call Joe so he can meet you in the driveway with your purse. Grandma and I have to continue on, so use your judgment about getting a later flight or whatever works." She understood the circumstances and dashed out to hail a cab. Mom and I proceeded through security and on to the gate. *How unfair*, I thought. After all those prayers I had requested that the outbound flight leave on time, now I needed a thirty-minute delay. *It's up to you, Wendie*, I thought as I glanced upward. *Jerry will be with you soon enough. Can you grant us this reprieve?*

Within minutes, an announcement came over the intercom. "Attention, passengers on Delta's flight to Atlanta." I held my breath, fearing the worst (a flight cancellation) and hoping for the best (a short flight delay). "There has been a gate change. Please gather your belongings and head over to gate twenty-five. There should only be a half-hour delay."

I had chills all over, and the hair stood straight up on the back of my neck. *Oh, my God, Wendie. You rock.* I thought. I repeated aloud the gate change information for Mom. We collected our purses and coats and walked down to the new gate. Just as we were getting settled, I saw Angie.

"I made it," she said. Indeed she had and probably not without some divine intervention or Wendie's amazing hand.

Emotionally I was all over the map. I was thrilled that Angie had made our flight, grateful it hadn't been me who had left her purse at home, sad about what awaited us at hospice, and devastated for my mom that she was burying yet another child and in the same year as her husband. I was mystified by Wendie's intervention, if indeed she had been instrumental in all this. Wendie, however, was just warming up. Her flight-delay trick was just a prelude. She hadn't even begun to show me what her angel friends and she were capable of, as long as I believed and let her guide me.

Upon our arrival in Atlanta, we navigated through the airport following the signs to ground transportation. The next decision was rental car versus cab, the former allowing us more control over our visiting time but causing me pre-GPS navigational stress, or the cab, providing an instant, stress-free arrival at Jerry's hospice facility but requiring an earlier exit to get back to the airport. *Okay, Wendie, you're on again.* I didn't dare even whisper lest I be overheard. I looked at the rental car booths—three to four people deep. *Okay, cab it is.*

"We'll take a cab," I said.

"I'll just follow you, Elaine," my mom said. Angie made sure Mom didn't get separated, sandwiching her between us from behind.

The next cab in line was a minivan, and the driver was Pakistani or Indian, perhaps. I handed him a prepared card with the name of the hospice facility and address. The sky was slightly overcast and the temperature in the low fifties. The three of us ladies chatted a little about Jerry. I was extremely cautious so as not to trigger tears for Mom. I was barely holding it together myself and certainly didn't want her to break down. Honestly, I suspected that she was in shock. I know I would be crying my eyes out if I were about to see Angie or Christie at an end-of-life hospice facility. The cab driver pulled into the gravel parking lot about fifteen minutes later. The building was nestled in woods of tall trees, the forest floor heavy with fallen leaves. As I paid the cab driver, he handed me a scrap of paper.

"It's my cell phone number. Call me when you're ready to leave, and I'll come back." Stunned, I gave him my cell number as well. *Wendie!*

We ventured inside and found Jerry's room. He knew we were coming and I had said a prayer that he might be at his best for our mom. He was. Jerry was alert, funny, lucid, sitting up in bed, and chatty. He didn't look haggard and distressed as he had in the hospital just a few days before. His eyes were bright and clear. *It must be the wonder drugs*, I thought.

I let Mom and Angie hang out with him for a while. God willing, Joe and I would be back. This visit, however, would be their last. I just sat back. As usual, I watched Mom closely for indications of emotional collapse, not that she wasn't entitled. I knew she just wanted to enjoy this priceless and final opportunity with her son, plus it would be very hard on Jerry to see his mother break down in front of him.

Mom did great. Jerry did great. I was *so* relieved.

I left the room a few times to give them an opportunity to visit and meandered about the place. The central gathering area was a little dark and uninviting. I started redecorating for them in my head: change the paint color, brighten up the walls with pictures and mirrors maybe. *Hey, Wendie, they need you down here for a makeover*, I was thinking. Wendie had impeccable taste in furniture selections and accessorizing. She hunted for the perfect accent piece, and her effort showed. Wendie and Jerry's house in Norcross had been warm, inviting, and tasteful. Taken individually, I didn't care for some of the pieces, but brought together they blended seamlessly.

Jerry's private hospice room, however, had an incredible view. The side next to Jerry's bed was a wall of wide, full-length glass looking out onto a courtyard with bird feeders, shrubbery, and the remnants of seasonal flowering perennials, which had graced the grounds with their vibrant colors in the fall. Squirrels scampered over the grounds and up the oaks in search of acorns. I watched a pair chase each other with hilarious antics up, down, over, under, around, and through every branch of every tree. Wendie would have said, "What a hoot!" Those memories made my eyes well up with tears, and I had to quietly exit his room. It would not be me who fell apart that day.

About three o'clock, my cell rang. It was the mysterious cab driver. He was in the parking lot but said to take our time, that there was no hurry. He just wanted me to know he was available whenever we were. *You've outdone yourself, Wendie.* I have always embraced the concept of angels and I couldn't help but think of the magnificent angel my mom had stitched. Suddenly it occurred to me that the cab driver was not a real person; he was an angel sent by Wendie. It made me smile. Never one to be underestimated, Wendie was full of unexpected antics.

Eventually we said our good-byes to Jerry and boarded the cab. The ride back to the airport was eerily quiet. I sat behind the cab driver and pondered his existence. Was it just great, good luck that we had him that day and not some jerky driver grumbling about working on Christmas Day? Or had Wendie really masterminded this fortuitous outcome? I pictured her moving pawn pieces through a maze in heaven, closing and then opening doors to guide and direct us through a seamless journey. I chose to believe the latter. If ever we needed an angel, it was then.

Angie suggested we get sandwiches after checking in at the airport. Mom and I were oblivious to how hungry we were until we smelled the food, so kudos to Angie. Emotionally exhausted, I slept on the flight home. I think my mom did too. It had been the best, most wonderful Christmas present Jerry and I had ever given our mom.

## December 27–31, 2004

I don't really remember the specifics of conversations between Mom and me about our visit with Jerry at the hospice center and his obviously impending death. I know I was afraid to initiate any dialogue for fear of seeing her cry uncontrollably. Perhaps she kept her thoughts private for fear of the same, although I strongly suspected she was in shock.

After Christmas, once Angie and Mom were gone, Joe and I looked into booking a return trip to Atlanta. Angie and her boyfriend, Ryan, later her husband, had left for a week's vacation that would bring them back to our house on New Year's Day evening, hopefully in time to see her and Jerry's alma mater, the University of Michigan, play in the Rose Bowl.

We had just booked tickets for Monday, December 27, through Friday, December 31, when the phone rang. It was a hospice nurse inquiring if I might be coming back. She knew I lived out of state, but Jerry's status was declining rapidly and he probably had only a week. I gulped and replied that we would be flying out later that day.

I checked my e-mail for the last time, just before we left for the airport. My son-in-law Chris sent me an odd, generic message, which read that he and Christie were fine. They were waiting things out at the airport trying to rebook their flights. My daughter and son-in-law were teachers with the Department of Defense living in Seoul, Korea, at the time. I knew they had post-Christmas vacation plans to travel, but I couldn't remember where they were headed. Barely holding up under the weight of phenomenal stress, I felt reassured that they were safe, but also indifferent toward their trivial vacation snafus. I had survived one of the most emotionally raw Christmas Days ever and was about to traverse into the haunting abyss of my brother's eminent death. My stress trumped theirs, or so I thought.

---

Jerry was in and out of alertness on Monday but slipped into a coma on Tuesday. His friends in the area stopped by often. I had a chance to put faces with names and stories that Jerry had graced us with for years. In keeping with my promise not to sit at his bedside in vigil, I visited in the morning and then Joe and I returned together in the afternoon. While I was gone, Joe was busy sorting and packing. We stayed in Jerry's condo and borrowed his car, but his refrigerator was a disaster: seventeen bottles of white wine, a pat of butter, and a block of cheese. I laughed. I knew he didn't cook much, but not even toast?

My husband was the news junky, but, as Christie accurately described me, I lived in a cave as far as current events were concerned. I was wallowing in my own current events as I watched my brother die. Not only was I completely oblivious to the catastrophic meteorological phenomenon occurring in the Indian Ocean, but also to the fact that Christie and Chris were traveling in that direction. As I left Jerry's room late Tuesday morning, I caught a glimpse of news footage on the TV screen in the commons area showing a tidal wave of water. Just then I heard the news commentator say, "This is spectacular aerial footage of the tsunami, traveling at 500 miles an hour, pummeling the coast of Thailand. The popular tourist town of Phuket Island as well as ..." Chills instantly ran down my body. The vacation destination that my daughter and son-in-law were headed to was Phuket Island. Gratefully I knew my daughter was safe before I could worry, thanks to my son-in-law's considerate e-mail. *What a difference a day makes*, I thought. If they had left a day earlier, they would have been on Phuket Island when the postearthquake tsunami hit. We were all going through enough hell!

I talked to Jerry when I visited, having no idea whether he still heard me or not. I reminded him of stories from our childhood, goofy things we did, vacations we took, and I confessed my guilt in things he had been blamed for. I told him we could stay through New Year's Eve and would then be flying home to meet Angie and Ryan. Either Joe and I or possibly just Joe would come back. My husband was retired, but I was supposed to return to work on January 3. Joe had generously offered to camp out in Atlanta as long as it took so that Jerry would never be alone. Maybe Jerry heard me, or maybe Wendie was orchestrating events from above. I tended to think both.

On December 30, Joe and I arrived at Jerry's in the late afternoon. I pulled up a chair to his bed as I always did, and Joe sat near me. Jerry was extremely bloated. His face was ashen white, and his breathing was labored and shallow. I held his swollen, puffy right hand and squeezed it firmly. I released him again, saying, "I love you. I admire you for putting up such a great fight, big brother, but your time is soon and you don't have to hang around for me." Then I added with a touch of humor, "Plus, Wendie is waiting for you."

As I looked up, I could see out the wall of glass windows, past the natural courtyard and beyond, into the forest of tall, slender trees devoid of leaves. It looked like the woods formed a protective enclosure, shielding the occupants from intrusions from the outside world. It was a beautiful, peaceful, serene setting, and I savored our time with Jerry in silence as the seconds ticked away.

The sun was just starting its final descent for the day. Its light glistened through gently waving branches that moved under the powerful wind's control. Unique shadows were created on Jerry's blankets as the twigs danced back and forth, letting in more light or less. I just sat there, his hand in mine, staring at the slowly setting sun, when Jerry took his last breath. I waited. I said a prayer for him and my mom. I waited some more. Then I quietly told Joe that I thought he was gone. More time passed by while I held his hand. Finally I stood up, leaned over, and kissed him good-bye for the very last time.

Eventually, Joe stepped out to notify the nurse. She came in, and Jerry was pronounced. We waited silently for the coroner. It was dark by then. The end of this day had brought the end of his life.

I signed some papers, and after a few hours, we left. I was a wreck. I called my cousin Mike in Sedona and my aunt Dee in Chicago and left a message for Angie while she was on vacation. Then I called my mom's closest girlfriend, Shirley, and asked her to drive over to my mom's and tell her in person. I couldn't imagine receiving that news. I was struggling enough, and he wasn't my son. The parent–child bond never erodes, no matter how old your child is, and Mom had lost two. How grotesquely, unspeakably, brutal Mom's pain must be. I couldn't imagine and said a prayer that I never would.

I drove over the first weekend in January after Jerry's death to check on Mom. She was holding up pretty well, all things considered. "I didn't see him regularly, of course, but I got lengthy e-mails every morning," Mom told me through her tears. I couldn't do anything except hug her tightly and be there for her. I felt completely worthless at easing her sorrow. Gradually I took on a more protective role. Apparently I revved up a little too high and into hover mode, as sometimes she told me I was "bossy" and needed to back off.

"I'm a survivor," she said proudly.

Indeed she was.

### February 2005

Aunt Dee spent several weeks in Sedona at her son Mike's in February. After my dad's passing, Mom was free to travel so she had planned to go out for a week also. I took advantage of the overlapping visits to schedule a small memorial for Jerry in Sedona where Joe, Angie, and I would join everyone. Jerry was averse to winter, so warm Sedona made at least some sense. We arrived at Mike's beautiful home in its natural setting in the foothills.

I was barely in the door at Mike and Linda's place when Mike took me aside and whispered, "Aunt Betty thinks she's at Friendship Village. She asked this morning where her room was, number 342."

I should have been alarmed, but just like with Angie's concern about Mom's confusion over the Sydney Olympics, I chalked it up to stress and dismissed it. I shouldn't have—not regarding the Olympics and not regarding Sedona. It wasn't just stress. It was a warning sign. I held myself accountable for blowing off these cautionary concerns brought to my attention by family who loved and cared about her. If stress was a catalyst for dementia, Mom was certainly a candidate. I would always regret not addressing these issues earlier.

## Spring 2005

On the lovely, well-landscaped grounds of Friendship Village was an area designated as the Woods—literally a dense woods of tall trees and blooming shrubs with a blacktopped path meandering through it. Residents were permitted to plant additional trees or bushes in memory of their loved ones. After Dad and Jerry passed away, Mom selected a Norway maple, had it planted, and placed a plaque on the site that read, "In Memory of My Boys—Wayne, Jerry, and David." She loved walking and working out there.

Judy wrote, "Betty's heart was impassioned with the success of the woods. She had been a major contributor in sweat to its success."

# CHAPTER 25

## *Finicky Finances*

### June 2004

As Jerry's courageous battle against cancer was coming to an end, he asked me to be the executrix of his estate. I was both honored and overwhelmed by the prospect. Jerry was a wizard at finances, and although I understood home mortgages and checking accounts, I wasn't even close to his level. In fact, my parents had asked him to review their finances back in 2000, not long after they had moved into Friendship Village. Dad had retired as a financial controller for Borgess Hospital and Mom was a math major, so they both had math brains, as did Jerry of course. They told me they wanted a fresh financial assessment, and Jerry was the natural choice.

Jerry called me after he completed his doubtless thorough review of their financial position. "I looked over Mom and Dad's accounts, and they'll be fine," he told me when he called. That's all I heard. He definitely didn't just leave it at that, but whatever additional information he shared was lost on my financially deaf ears.

It wouldn't be until May 2005, when I had to step up, that I fully absorbed what he had said so casually to me years earlier. I had much to learn after he was gone, but gradually, with a lot of guidance from others, especially Joe, I felt reasonably comfortable helping Mom with money management. But it wasn't without drama!

## 2005

In my new role as Mom's everything—financial assistant (make sure she doesn't invest in a Jim Bakker evangelist scam), technology guru (get her an answering machine that actually answers), strategist (get her a key hook so she doesn't keep losing her car and apartment keys), travel agent (help her get to my house from Kalamazoo without actually allowing her to drive there)—I stepped up to juggle whatever other balls the future would throw at me. And there would be more than I could possibly imagine.

Mom scheduled an appointment for me to meet with her financial planner, Todd, on the Friday of Memorial Day weekend in 2005. I drove over early in the morning from my house in my Crossfire for an eleven o'clock appointment. It was a beautiful, sunny day, and I got there in record time. Could it be the little red sports car? About an hour before Todd was to arrive, I asked my mom for any account information she could locate.

"The Valic ones are in here," she said as she pulled out an old, plastic file-folder box. Indeed they were. On the manila file folder tab in her beautiful handwriting was written "Valic." I took out the folder and removed the most recent statement. Then she produced a different account folder and handed it to me.

"This account," she said, pointing to the Valic one, "Dad and I set up with after-tax dollars."

*After-tax dollars? What does that mean?* I thought.

"And this account," she went on, referring to the second statement, "is a retirement fund. I have a minimum distribution from it each year. When it is liquidated, taxes still have to be paid on it. Uncle Sam always has to get his cut."

She handed me the second statement and left the bedroom. I could feel my head starting to pound. It was a whirlwind of papers, statements, and after-tax and before-tax stuff. She was going to have to help me help her. I was clueless about what she had and what she was even talking about. I calculated the total between the two accounts in my mildly aching head. *Not bad,* I thought.

"Here's the one from Edward Jones," she said as she walked back in. "The taxes have been paid on this one too." I added this amount to the total of the other two. *Seriously? Where's the Tylenol?*

"Well, Mom," I began, "I'm not sure exactly what your monthly expenses are or if you have any other sources of income, but this is a pretty decent nest egg."

"Dad and I worked very hard to save and invest," she replied with a slight tear in the corner of her eye. "Sometimes I thought he made financial decisions to pay off the house early or save more money that limited us from doing things and going places. I didn't always agree with him, but it was something he felt we should do."

I pondered this revelation for a moment. "You know, Mom, Dad grew up in abject poverty. I remember using the outhouse at Grandma Ward's while your house had indoor plumbing. Maybe he was just financially prudent, given what little he grew up with."

While I was yapping, she was hunting for something, although I think she heard me. The next thing I knew, she was handing me yet another statement, the fourth. "This is the last one. It's a retirement fund also—you know, where the taxes aren't paid on it yet."

I recognized the four interlocking hands on the logo. What might this statement reveal? As I peeled away the first page to unmask the second, the proverbial bottom line stared at me in huge black numbers. I remember sitting down on the bed, groping for yet another Tylenol as my head throbbed. I collected all four statements, jotted down the totals of each one, and then literally felt my jaw drop as the reality of her healthy financial picture started to sink in.

"Wow, Mom. This is a pretty impressive estate," I finally said as I heard Todd knock on the door.

Our exchange was pleasant and fairly benign. I took notes, trying to sort out what all the jargon meant. Mom seemed to be keeping up with Todd. He did make some recommendations for "next time," which I noted. We scheduled the subsequent meeting for late summer, just not on a golf Thursday. When he left, I asked my mom if I could make copies of her financial papers, but she suggested I just take them with me. "I get new ones every month," she said.

I drove home later that day in my little red sports car somewhat numb and yet pleased that she was so comfortable financially. Now I understood what Jerry had meant years ago by "They'll be fine." I guess! Good job, Dad. The man who was born into a life of poverty and was determined to make his adult life better had accomplished that and more.

My husband reviewed the statements with me at home and was also a little stunned that my dad could have amassed a virtual small fortune on what he probably made. My mom had worked full time but only for twelve years. Joe patiently explained to me the need-to-know details of each account. Then the proverbial light bulb went off in my head: Microsoft. Dad had invested in Microsoft at some point, apparently, and had made a financial killing when he sold it. I vaguely recalled a conversation years ago that I had only half listened to when he rambled on in his poststroke, slightly dysarthric speech about investments and Microsoft. What a quiet, lucky genius he was. My dad didn't know how to be a play-on-the-floor parent, but he was a great provider. Because of his commitment, my mom would have a very good life, at least financially, anyway.

## Spring 2006

Todd, my mom, and I met once more in August 2005. I still didn't know what I didn't know, so I just sat there furiously taking notes. I went over them with Joe later for his thoughts, assuming I could still decipher them. No financial alarms went off from Joe's perspective regarding my mom's money matters.

Sometime in the spring of 2006, Joe and I drove over together to visit and take Mom out to dinner. In addition to generic chatter about kids, Joe's retirement since 2004, and so on, we always provided Mom the opportunity to go over her finances and answer any questions she might have. My hubby did a much better job than I about understanding and explaining the details to her. As I sat on the floor rifling through the assortment of financial statements, bank as well as investment accounts, Joe and Mom sat next to each other on the couch to look over her list of questions. I had collated the statements into color-coded notebooks, more for my benefit than hers. She had a few miscellaneous pieces of paper already separated to one side for Joe's review.

"What is this one?" Mom asked Joe.

"This is confirmation of an account transfer. You must have moved this account here," he said as he pointed to the paper she held between them, "to this one. The new account is now invested in an annuity. It—" Joe was quickly interrupted by a sudden outburst of, "What annuity?"

"I didn't agree to any annuity. Dad and I loathed annuities, and I never would have agreed to it." She was hot. The sudden change in her voice pitch and prosody was completely uncharacteristic for her. I got up off the floor and pulled over a chair to see what she was so upset about. I had no idea what an annuity was and felt puzzled but also concerned.

"This is dated February 7, 2006," I offered. "I think I remember you telling me that Todd had been here in February, but I know I wasn't."

I had copious notes from all of my visits and was scanning them for anything that could shed some light on this annuity thing that was upsetting her so much. I always transcribed them from my scribbled handwritten notes. I found an entry confirming that Todd had met with her in February 2006, but I wasn't at that meeting. I remember Joe explaining to her that, although an annuity at her age was quite unusual, it was guaranteed for a reasonably decent rate of return. I don't think she heard a single word he said, although I was paying attention.

"I didn't want this. I didn't sign this. That Todd …" she was miffed.

I didn't really know what to say to reassure her. I hadn't been there in February so I didn't know what had been discussed. I didn't have a reason to suspect malfeasance, but clearly she was fuming.

"Todd must have forged my signature. They can do that, you know." Her voice had suddenly taken on a sinister, eerie tone.

I could hardly believe my ears—"forged my signature"? Maybe Todd hadn't been very clear or perhaps she hadn't understood him or both, but Todd had not forged her signature.

"Mom," I started. I held her hand gently and looked right at her so she could both hear and process my remarks. "I don't know whether the annuity is a good financial instrument or not. And I'm sorry I wasn't here when you and Todd met, but he did not forge your signature. He certainly may have been misleading, but not illegal. How about if Joe and I get into this a little more? Could we borrow the contract so we can review it?" I kept my voice calm and steady.

Almost instantly she settled down. "Of course," she said as she handed Joe the folder.

She seemed to accept this idea as reassuring. I took advantage of the lull in the drama to suggest we go to dinner.

Joe carefully reviewed the contract terms of the annuity after we returned home and reiterated that it was an odd choice as a financial instrument, but he found no indication of fraud. Of course, he agreed with me that there was no way Todd or anyone else forged her signature. For my mom, however, it was a tender subject that triggered instant hostility, and eventually she lobbied for a change in advisers. My financially savvy and connected son-in-law Ryan provided Mom with a short list of individuals in her area. She interviewed them on her own, without me, and apparently felt she connected well with Jeff from Merrill Lynch. She appreciated Jeff's willingness to correspond with her via e-mail, plus he was local. At least one dilemma was resolved.

# CHAPTER 26

## *Pretty in Pink*

### Winter 2010

The way I drove, the trip to Kalamazoo took two hours, driveway to door. My brother and I had agreed several years before, especially after our dad's stroke, that one or the other of us would make the Kalamazoo journey at least every four weeks. And we did until Jerry couldn't any longer. After that, I was religious about getting to my mom's or having her at my place every month.

My husband joined me sometimes, but usually I made a day trip by myself. My mom recovered fairly well, all things considered, after my dad's and Jerry's deaths. She had prepared herself for a long time. "Death by inches," she called it, referring to Dad's slow but progressively downward nine-year trek to his death poststroke. She had been an unwavering caregiver for him and I admired her ability to sustain the promise she had made over fifty years earlier when they were married. "For better and for worse, until death do us part."

After Mom's Christmas packing debacle, I was more observant of her clothing choices and suspicious of her laundry skills. She had mentioned months earlier that Friendship Village had gotten new washers and dryers on each floor. I strongly suspected that she might not be able to transition to new appliances.

"What do you think of them?" I asked. "Are they better?" I was curious about how revealing her responses might be.

"I guess," she answered. "I still have to refer to the manual."

Alarms went off in my head. *Refer to the manual?* I seriously doubted that she could read and process the directions for the washer and dryer, especially after seeing her in a trance with the company cauliflower recipe. I visually scanned the clothes she was wearing for stains or soil marks like an airport screener looking for evidence of weapons. She passed, at least this time. How tragic that the person who used to be so tastefully dressed could not recognize a dirt spot on a sweater or chocolate dribbles on her pants.

The clothes in her bedroom closet were the first on my scrutiny list. I pawed through everything hanging there—each pair of slacks, every blouse, sweater, and jacket. Items that failed the clean wardrobe test were confiscated for laundering. She protested at first. "I can do my own laundry. You don't have to do it." But then she relinquished the clothes since she saw that I was not budging. I would scoop them up, wash them at my house, and return them on the next visit.

Mom always looked pretty in pink, except when that's the only color she wore. Despite an abundance of clearly clean clothes in every other color and style, I often saw her in pink. Deteriorating circumstances required that I make more frequent trips to Kalamazoo in 2010 and every time I visited, she was in pink. I wondered that she might actually be wearing the *exact* same pink outfit over and over and it wasn't getting washed. I made mental note to check specifically which pair of pink pants and blouse she was wearing. When I saw her yet again in the same, but clearly soiled pink clothes, I flat-out asked her to change into something else. She averted the suggestion—which, in fact, it wasn't really—by changing the subject. After a few minutes, I asked her again, but she started to become annoyed. I tried a more direct approach.

"Mom, can't you see the pants are dirty and the blouse is too?" I pointed to the stains.

"I'll wash it later, tomorrow." Her voice pitch was escalating. I knew she wouldn't launder it, but she was also becoming testy at my inquiry. I dropped it but only temporarily while I pondered alternative strategies to handle the situation. Several minutes passed, and she seemed oblivious to the previous conversation. I brought out a pair of clean, deep-green slacks and a coordinating pink and green blouse and jacket, ones that I knew she had always favored in the past.

"I haven't seen you wear this in a while," I said. "It has always been a favorite of mine."

"Mine too," she replied.

"So maybe you could try it on and see if it still fits," I said. I watched her facial expression carefully, knowing I might elicit an avalanche of hostile emotions.

"I think it still fits, but okay," she said.

And with that placid suggestion, she complied—changed out of the dirty pink and into the clean green. I quickly scooped up the soiled clothes, lest she put it on the next day, so I could sneak them home for laundering. I would need these intervention techniques and many more as time went on: listen, wait, and redirect.

# CHAPTER 27

## *Undercover Daughter*

February–March 2010

It would be a tricky operation to mastermind and execute, but I was up to the challenge. In mid-January 2010, after visiting Woodside (the assisted-living facility that Judy had recommended) Joe suggested perhaps Mom's wonderful internist, Dr. Bradtke, in Portage might be a good person to communicate with in her behalf. I had been struggling to balance what Judy was telling me about my mom with what I experienced when I was with her. I saw Mom differently—goofy at times, but not frequently hostile or unsafe. Of course I wanted to do the right thing by her, but I wasn't sure what that was, exactly.

With all of the HIPAA laws and confidentiality policies in an increasingly litigious society, I knew I couldn't just pick up the phone and expect Dr. Bradtke to chat with me. Actually, I had not met him, further complicating the possibility of any meaningful dialogue even if I could get past the insulating wall of receptionists, secretaries, and nursing personnel.

"I'll have to make an appointment for my mom with  Dr. Bradtke and accompany her," I informed Joe.

"Will she welcome you, or perceive your presence as intrusive?" he asked.

I started laughing. "Oh, she'll be miffed all right. I'll have to

160

come up with a ruse. She doesn't drive anymore so that helps as far as providing transportation, but she'll object to my actually going in with her to the appointment. At least I think so, anyway."

Mom had been very protective about her independence, although I had seen cracks in that resolve already. She had gratefully handed over her checking account to me just after Christmas. Assistance in Living had been doling out her medications for more than a year, and she had just relinquished her car and driving without being prodded.

If I orchestrated the events carefully and was creative with my reasons for accompanying her, I could probably mount a successful coup and maneuver myself into the doctor's office. I felt like an espionage agent, crafting an alter ego and practicing my story so I wouldn't get caught in a lie. Although I considered the possibility that she might not be astute enough any longer to catch me in one, I wasn't about to underestimate her either.

I called Dr. Bradtke's office the next day. I explained succinctly to the receptionist—responsible for making appointments and the first line of defense in protecting her boss from attack—the five W's: who (I was), what (I wanted), when (I needed it), where (she/I lived), and why (I was calling). It worked. She would have Dr. Bradtke's nurse Susan call me back.

When Susan returned my call a few hours later, we had a wonderful conversation. She commiserated with me about my concerns from her own personal experiences. She was totally in cahoots about getting me in to see the doctor without ticking off my mom or demeaning her. I could handle covert operations if the office played along. As Dr. Bradtke did not see patients on Friday afternoons, Susan suggested that we take the last appointment on a Friday morning so that he could spend more time with us. I thanked her and was very appreciative of her cooperation.

Mom's appointment was scheduled on a Friday for mid-March 2010 at 11:30 a.m. I e-mailed her with a fabricated story, saying that Dr. Bradtke's nurse, Susan, had contacted me because she had not been able to reach Mom by phone, a very plausible situation as my mom never seemed to answer even her CapTel phone any more. Mom had a newer captioned telephone that instantly transcribed into readable text what the speaker was saying. She could read the screen and then answer verbally. It worked much faster and better than the previous ticker-tape-like device. Mom had successfully used the CapTel phone for several years to set up her own appointments but that skill had waned like many others.

March could be such an ugly, gray month, and this early morning drive over from my place to hers, wasn't any different. At least it wasn't snowing, a distinct possibility with Michigan's unpredictable winter weather. My thoughts wandered in anticipation of various scenarios, comments, or questions that Mom might come up with. Good thing too. I was practically met at the apartment door with her suspicious tone.

She started right off with, "I don't understand why they called you." Calm, but probing.

"Dr. Bradtke's nurse told me their office has been trying to reach you, but you never answered your captioned phone." I waited a moment. It seemed to be working so far. "And honestly, Mom, I also have tried to reach you by phone occasionally without success." So far it was going okay.

"I don't talk on the phone much," she said. I doubted she had initiated any appointments with Dr. Bradtke in some time. Friendship Village's nursing staff would have contacted his office for prescription refills in Mom's behalf once they started handling Mom's medications.

We hung out at her place for an hour while I did my routine paper-sorting ritual. I had established a program in which I asked Mom to carry out specific assignments so we could work together. "Could you please staple these papers?" "This goes in the black file box next to you." She felt useful and was indeed helpful. Sometimes she had strange responses to the directions, though. I remember her staring at letters, glossy newspaper ads, and pieces of just junk mail for an inordinate amount of time. She looked stuck, like she couldn't move past that moment in time. If it lasted too long, I would prompt her with, "Is that something you would like me to look at too?" Usually she just put it down and went on to something else. I also observed her remove papers from the trash occasionally and set them aside. *Odd*, I thought, but it was more than odd. These were the types of behaviors, taken collectively, that Judy saw and could interpret as indicators of underlying dementia. She understood the significance, but I did not, at least not quite yet.

The fifteen-minute drive over to Portage for her appointment with Dr. Bradtke was easy. We didn't even have time to sit down when the nurse Susan came to get both of us. I was again navigating in uncharted waters. Would Mom let me accompany her into the exam room? If not, I had a backup plan. But the nurse was in collusion with me and simply said, "I'll have your daughter come in with you for now." Seamlessly Mom and I walked in together. Susan's smile discreetly met mine.

Dr. Bradtke came in the room and enthusiastically greeted my mom and introduced himself to me. I liked him instantly. His presence could fill a room. He was funny, appropriate, and just "got it." He reminded me of Dr. Dowd, our family doctor when I was a kid.

Dr. Bradtke asked my mom permission to speak with me while she was sitting right there. He was polite and validating to her. I briefly explained, although he had already been clued in, that I was having trouble gauging the need for more supervision for Mom and that if she did need it, as the Friendship Village staff felt, then I would seriously consider relocating her to the east side of the state. Mom's close friends, husband, and sons were already gone, so any decisions rested on my shoulders. Addressing Mom's evolving situation and possibly uprooting her would be tricky, but he was completely on board.

Then he turned his attention to my mom. When asked, Mom knew about what time it was (noon), what month it was (March), and the day of the week (Friday). She was iffy on the date (me too) and of course knew her name, my name, and his. He asked who the current president was (Obama), the governor (Granholm), and some other random questions to assess her orientation. She did very well on these. He finished his exam, and we chatted a little more about her general physical health. He talked to and with her throughout the appointment and periodically couched a discreet, probing question my way. "Does she still drive?" (No.) "Does she need to cook for herself?" (No.) "Handle her finances?" (No.)

I walked out with Dr. Bradtke while Mom got dressed. He indicated that she certainly may need an environment that provided more supervision and greater assistance eventually, but it did not appear that she required it then. I felt relieved that we viewed her condition similarly, albeit mistakenly. But based on what we both saw—and he knew her very well—Mom appeared medically stable and adequately oriented. In his setting, for an hour's appointment, or when I hung out with Mom for a day, her strengths surfaced. It was in everyday life that she was failing.

Then Dr. Bradtke made me a generous offer. "Now that we've met, we can dialogue in the future if things change for your mom. You can call me anytime." I felt so humbled. I also felt extremely appreciative that he opened the door of reciprocal communication for me and I would use it in the months ahead.

Mom and I went to lunch. At the café, we discussed her long history with Dr. Bradtke. She told me how she and Dad had first started with him, details of subsequent appointments, this and that. I was spellbound, not necessarily because of the information but because of the fluidity and consistency of her dialogue, her facial expressions, and her hand gestures that were so familiar.

She grabbed the check, which she hadn't done in a very long time. She and Joe used to pretend arm wrestle for it, but he always let her win even though he felt his mother-in-law shouldn't pick up the tab. When the waitress returned with my mom's charge slip, though, things fell apart instantly. Mom didn't remember having pulled out her credit card and didn't know where to sign or why. I guided her through those steps, including helping with the tip calculations. She stared at the printed name on the Visa card in front of her.

"This says Elizabeth O. Ward."

I was puzzled at why she was puzzled. "Yes. Is there a problem, Mom?" I asked.

"This is my name." Mom's previously soft, pleasant voice tone was gone.

"Yes. This is your Visa card."

"How did it get here? Did they steal my card?"

I responded quickly to defuse any further escalation of her emotions. I could picture a sudden outburst of accusations in the restaurant.

"Mom," I said, putting my hand over hers, "you got out your charge card to pay the bill. The waitress just returned it to you. That's why you are holding it in your hand. That is your card." If I didn't need to say any more, I wouldn't. Less was better.

"Oh, I did? I don't remember," she said. "It's hard to remember a lot of things."

No truer words were ever spoken. Intermittently my mom knew her memory was sketchy. We were just getting in the car when the waitress ran out, waving Mom's credit card in her hand to get our attention. Mom had left it on the table. I was rethinking how accurate Dr. Bradtke's assessment of her was after all.

# CHAPTER 28
## *The Ugly Truth*

February 2010

My parents moved into their one-bedroom apartment at Friendship Village in October of 1999. Every ten years, residents were eligible to have their places decorated. Mom's tenth anniversary was in October of 2009, but nothing tangible had occurred so far. She and I occasionally talked about what she might want: change up the paint, maybe get different drapes or a wallpaper border.

"I'm so tired of these boring, white walls," she had said several times. "I wonder how long I'll have to wait before they decide to do my place."

There was a distinct tone of sarcasm in her voice. I was hearing it more often. I downplayed it, staying on point.

"Do they initiate arrangements for repainting, or do you have to fill out a requisition form?" I asked. Whenever residents needed maintenance to replace a light bulb, repair a broken handle, or hang a heavy picture, they completed a requisition form available at the reception desk.

"I'm sure I'll have to keep on them to get it done," she replied. It sounded like she was growling under her breath.

I did not respond. I was not exactly sure what to suggest that would be productive but not provoking. A few seconds passed, and then she added, "I'd like these walls green, and the bedroom pink." *Yuck!* I thought.

"Sounds very pretty, Mom," I managed to say without rolling my eyes. "Are you thinking of a green like this," I said, poking at a the tapestry weave of her couch, "or something more like this?" I was trying to steer her toward the subtle hues of gray-green and not the stronger, in-your-face blue-green.

"I think this is too dark," she said as she pointed to a deep green accent color in the floral pattern. On this we agreed.

"I have a paint color chart at home and will bring it with me next time so you can look at some ideas," I said.

Mom's journal was always with me. It got heavier every month. I summarized the day's events and made a note to bring the paint card samples on my next visit.

March 2010

"Well, isn't that the cat's meow." Mom was clearly thrilled with the paint samples fanned out in front of her. I suppressed a little snicker. She had a lot of colorful idioms, but this one was just goofy—not that she had made it up, but she used it enough.

From what I could determine, the redecorating project had stalled, but Mom's answers to my questions were inconsistent and misleading. Sometimes she claimed that the project manager, Mike, "was too busy with empty units" to do hers or said, "I think they're deliberately putting me off."

*Enough already*, I thought and I decided to take control. "I'll be right back, Mom, okay? Then we'll head out to lunch."

"Sure, honey."

As I made my way to the front desk to talk to Mike directly, I heard a deep sigh; it had come from me. Again I was stymied by the paranoid tone of Mom's answers. It was increasingly more difficult to ascertain any specific facts, even face-to-face. Mike wasn't available then, so I left him a brief note and my contact information. When he called a few days later, I was a little taken aback when I heard his side of the dragging decorating project.

"I've been up several times to talk with your mom," he said. "Either she isn't there or, if she is, she won't make a decision about what she wants, so that's why nothing has been done."

I could understand the "she wasn't there" part since she missed appointments and didn't always know when I was coming, but I didn't understand the "won't make a decision" part. She had been pretty clear about the paint colors. I made a plan to meet with him at my mom's apartment at the end of the week.

She was quite specific when we reviewed the paint plan. Should the kitchen be green? Yes. Paint the bathroom? No. End the pink here? Yes. When Mike arrived, we sailed through paint colors, and then he set down two boards of carpet samples in front of her. Instantly, like a light switch that had just shorted out, she was gone. She couldn't comment on Berber versus plush, light versus dark, anything.

"I don't know," she said. And she really didn't know. This wasn't, "I can't decide because there are too many choices" or "I'm not sure which one will look best." This was, "I don't know what we're doing." Her expressions and nonverbal body language changed from clear and with it to dark and in pain so fast that it was scary.

I tried to jiggle her light switch with cautious remarks like, "The Berber is nice, but in the past you've liked plush carpet. I think maybe the plush?" It wasn't really a question but phrased such that it left the door open for her should she suddenly return to the project at hand and render an opinion. Nothing. I removed the Berber samples from view. "Are there any of these you like?"

"Something neutral?" she said eventually. Progress.

There were maybe sixteen different three-inch-by-three-inch carpet samples on the floor. I quickly grabbed a couple of file folders lying around and used them to cover up two rows of darker carpets and used my hand to mask two more, leaving six neutral ones. With my other hand, I spread my fingers apart and rested them over three contenders and said, "These are good colors for this room, Mom," and then I pointed to one and added, "but this one might be the best." I glanced up at Mike for any input he might have; he nodded in agreement.

"Sure. That's fine," she said. Her voice was flat, but at least she was back. She got up to go lay down on the bed, and I wrapped things up with Mike. He scheduled the project for early April. I would be in Germany then, but Mom had already refused many times to come over to my place while the project was underway. She was *adamant* about being there. After Mike was gone and Mom had gotten up, I made sure she wrote the project date on her purse and wall calendars. They had literally been her lifelines, but she wasn't able to use them very effectively anymore. There were a few more critical details to go over with her.

"Mom," I said, looking right at her, "this will be a disruptive week for you while this project gets done. You will be staying in one of the guest rooms when they paint and recarpet."

"I know. It will be a bit of a mess, but it will be fine," she replied.

I *so* wanted to believe her, but I really should have known she wouldn't be fine. I had just seen her space right out when the innocuous task of picking a carpet befuddled her. This on/off, in/out, up/down behavior of hers was so erratic and mystifying that it clouded my judgment at my mom's expense.

Judy had already suggested that perhaps the chaos of such a project might not be in my mom's best interest. Unfortunately, I was part of the problem. I saw my mom as a glass half full, mostly together except for some episodes of disorientation when, in fact, she was more half empty with fleeting moments of lucidity. I wasn't seeing the day-to-day blunders, errors in judgment, outbursts, confusion, obsession, and paranoia, just to name a few. If I had really seen them, if I had really grasped the depth of her situation, I would *never* have sanctioned such a massive, disruptive decorating disaster. Consistent with the expression "Some things happen for a reason," it would be the ugly culmination of this specific project that would finally enlighten me to my mom's condition.

As a parent, you question, think about, and muse over your child's pleas for a puppy and your teenager's request for the car or a delayed curfew. But as the adult, the nebulous abyss of being a parent to your parent is a delicate responsibility. Balancing respect and autonomy and naturally expecting them to be accurate when they tell you, "I'll be fine" is a daunting challenge. Somewhere deep down, you know it's not true. They are no longer "fine."

### April 2010

The first sign of trouble was an e-mail I received from Judy. I was in Germany visiting my daughter Christie, son-in-law Chris, and grandson Isaac at Easter. Judy had arranged for some staff to pack up my mom's things so her curio cabinets and such could be moved for the painting project and carpet removal. Between e-mails and a phone call to Michigan from Germany via free voice-over-Internet, I had learned that my mom had become very upset—more like ballistic, frantic, agitated, and accusatory—that people were taking her things. She thought her lamp had been stolen, couldn't understand why strangers were in her room, and demanded to be shown where her lamp was—more than once actually. Honestly, a lamp?

I literally could not even begin to imagine how catastrophically out of control she was already, and it was only Tuesday. The redecorating project had just begun. Collectively, Judy and I decided to cancel the new carpet as Mom probably wouldn't even notice the difference. I had no idea to what extent she had emotionally unraveled over her furniture being moved in order to paint, how threatening she had interpreted unfamiliar faces in her room to be, how all encompassing her personal crisis was. I was just sitting on the floor at my daughter's in Germany, playing with my grandson, oblivious to the nightmare my mom was living.

Just before I flew home, a follow-up e-mail from Judy indicated that the painting was finished and that Mom liked it, but she wanted her original drapes back, the ones on the traverse rods. Judy asked if I knew where they might be since Friendship Village didn't have them. Judy added, "Betty's apartment painting project had produced huge levels of anxiety and frustration. She came down to the desk or my office with increasing frequency and fervor and was considerably more agitated."

---

"I have no idea what drapes she's talking about," I said when relating the decorating drama to Joe after returning from visiting the kids. Only my version was considerably more benign than the truth. "Mom had those ugly, green, swag sheer things, which aren't going back up, but before that there were white ones."

I was absolutely positive, after really giving it some thought, that there had only been two different window coverings in her apartment over the ten years. I had spoken with Mike a few times to that effect, but he said my mom was adamant about missing traverse draperies, so they kept looking. Mom was fragmenting more and oriented less. Details from her past took center stage and became her present, blurring her reality and pummeling sound reason and judgment to near death. She also had less energy to fight the demons ravaging her memory.

"I can only recall the green sheers," Joe said. "Well, when you're there next week, I hope things get resolved."

Not even close. There was no resolution forthcoming in our Ouija board. I drove to Kalamazoo at the end of the week.

"Do you like the wall color, Mom?" I asked.

She just beamed. "Yes. It's perfect." She loved the color of her apartment. I thought it was hideous. I am not a fan of baby pink, nor the green of the living room, but all that really mattered was that she liked it. Then suddenly, without warning, she ranted, "But I want those drapes back. They say they can't find them, but I bet they lost them." She reminded me of a rabid dog.

I took a deep breath and reached my hand out to hers,

cautiously. When she stopped spouting, we sat down on her couch. I kept my voice very calm and started slowly, one query at a time.

"Mom, what drapes are you talking about?"

"The traverse ones …" She rambled on and on about phantom drapes that had never existed, but I let her finish and was careful.

"Mom, I don't believe you had traverse drapes in this apartment. When you and Dad first moved in, there were white ones with cascading side panels."

I went on to illustrate them carefully and accurately. I clustered the descriptive words together and paused after each grouping slightly, hoping she could envision them in her mind as I spoke. Unbeknownst to me, it wasn't working. "A few years back," I continued, "you had them replaced with the green sheers." No response. I waited. She didn't appear to be pouting, just staring blankly. Then she spoke, not even looking at me.

"They won't give me my drapes back." Her voice resembled a hiss.

From my warped perspective, I thought that if I could convince her that traverse drapes had never existed in her apartment, she wouldn't feel so paranoid and angry that someone had lost them. Wrong! I was attempting to apply reasoning and logic to someone who was no longer capable of higher executive thinking.

I made one more disastrous attempt. "You never had traverse drapes in this apartment, Mom." Calm but too confrontational.

Immediately, she burst into tears and buried her head in her hands, her shoulders shaking hard in an emotional outburst. She mumbled something completely inaudible. I knelt in front of her, wrapped my arms around her, and hugged her tightly. Baffled, stressed, and utterly mystified by her tearful explosion, I genuinely didn't know what to do next. Finally, after what seemed like forever, her crying subsided and she lifted her head. I relaxed my comfort hold on her and rested my hands on her still quivering shoulders.

She looked right at me. "Why don't you believe me, Elaine?" she asked.

My first reaction was to reassure her that I did believe her and to try again to explain the nonexistent traverse drapes. A flood of conflicting ideas and approaches was whirling in my head. Then, suddenly, abruptly, and with stunning clarity, I got it! With her words and in that instant, I had an epiphany. For the first time, it all made sense to me, and I really understood with complete clarity how severely compromised she was.

Her memory demise was so substantial that her past and present were entirely blurred. She was thinking about our house on Olney Street. *That* house had traverse drapes everywhere. She had sewn most of the original drapes herself. I felt so stupid and yet oddly relieved. Judy had been trying to tell me for some time how flawed my mom's judgment was, how paranoid, confused, and challenged Mom was most of the time. I had indeed witnessed all of those behaviors, but intermittently, not daily, because I was there intermittently, not daily. Floundering along without a plan did not bode well for me, but I was quickly developing a new strategy.

First, I projected a reassuring tone and responded to her last accusation. "I do believe you, Mom, but I need you to trust me." My hands had not left her quivering shoulders, but slowly I could feel her trembling subside slightly.

"I do trust you," she said. Her voice was reaffirming. The emotional tables had flipped, and now she appeared to be comforting me, possibly shaken that she had inadvertently projected an element of mistrust in her daughter. It was perfect. Then I strategically skirted her original assertion: "The old drapes wouldn't look good in here anyway, Mom. Let's get someone to come out and measure for new ones, whatever you want. I'll take care of it."

A smile was forming on her face. "Sure," she said.

I couldn't help but think about the ironic analogy of traverse drapes being pulled open by the cord, revealing the brightness of a new day. It applied to both of us, albeit in different contexts. With the promise of replacement drapes, she was calm again. With newfound incredible clarity, I could carve a plan. Judy had projected perfectly back in January that she expected my mom to need Woodside by September. How did she know? Why didn't I?

There were some surprisingly lucid and revealing moments that day. Seemingly out of nowhere, she admitted, "I know I'm having a lot of difficulty remembering things, Elaine. It's terrible knowing you're not with it sometimes. I hope that if this is genetic, your brothers David or Jerry inherited this gene and not you." It took everything I had to suppress the tears and let her continue. I was sitting down next to her. "I don't know how much longer I will be able to stay where I am. My close girlfriends are already gone so ..." She didn't finish as her voice trailed off.

I took advantage of this perfect opportunity and responded, "Mom, you are right. You might have to move, and if you do, I want you closer to me."

"That would be fine. I would like to see you more often."

With that, I had her permission to launch into making some proactive decisions. Mom would have to be moved. I wasn't sure exactly where that would be, but most likely it would not be Woodside. The two-hour drive home that evening afforded me lots of time to decide that the two-hour drive sucked. I most certainly would investigate options nearer my home, but for now, the drapery project would proceed. I didn't know how long it would take before everything else would fall into place. A peace came over me. The day's clarity solidified my acceptance, which in turn helped me develop a plan. The tranquility wouldn't last long and I would have to take each validating, positive moment and savor it to power through the torturous times ahead.

Judy said of my mom, "She knew her memory was weakening. A resident once told me a story about Betty. Betty said that she walked and walked so she could strengthen her mind because there was a history of Alzheimer's in her family and she wanted to beat it."

There was no way to know for sure, but I wanted to believe that perhaps her generally good physical health reinforced through her daily treks about the Village complex and the Woods, her lifelong success with weight management, and her bright, positive attitude had at least stalled the ravages of Dementia.

# CHAPTER 29
## The Spirit of Oberon

Late April–Mother's Day 2010

"That's so sad. It's such a shame to see a vibrant, intelligent woman fall apart like that." Joe shook his head.

On my drive home, Joe had called me on my cell and asked how things had gone. I had recapped for him the unbelievable drape drama that had unfolded earlier in the day and Mom's catastrophic emotional breakdown. He could tell I was also struggling and a little tearful. It certainly hadn't been a fun day, just very revealing.

We agreed that having a lengthy conversation while I was driving was not a good idea, so the details would wait until I was safely home. When I walked in the door, after being welcomed by Bailey's craving for ear rubs and Maddee's hello barks, Joe just hugged me tightly. I was about to break down in tears, but something caught my eye and I started laughing instead. On the buffet in our foyer off the garage, Joe had placed a Bell's Oberon and the bottle opener. Oberon was one of my favorite brews. Ironically, it is made in Kalamazoo.

"You sweetheart," I said sniveling.

"I thought you might need it." Indeed I did. We sat down at the kitchen island and went over all the gory details of a difficult day.

"As I've said before, she's welcome to move in here ..."

I waved him off. "She has both the financial resources and a well-documented personal desire not to live with her kids—well, me, actually."

The Italian side of my husband favored family caring for family. It was admirable but misguided in this situation. My mom talked openly about quality-of-life issues. Although she embraced Catholic values and would not advocate proactive measures to end her life, she was adamant about not prolonging it either. I, on the other hand, would have preferred a shot of heart-stopping Digoxin rather than endure the confusion and terror that Mom was yet to experience.

"I know you," Joe added. "On the drive back, you've been thinking about what to do next."

My favorite brew was becalming. "I'll start looking at places in our area," I said. "If she has to be moved, it doesn't make sense to keep her at Woodside, still a two-hour drive away, when I could have her closer to us." Joe was totally on board.

"My internist's mother is at Hearthstone," I continued. "I'll make an appointment to see it and Google to find out what else is available." The hunt was about to begin.

I had announced my retirement in April to be effective at the end of the 2009–10 school year in June. I loved my job, the students, and my coworkers, and the Special Education Department in Taylor had been wonderful to me. I wrestled with the decision constantly until I found myself answering "No" to the simplest of questions: "Do you want to work next year?" After waffling for months, it was finally clear to me that I was indeed ready to leave. Although my mom's ongoing issues did not weigh in on my decision, I was eternally grateful that I had the time for her when she needed it, and that need would increase substantially in the months ahead.

I love Google—the word, the search engine, and the cute, seasonal pictures added to the home page. Besides Hearthstone, many possibilities within a thirty-mile radius popped up when

I Googled assisted-living centers. Mom would be a private-pay individual, and those facilities afforded many amenities and a better staff-to-resident ratio.

Hearthstone was my first stop. It was a beautiful, sunny spring day when I visited. The director was very accommodating and gave me a full tour along with a detailed price sheet and brochure. I liked everything about it except that the rooms were studio style. As Woodside was the only assisted-living place I had toured prior to Hearthstone, and they had several one-bedroom options, I was disappointed in the studio arrangement. We had literally just completed the megadrama of having Mom's place repainted, so I was holding out for a one bedroom and hopefully one with a similar layout. I added a filter on my next Google search to exclude studios.

*If* there were any fragments of doubt remaining in my mind about moving her, they would completely evaporate after the upcoming Mother's Day weekend.

# Chapter 30
## Macabre Mother's Day

May 8–10, 2010

"I put labels on the doors upstairs for her as well as a note on the bathroom mirror," I explained to Joe. "I hope that helps." After the decorating disaster at Friendship Village, I was extremely concerned about her flipping out at my house even though it was familiar. It seemed like virtually anything that disrupted her routine and took her out of her comfort zone was a potential pitfall for trouble.

"It's so sad," he acknowledged. He started to add more, but I waved him off. He didn't have to finish. I knew what he meant.

I held back a tear. My mom was coming for Mother's Day. She would arrive via limo per usual, and Joe would take her back Monday while I was at work. The previous December, she had become confused about which room was hers upstairs, so I was trying some visual cues. There were three bedrooms and a bath on our second level, so I made four signs in big, eye-catching print: "Betty's Room," "Bathroom," and two that read "Empty." I taped a longer, more detailed reminder on the bathroom mirror that said, "Mom, you are at our house, not your apartment. I'm downstairs. Love, Elaine."

Later Saturday evening I went over the notes with her. Mom nodded in understanding, but I doubted she was really absorbing the information. After her suitcase debacle at Christmas, I had called Friendship Village and asked if someone could help her pack, which they did.

When she called it a day at about nine thirty, I hung around upstairs for a while to make sure she was settled and reminded her again of the door signs. She nodded in clear comprehension, but her retention was anything but clear. I so wanted to believe the notes would guide her from her bedroom to the bathroom and back again. Sadly I was wrong.

I poured a glass of wine, plopped down on our bed to watch something mindless on TV, and beckoned Snoopy. I felt drained and welcomed an alcohol-induced escape from reality, if only for a few hours. It was well into the witching hour when Joe called for me from the living room, where he was reading the paper. Quickly I got up and came out. My mom was standing on the catwalk upstairs, peering down over the railing.

"Where am I?" she said in a soft but definitely apprehensive voice.

"You're at our house, Mom," I answered reassuringly while looking straight up, but I knew she wouldn't have her hearing devices in and was stone deaf without them. I waved my hand toward the living room, hoping the visual cues would guide her to a comfortable reality. It did not. Immediately I went upstairs. She was frozen, still staring downward. I didn't want to frighten her more by touching her unexpectedly, so I walked past her, turned, and leaned my face forward so she could see me directly. She was absolutely devoid of expression. She was so ashen and motionless that, for a moment, I thought maybe she had just died and would collapse to the floor in front of me in the next millisecond.

Then I heard, "Hi." My presence seemed to help her out of the trance-like state of immobility. "Hi," I said back.

"Where's my room? I'm looking for 342?"

I knew she couldn't hear a thing I was saying, but I responded automatically with, "You're not at Friendship Village, Mom. You're at my house." It literally fell on deaf ears.

I extended my hand, and she let me guide her back to her room. I didn't really try to explain anything more to her, but as she got back into bed, I ripped the note about her being at our house off the bathroom mirror and took it over to her. In only those few seconds, though, Mom had fallen asleep, so I just closed the door and went back downstairs.

On Mother's Day morning, she didn't come down until after ten o'clock. I had peeked in on her once, just to make sure. That expression, "just to make sure," presented an emotional quandary that gnawed at me when she stayed at my house. In the event she wasn't breathing, what should I do? What *would* I do? Those questions held me hostage as I carefully opened the door to peer in. She had made it clear in numerous conversations, as well as in writing via her living will and power of attorney documents, that she didn't want any heroics. She had a Do Not Resuscitate order also. But she was my mom; she was at my house, and it wasn't that simple. Fortunately, she was breathing.

Mother's Day was pleasant and, compared to the drama of the night before, benign. It was cool outside but sunny and breezy. She petted the dogs, especially Bailey's coveted, soft ears. Barely a month before, we had picked up a two-year-old rescue dog from the animal shelter. We renamed her Maddee. I supplied their names frequently throughout the day since she couldn't remember them, and not because they looked similar to her. She hadn't remembered that our cat was, in fact, a cat. The vibrant, intelligent woman I had known was no more.

At times the ebb and flow of her remarks were spot on. Joe would ask what she thought about something, or she might comment on a newspaper headline. And then, like blowing out a candle, with one poof, her brightness was gone. She wandered the house, took catnaps, asked over and over about the dog's names, and asked if she could have Bailey's ears when he died, a request that made me cringe.

We made company cauliflower, only this time I was more prepared and took into consideration her limited ability to stay on task. I had her sit down at the kitchen table and brought her specific ingredients, tools, and one-step directions, "Could you chop the green pepper slices?" "Could you break the cauliflower apart and put it in this pan?" To every request she answered, "Sure," sometimes followed by, "What are we making?"

My gracious husband had offered many times to house my mother at our place, but she always declined. He took advantage, however, of a lengthy period of lucidity during postdinner coffee—decaf for Mom—and mentioned it to her again. For as wacko as she had been most of the day, she was right on point with her response: "Thank you, Joe, but no. You deserve your life and your plans. I would not want to move in with any of my kids."

Her last four words were strange: "any of my kids." Did she not realize that I was it? Did she forget Jerry was gone? If so, I figured, how much the better. Ignorance is indeed bliss.

The plan was for Joe to take Mom back to Kalamazoo on the Monday after Mother's Day since I was still working. My husband was very good to her, respectful and patient. In the not-too-distant future, he would be asked to step up and problem solve in her behalf well beyond the scope that many people, especially men, could accomplish.

Before my mom went to bed, I reminded her that Joe was going to take her back to her place and that I would be leaving early in the morning for work, so I wanted to say good-bye to her then. She had slept in past ten that morning, and I know she had missed events at Friendship Village because she slept through them. We hugged good night. She acknowledged recognizing who was doing what, but I doubted she would recall the details, although Joe was quite prepared to handle her confusion.

On Monday morning, I finished pouring coffee into my travel mug, secured the lid tight, and grabbed my lunch. I butt-shut the refrigerator door and turned to leave the kitchen when I was literally startled by the sight of my mom standing in the hallway at the threshold of the kitchen entrance. It was 7:45 a.m. She was fully dressed, with her purse slung over her shoulder. The look on her face was nothing short of confused, unadulterated terror. Her piercing eye stare was frightening, like she was looking through me while simultaneously looking at me. Her face clearly communicated alarming distress and complete disorientation.

"What are you doing here?" she asked. She was irked but also puzzled.

I approached her slowly as her body language was honestly threatening in a scared and protective way. "I live here, Mom. You are at my house." I spoke firmly and calmly and enunciated every word.

"Isn't this Friendship Village? Didn't Joe take me back already?" Some of her defensive posture was relaxing. A glimmer of lucid recognition was peering through.

"No. Joe will take you back today. This is my house."

"Oh. Okay. I get addled at times," she said. "I thought Joe had already taken me back."

*That was really bizarre!* "Coffee?" I offered.

"Sure." Her face and her rigid posture started to relax.

I excused myself for a quick moment and took a cup of java into the bedroom for Joe. I made him aware of what had just transpired. He was good for trying to diffuse stress with humor, saying, "Well, if I've already taken her back, then I guess I don't have to go." I finally found a smile and kissed him good-bye and then my mom.

Driving afforded me the opportunity to just think. I was replaying the morning's bizarre, inherently contradictory dialogue, trying to make sense where there wasn't any really. How frightening it must be for anyone to live with the insidious disease of dementia. Mom remembered Joe was taking her back home, but didn't realize that he had not done so already. She knew I didn't belong at Friendship Village, but didn't recognize that she was at my house. How did she view her immediate surroundings and not absorb that they looked nothing like her apartment, especially with her gaudy green walls? I couldn't help but consider that her dementia-riddled mind was trying to assemble a puzzle, without a clue as to the finished picture, from random pieces belonging to a thousand different puzzle boxes. Everything I witnessed reaffirmed her need for more supervision.

# CHAPTER 31

## *The Hunt Is On*

Mid-May–Early June 2010

In the course of a series of phone calls with my friends detailing my search, my girlfriend Val mentioned that a mutual friend's mother-in-law was at Hunter Place, in Napier, "in the Memory Care wing, which is expensive, but she's been very pleased there." Back to Google, where I found two other Hunter Places in Castel, even closer to me than Napier by about fifteen miles. I made an appointment to tour the Castel site that offered one-bedroom apartments where I met the lovely marketing director, Carolyn. The only drawback to their center was the waiting list. As there was no way to predict when a vacancy would occur, I was reluctant to basically postpone Mom's move indefinitely. Carolyn encouraged me to see the premises of the other Hunter Place in Castel anyway, since I was so close. There, another attractive young woman escorted me around. They had immediate availability but only offered the studio design.

"Hunter Place in Napier has one bedrooms," the woman said, "and I don't believe they have a waiting list. If you would consider that geographic location, I can give you Heather's number."

"Yes. Coincidentally, an acquaintance of mine has someone there," I replied. "I will contact her. Thank you again for your time."

I distinctly recall reaching Heather just before Memorial Day weekend of 2010. I detailed my mother's situation, and we discussed my previous tours at the two Castel sites and my desire for a one bedroom.

"We have openings here in both independent and assisted living with one bedrooms. There is one unit in particular with a balcony overlooking an enclosed courtyard with a gazebo, pond, and flowers. It's available immediately, if you would like to see it." I told her I would be out after work.

The entire grounds of Friendship Village were beautifully manicured. My parents' apartment had a view of the inside courtyard with its majestic blue spruce in the center, surrounded by deciduous trees and an endless variety of scrubs, bushes, and flowers with seasonal blooms. I had accepted that Mom would not likely be so fortunate again, but I was feeling more encouraged that a solution might be on the horizon. I drove out after work to meet Heather and get yet another tour.

It was a very sensitive undertaking, picking out a place for my mom without her input, without her knowledge, and yet I knew I had her permission from the multitude of conversations we had had over the years. I felt the weight of making life-changing decisions for someone else. I so wanted to just pick up the phone and call my brother to run things by him, but of course I couldn't. He was gone, but I found myself having increasingly more conversations with him in my head. What did he think? What would he do? What should I do?

I knew of too many families in which the dynamics between siblings disintegrated, leading to hostile, territorial wars because of splintered ideas about their parents' care or finances. I reconciled that I would rather take on complete responsibility for every issue related to my mom than to have a contentious relationship with an adversary who was undermining me at every turn. My cousins Mike, Jan, and Maggie worked very well together in behalf of their mom, my aunt Dee. I felt confident that Jerry and I would have made a great team for our mom if he had lived. I missed him terribly. However, despite the complete support of my family, the ultimate decision rested totally on my shoulders. It was intimidating to yield such power and yet feel so powerless.

Hunter Place in Napier was off the perimeter drive that encircled Oakwood Mall, my favorite shopping mecca. How convenient. Maybe it was a sign. When I arrived at Napier's Hunter Place, the receptionist, Mary, welcomed me with her beautiful smile and inundated me with brochures and price sheets. Residents were playing putt-putt golf in and around the inviting lobby. It made me smile, and I thought that was something my mom might enjoy.

Heather was as lovely as her voice. Hunter Place was 3–0 for marketing directors. She went over the services, fee structure, and so on. We discussed independent versus assisted living for my mom. Clearly I was there only because Mom needed more supervision, not less. Although the complete picture eluded me, I was honest about what I knew. Mom was independent with all self-care but needed guidance in selecting her clothes, as her default choice was pink. She was disorientated when it came to time and thus would need assistance with her medications and instant reminders for activities and meals. Hunter Place offered an enhanced package in independent living that provided all those needed services.

Heather escorted me to the available room. I felt an immediate connection the moment she opened the door. It was almost exactly the same layout as Mom's current apartment, with the kitchen and living room on the right, bath and bedroom on the left. The balcony off the living room had a beautiful view of the courtyard, just as Heather had described, and the apartment could be repainted. Of course, I might mute the gaudy green a bit this time. With the Enhancement Option Package, I figured Mom would be safe and not require another disruptive move, or so I naïvely thought.

A deposit check secured the room until Joe and I could return the following week to finalize the contract. I was leaving for Colorado over the upcoming Memorial weekend with my girlfriend Pat to visit my daughter Angie and her husband Ryan. It was mostly a girls' weekend, and I was very much looking forward to all of the shopping, restaurants, and social amenities the getaway afforded us. Plus, my son-in-law Ryan was an amazing bartender, and I had already preordered mojitos. It would also give me ample time to update Angie on her grandmother's dynamic situation face-to-face.

I had made a decision without making a decision. I still felt an overwhelming need to validate Mom's impending move. Jerry would have been my first choice, but except via telepathy, that wasn't going to happen. On the sunny thirty-minute drive home to our house, I called Judy for her professional input. I remember how hopeful I was that she might actually be available to talk with me right then. Judy was in. Maybe Jerry was helping out from above after all.

I summarized the various sites and what I had tentatively decided on, and I asked her point blank, "What would you do if this were your mother?"

I was fairly certain Judy would support relocation, but there were distinct advantages to staying at Woodside also. My thoughts were like ping-pong balls smashing at lightning speed, ricocheting against the inside of my skull with contradictory ideas. As Judy and I concluded our lengthy and in-depth conversation, she answered my query with, "My mother lives on your side of the state, and if or when the time comes, I would move her here." The deal was sealed with her endorsement. Then Judy recommended the book *The 36-Hour Day* by Nancy L. Mace and Peter V. Rabins. "It's not a fun book to read," she said, "but it should be helpful and provide insight on dementia."

My head nodded and bobbed in agreement as I pulled into the garage. After months of stress and indecisiveness, as far back as January when Judy first warned me, "Your mother will need Woodside by September," one dilemma was resolved. As I packed for the Memorial Day weekend trip, I updated Joe on my find and confirmed that he would be available to join me the following week when I would sign the papers, which I stuffed into my carry-on.

---

In Colorado, I located the book Judy had suggested, subtitled *A Family Guide to Caring for Persons with Alzheimer Disease, Related Dementing Illnesses, and Memory Loss in Later Life,* in a Denver bookstore, a fortuitous find. I smiled, looked upward and then at Pat, and said, "I think Jerry and Wendie are guiding me from above."

"I'm sure they are," my good friend said as she put her hand on my shoulder.

On Saturday mother and daughter sat across from each other on Angie and Ryan's new couch. It had been a wonderful and much-needed getaway, but Angie both wanted to know and could handle the Grandma facts. Angie and I usually corresponded via e-mail or text, due in part to the two-hour time difference and the complexities of our respective schedules. She had just finished her second year of law school. Not surprisingly she was completely supportive, which I appreciated. At the end, to lighten the moment, she added with humor, "There are gorgeous places in Boulder, Mom, nestled at the foothills of the Colorado Rockies, if you ever need one."

"Well, like Grandma, I would not want to alter my children's lifestyle by living with either of you girls." With those words, I suddenly recalled a remark my mother had made years before, probably around the time my dad's dad, Grandpa Ward, was placed in a nursing home after suffering multiple strokes in 1963: "One of the greatest gifts a parent can give their children is their financial independence." She and my dad had done that for Jerry and me.

Not a single person ever questioned my motives, judgment, and decisions or the love I had for my mother. It was indeed awesome to have such unwavering strength of support behind me, and I would need all of it and then some. I had no idea what else lay ahead.

# CHAPTER 32

## *The Calm before the Storm*

June 2010

Memorial Day Monday brought me home from a great weekend in Colorado. I had read significant portions of *The 36-Hour Day* at Angie's. It provided an insightful perspective on the behaviors common to many ravaged by dementia. Their abilities fluctuated. They insisted they were fine when they were not. They couldn't process written directions even though they could still read the words. Their sense of time was shattered, and they were adept at masking deficits. Most of the book applied to her, as well as the recommended strategies: listen, acknowledge, and redirect.

Although technically the wheels were already in motion, I felt the need to network with Mom's wonderful, long-time internist, Dr. Bradtke. He had offered me the opportunity to talk with him and, in part because he would be receiving documents to sign from Hunter Place, I called.

Remembering that he saw patients only in the morning on Fridays, I contacted his office and left a detailed message with his nurse. As he had promised, Dr. Bradtke called me back around one o'clock on a Friday in early June. I reviewed the key events that had solidified the need to move my mom and my decision to relocate her closer to me, reasoning that any move would be disruptive. I wanted, and she deserved, to have me more involved

190

in her care. Was there anything pertinent that I was inadvertently overlooking? I asked him. He made generic supportive remarks until the end of our conversation, when he added, "I wish I had a daughter like you." I was stunned. His gracious remark was a very genuine accolade, and I thanked him. After all of the teenage rebellion I had put my mother through, I smiled at his assessment of me. It was a *real* compliment.

After Jerry died, Joe and I kept his two high-end pens. Joe used the Montblanc, and I kept his engraved one. I carried mine in the zipper compartment of my purse, always. Joe and I both used our special mementos to sign important papers. I thought about Jerry often, but certainly the frequency had increased lately. On the drive out to Hunter Place to sign the contract, I groped in my purse for Jerry's pen and palmed it tightly. Privately, I thought, *If you aren't okay with this, you have to show me.*

Joe and I met with Heather in the conference room. I was just getting ready to put my signature on the contract documents when I thought again, *Okay, Jerry, this is it. Show me now.* His pen worked beautifully. I interpreted the smooth flow of the ink as an indication of Jerry's endorsement. It was eerie to sign my name next to the Do Not Resuscitate line on behalf of my mom, but inexplicably, I never hesitated. I checked boxes, filled in blanks, wrote checks, and initialed everywhere.

---

June was mostly a fun and exciting month, the calm before the storm. Joe and I hosted a blast of an end-of-the-year, end-of-a-career, nonretirement party at our house. Our third grandchild was due in late June. Joe's son had ten-month-old little Mia. My daughter in Germany had two-year-old Isaac, and baby Lillian was born June 26, 2010. I was on a plane a few days later for a brief but singularly important visit. Grandma Elaine had to see her new granddaughter, and it would be the only opportunity until my return visit scheduled for September. Isaac had been five weeks old when I held him for the first time, but I cradled newborn Lilli in my arms at five days old. It was an insanely expensive flight but an extraordinarily important visit to me. *Thanks, Jerry,* I thought, as I had inherited a portion of his estate.

My mom's prodigious move was scheduled for the weekend of July 10, 2010. Mike had provided me with paint samples of her new wall colors so I could duplicate them, although I had decided I might order a more subdued, tasteful green. My girlfriend Michelle and family had relocated from South Carolina to southeastern Michigan and had tons of great moving boxes for me to use. My usually phenomenal multitasking skills were revved up into high gear as I made lists, planned ahead, purchased packing tape and yellow and black highlighters, and networked to arrange for people to help me pack at the Kalamazoo end.

I navigated the uncharted waters of Mom's impending move with Judy's input. Should I tell Mom ahead of time? "Probably not." I already knew that my mom shouldn't help pack. Should Mom have an opportunity to say good-bye to her friends at The Village? Again, "No." That decision, however, would prove to be problematic for Judy, as many people were upset that they were robbed of the opportunity to say good-bye to her. That said, it also could have been disastrous for my mom. I could envision her refusing to leave, denying she was moving, exploding, and unraveling. No doubt Judy's suggestion was made with Betty's very volatile state in mind.

Angie said she could fly in and help, and I accepted her gracious offer. With three available adults, I thought through, tweaked, and finalized the details of the big move. I would drive over Saturday, July 10, and spend the night at my mom's. On Sunday, Mom would take the sedan limo to our house, under the ruse that I already had plans with my friend Barb who lived in the area, but that Angie was flying in to visit with her grandma at our place.

Joe, Angie, Mom, and the pets would hang out at home on Sunday while I pitched and packed in Kalamazoo. Angie could be her grandmother's ears and escort during the night if Mom wandered around upstairs. Back at Friendship Village, the movers were scheduled to come at 8:00 a.m. on Monday. When everything was packed and Mom's apartment was emptied, I would drive out to Hunter Place, where Angie would meet up with me in Napier to help unpack and reorganize. If all went well, Mom would stay in her new room at Hunter Place on Monday night, and I would sleep on the couch. What a plan! And except for some anticipated emotional Mom reactions, it worked perfectly. No plan in her behalf would ever be as flawless and efficient as that one.

# Chapter 33
## *Precision Pitch and Pack*

Saturday, July 10, 2010

My multitasking, flawless organization, and precision-planning skills were about to be put to the test like never before. The back of Joe's Ford Escape was stuffed with empty moving boxes, tape, markers, and an overnight bag with my things, which included a back-up Oberon. I arrived at Friendship Village about seven o'clock Saturday evening. I carried my bag to Mom's apartment, the infamous number 342, and went in. Mom looked very nice and bright eyed. She seemed especially together, and gradually I started to detail what Sunday's arrangements would be.

"I have plans with Barb tomorrow in this area, but Angie is flying in to visit with you. The limo will pick you up in the morning at ten and take you to my house." Of course, I wasn't meeting Barb; it was just my cover story.

"Angie's coming? Oh, how nice," she replied. "What is she doing now?"

"She just finished her second year of law school," I answered. Before Mom had forgotten, she knew that Angie was pursuing a law degree.

"She's coming here?"

"Not your place, Mom. Angie is flying in to our house Sunday. The limo will pick you up tomorrow at ten and take you there."

"Where's Joe?"

"He stayed home with the dogs. He'll be at the house tomorrow when you get there."

"Bailey," she said. "I can rub his ears."

*And they aren't coming off, either, Mom,* I thought.

We were sitting in matching burgundy side chairs. She set her decaf coffee down on the glass-topped table between us; she only drank decaf. I scanned the room as I had done a few times already, visualizing how best to arrange her furniture in her new place. Joe had discreetly taken measurements of her dressers, couch, curio, and server when he had taken her back after her Mother's Day visit. Together we had made a preliminary floor plan on graph paper. Mom had a heavy mirror requiring a daunting reinstallation process, so Joe had studied that as well.

The brief silence was broken with a stunning revelation. "What's going on," she said.

"What do you mean, Mom?"

Her face communicated suspicion. "I feel you are planning something." She was very together.

I was dumbfounded, to say the least. Did she really suspect something was brewing? *Let's see where this conversation goes,* I thought. *She could rapidly derail.* "What would I be planning?" I asked. It started to feel like a chess match with clock timers. Your turn—ding.

"I don't know. Are you?" she asked.

Okay. It was time for the Oberon that was chilling in her refrigerator. I got up, opened it, took a sip and sat back down. Then I invoked Wendie as she always had the right words, and began, "Well, you've told me many times that you don't have any close girlfriends here anymore."

"Yes. The people are nice here, but my really close friends are gone." She was referring to Helen, Ann, and her closest girlfriend, Shirley, the person I had contacted after Jerry died. They had all passed away. Shirley's death was the most recent of the three and had further rocked Mom's already compromised world. "I feel so lonely," she had said after Shirley's death.

Were we really having this amazingly lucid conversation? If so, I would take advantage of every second. "You told me it would be okay if I moved you closer to me."

"Am I moving?" she asked.

If I answered honestly, what would she say? Would she remember the conversation tomorrow? I took another sip of Oberon and assembled every ounce of evasive finesse I could muster.

"Honestly, Mom, I have looked at places like this closer to me." How was that? Truthful, but not too direct. *Let's see if that triggers a change in cooperative dialogue*, I thought.

"Are they nice?"

"Yes, Mom, very nice."

"I would be okay with that," she replied.

"It would be better to have you closer to me. I would like to see you more often, but the drive over here is long." So far, I was on a roll, as was she.

"That would be nice." Pause. "Am I moving soon?"

"Yes. I think that would be best." I ventured out a little farther on the limb. "What do you think?"

"That's fine."

As the Oberon's effects lightened the mood, the back-and-forth conversation continued for at least another half hour. She probed gently for more factual information, but I avoided telling her outright what was happening. Her short-term memory was so unpredictable; I couldn't know what fragments of the conversation she might recall or how twisted her brain might rearrange them, from fact to fiction.

Finally, I said, "Do you have your bag packed for tomorrow?" I didn't even give her a chance to respond and burst my bubble with some blank stare. It had been so long since we had an easy, meaningful chat. I didn't want to see it dissolve. I directed her with, "Let's make sure you have what you need for your visit to my house. Angie flies in tomorrow."

Together we went into her pink bedroom. Her suitcase was mostly packed, but I strongly suspected that Friendship Village staff had had a hand in that. Despite the amazing clarity of our just completed exchange, I really knew how impaired Mom was. It was getting late, so I kissed her good night and left with my bag for the guest room down the hall. I preferred not to sleep on her couch, which I had done a few times before. That night I really needed the alone time to decompress. I called Joe and filled him in on our surprisingly lucid discussion and then wished him a good night.

I lay on the bed in the guest room, channel surfing and reminiscing on so many red-flag situations of her past that had completely escaped me. Hindsight was indeed twenty-twenty. All the goofy, unexplainable, bizarre events speckled here and there over the years were indicative of a mind slowly eroding from dementia, one brain cell at a time.

She described my dad's poststroke demise as "death by inches"; so was this. The subtle inconsistencies baffled me the most and greatly contributed to my ignorance. Her accusations about stolen brown pants and missing nail files and stamps were paranoia. I never thought anyone had taken two pair of pants for their kids. It was absurd. I just couldn't understand why Mom thought they had been stolen and rejected more logical explanations such as having donated them. In my distorted thinking, if I didn't believe her account, then she must be lying.

I chuckled a little as I recalled the multiple birthday cards—three in total—that she had sent to Joe in September 2004. What I chalked up to stress after my dad's death that year was just the preamble. She habitually lost her car keys, and I explained away the multiple episodes due to her inability to hear the clink on the ground. Not so. She was misplacing them, setting the keys down in strange places and completely forgetting about them.

Her irrational complaints about other residents or staff were completely suspect to me now. They were mostly the product of her delusional mind. I recalled other stories like her money-handling debacles involving writing nine checks for her car insurance and her inability to write any checks at Christmas.

Mom was always on her soapbox to rectify some injustice. To forward her mission to stop resident mumbling and enunciate when they spoke, she slapped a sticker on her blouse to get their attention. Per Judy's account, as Mom's impatience increased, her judgment decreased. When Mom wanted something from the local store, she wouldn't wait for a driver. She was so adamant about her independence that she walked the mile-long round trip to Walgreens, maneuvering around the massive road construction equipment. Somehow, she managed to find her way back to Friendship Village but then couldn't get inside the building. She crawled through the shrubs and banged on the windows until someone let her in. Initially, I identified my mom's wanderings as consistent with her determination to remain independent and her little snub to others whom she perceived as trying to corral her spirit. It wasn't until she accused "them" of locking her out that I realized the demise of Mom's reasoning and judgment.

Mom got lost in the halls she had walked repeatedly for over ten years. And these were the stories I knew about. I literally could not fathom the numerous other parallel situations reflective of her decline.

I envisioned the early stages of Mom's dementia as a cunning, smoldering fire, its smoke whirling up and down, in and out, around and through her brain. Occasionally it would choke her orientation to time, sometimes cloud her vision or pretzel-twist her gray matter. It always lay in wait, concealed in the crevices of her short-term memory centers, fogging judgment, reasoning, and logic. For a while, it would remain dormant, having already ravaged parts of her mind permanently until, like wildfires, something sparked it to flare up, engulfing and consuming its insatiable appetite for brain cells. Mom would never get better. All I could do was be there for every step of her journey through hell and pray that was enough. She deserved better; everyone did. She deserved to go out with her boots on, not have her mind chipped and chiseled away piece by piece.

## Sunday, July 11, 2010

Sunday morning went smoothly. We had breakfast together in the café, a welcoming dining area decorated to look like a patio with a view of the magnificent roses and courtyard. That was the aspect of Friendship Village I would miss the most, lingering over the third cup of coffee and peering outside on a sunny day at beautiful grounds. For years, Mom had been very dismissive of breakfast. "I don't really like breakfast," I recalled her saying frequently, but since she didn't remember not liking breakfast, there we were, enjoying the view and crispy hash browns. "Every cloud has a silver lining," she would have said if she had remembered.

My mom voiced nothing that indicated any awareness of the previous night's conversation. I suspected as much. We went back to number 342, Mom's last time, got her bag, and met the sedan limo at the reception area. I reviewed with my mom again the details of the day, gave her a note to that effect, as well as shared the information with her driver. I just kept repeating and reassuring her with reminders of Angie's impending visit and hoped that was enough.

After her trip was underway, I called Joe to say good morning and get a boost of supportive encouragement. He wished me well, and we agreed to update each other as the day unfolded. I had put the Escape in Mom's garage the night before, so I borrowed a flat cart and headed to the garage, where I had clandestinely stashed packing boxes on a previous trip. Once loaded, the cart was unwieldy to steer, but I slowly maneuvered the beast from the garage to her apartment.

The actual sorting, pitching, and packing project, especially with several hours of help from the paid volunteer Judy had arranged for, went incredibly well. I found a set of missing car keys, Mom's long-lost diamond earring, Aunt Dee's misplaced letter, and more "stolen" items. There were unopened envelopes slid between the bed and the nightstand, financial statements in the kitchen towel drawer, and documents between the pages of magazines. By seven, we were nearly finished. Boxes were stacked, taped, and marked. I packed the Escape with some hanging clothes and Mom's most valuable crystal and figurines. I scanned the room and sat down in the burgundy chair to kick back. I had had a very productive and successful day. Joe, however, had not.

---

"Your mom rode with me when I picked Angie up from the airport," he said. "We had a light lunch, and then your mom took a short nap. When she got up, though, she was very agitated and disoriented." Joe was updating me at midafternoon on the day's events to that point. "She asked where Wayne was, Elaine. She said he had been in the cab with her, sitting in the backseat on the way over, and was upset that she couldn't find him. She asked me what I did with him."

She had *never* done that before that I knew of. She had never drifted so far back in her memory that she thought Dad was still alive, let alone sitting next to her. I had highlighted segments of the book *The 36-Hour Day* for Joe to read, which he had, to help him also know how to respond. "What did you say?" I asked.

"I told her she had come in the cab by herself and that Wayne wasn't here. She looked through the house and asked several times. Finally I offered her some of the cookies you made, and she settled down."

There was no perfect response to someone anguishing with confusion and unhinged by events she believed were real. Joe had a harder job than I did, staying with his unpredictable mother-in-law and running interference with two big dogs. I knew he would have preferred to help me pack, but I had made the best arrangement I could to expedite the moving process.

In contrast, Mom was fairly lucid while talking about her past with Angie, describing how she worked as a chemist at Upjohn Company in the mid-1940s. I had cautioned Angie about her grandmother's strange behaviors over Mother's Day weekend, so Angie was alerted to Mom's probable nighttime wanderings. Not surprisingly, sometime around four o'clock in the morning, Angie became aware that Mom was indeed moving about upstairs. Angie got up to find her grandmother in the walk-in closet off the bedroom and redirected her back to bed. It takes a village to raise a child or guide an elderly one.

## Monday, July 12, 2010

The movers were there before eight thirty, and by noon all of the boxes and furniture were loaded either into their moving truck or the Escape. I turned the apartment keys in at the desk and was on the road to Hunter Place. I glanced in the rearview mirror as I drove away, recalling all the trips I had made to Kalamazoo—too numerous to count. It was a strange and nostalgic feeling.

I called Angie when I was thirty minutes away from Napier. She borrowed my car and drove up to meet me, and we started the unpacking process together. The movers arrived midafternoon, set everything up, and were on their way. About five o'clock that evening, Joe gathered Mom's things, helped her into his F150, and drove out to meet Angie and me at a restaurant halfway between Hunter Place and our house.

After dinner, as we all gathered in the parking lot, I cautiously started to prepare Mom for what was happening next. She was inquisitive, but I was vague. I didn't want her flipping out suddenly and possibly refuse to get into the car with me. We hugged and said good-bye to Angie and Joe and moved Mom's suitcase into my trunk. On the way back home, Joe dropped Angie off at the airport for her 7:30 flight, and I drove Mom out to her new apartment. The quiet ride in the car afforded me time to decompress and try to prepare for anything. I parked, got her bag, took a deep breath, and led her through the wood doors of Hunter Place of Napier, her new home.

"This is the place I've told you about, Mom. It's much closer to me than Kalamazoo," I said.

"It was a short ride." This would be one of very few calm and on-point remarks for months.

I ushered her toward her new apartment and unlocked the door. There were still boxes stacked in the kitchen, but for having literally moved just hours earlier, it looked fairly organized. She made no remarks that indicated she even recognized her own furniture, clothes, bedspread, pictures, or wall colors.

"Where are we?" she finally asked.

"You are at Hunter Place. This is your new apartment." I jotted it down—not that it would really help her anymore, but maybe it helped me in my efforts to calm her.

Overall the initial introduction to her new home was fairly benign; it just wouldn't remain that way. I stayed the night on the couch. I didn't sleep much, but I was aware that my mom was sufficiently oriented to use the bathroom during the night and return to bed without incident.

In the morning we went over details, again. I showed her around a little, introduced her to a few staff members, even though I knew she wouldn't remember their names. Mom was pleasant and said hello appropriately. Stephanie, the assistant director of independent living, met with us for a short time. I had already set up my mom's medications and went over the schedule with Stephanie. Mom would have timely escorts for meals and social activities, and I would scoop up her laundry to do at my house.

By early afternoon Tuesday, I could tell I was approaching the point of complete exhaustion. I struggled to remain patient and reassuring. Not surprisingly Mom was starting to recycle questions and couldn't remember the answers. I knew there was nothing I could say or do to comfort my mom in a way that would sustain her. I sat across from her on the couch and told her verbally and wrote down for her that I was going home and would be back the next day. I thought I was frazzled then, but the next few months would escalate literally beyond belief.

# Chapter 34

## *Dementia Demons in Disguise*

July–Early September 2010

Wednesday, July 14, 2010

"How is she? How are you?" Joe asked as I practically stumbled into the house Tuesday afternoon. I wanted a shower, a hug, and chocolate, not necessarily in that order.

"Okay, I guess. She can navigate to the bathroom and back, which was one of my concerns. Of course, I barely slept with one ear on her."

"Well, you just get some rest," Joe replied. And I actually did take a catnap that afternoon, with the cat.

The next morning Joe and I went out together to continue unpacking, hang pictures, and install drapery rods. When I suspected earlier that Mom would have to be moved but before any final decisions were made, I had contacted the drapery maker to postpone any further sewing. Fortuitously, the fabric had just arrived and no work was underway. Joe had taken window measurements at Hunter Place, and, given the completely different dimensions, Mom's very accommodating drapery lady was still able to make traverse drapes for Mom's new bedroom and a valance for the living room. When completed, she had dropped them off at Friendship Village, thoroughly wrapped in protective plastic. That was in late June, just weeks before the big move. I had carefully laid them on top of the boxes in my Escape before leaving on Monday.

Mom and I worked together to unwrap her breakables, but not once did she acknowledge her Hummel figurines, her Waterford crystal, her cross-stitch, or pictures of Jerry, her granddaughters or me. *Strange*, I thought, but as long as she wasn't hostile or recycling the same question every few minutes, it was fine. After three hours of unpacking, she sat down on the couch, tilted her head back, and closed her eyes. We took our cue to exit—enough for one day.

Friday, July 16, 2010

Joe and I returned to Hunter Place on Friday to meet Dr. Tashka, the internist available to residents there. Mom had loved Dr. Bradkte, and deservedly so. Whomever we selected as her next physician would have big shoes to fill. Dr. Tashka's feet, however, were small and narrow, as she was slender and of average height, maybe five feet, six inches.

We arrived a few minutes early for our eleven o'clock initial meeting. Dr. Tashka was already there, and my mom was talking her ear off, complaining about being relocated and wanting to return to Friendship Village. Her short-term memory issues were exacerbated under stress, and the move ranked in the Big Three of disruptive experiences.

"I've listened to you for a while," Dr. Tashka said to my mom respectfully. "Now I'd like to hear your daughter's version."

I liked her instantly. She was friendly, professional, and spot on when it came to evaluating my mom's situation in a snapshot moment. I tried to collect my thoughts quickly to give her "my version." How many hours did she have? The move had been physically and emotionally draining, and my mom's understandable but definitely out of character accusatory remarks made being patient difficult. I knew Mom wasn't herself, and most of the time I did pretty well giving her the validation she needed and the repeated explanations she required in a nonconfrontational voice.

"We moved her on July 12 from a senior independent facility in Kalamazoo. Her close girlfriends have all passed away, and since Friendship Village had been recommending more supervision for some time—"

"You don't understand," Mom interrupted. "I was on the resident council there. I couldn't be on the board if I needed so much help." She was clearly frustrated, and her voice cracked. Indeed, she had served on the board, although it had been years ago, but I kept quiet.

"I'm sure you were." Dr. Tashka's tone was perfect, validating without encouraging more flawed recollections and polite without being condescending. She had broken off her gaze with me to address my mom and then added, "I listened to you for a while, Betty, and I would like to know what your daughter thinks. She obviously cares about your best interests."

Mom seemed to calm down a bit with those words and let me continue.

"We need to get established with a new internist for her, and I wanted to meet with you first." There were a gazillion things I wanted to add, like, "My mom won't remember your name, but she used to teach high school math," or "She's a very kind woman and never used to raise her voice," or "She told me many times that it was okay to move her closer to me." There were so many things I wanted Dr. Tashka to know, but somehow I had the distinct feeling that she had a very good picture already of what was really going on with my mom. Dr. Tashka would get medication scripts switched over to her from Dr. Bradtke. She would be back again and told my mom as much. I furiously took notes, as I had been doing for years.

"I'm a little surprised Betty is here and not in assisted," Dr. Tashka said as we walked toward the door together. Her remark surprised me, but like many things, it would prove to be an accurate prediction of what lay ahead.

"I have arranged for escorts for meals and medication assistance," I said. I was not defensive, just explaining briefly. Still, Dr. Tashka saw something I didn't. From my viewpoint, Mom appeared to have adequate help available. However, Dr. Tashka's remark would prove to be prophetic.

With limited exceptions, the theme of every subsequent visit over the next several weeks was a carbon copy. Mom couldn't remember where she was or why she was there. Sometimes she greeted me calmly with "Hi, Elaine," but typically she nailed me as I walked in with, "I want to talk to you!" Intellectually I could rationalize that she was in unfamiliar surroundings, that faces were new and her routine had been altered. It still mystified me, however, that she didn't acknowledge the familiarity of her green and pink painted apartment, her furniture, her family pictures, and her clothing. Maybe I had tweaked her bold green wall paint too much!

## Late June 2010

"I wrote a letter to Mary Agnes, but I don't have any stamps!" Mom said as I walked in, miffed and glaring.

"You do have stamps, Mom," I said. "They're right here in the drawer marked 'Stamps.'" I had purchased several sets of small drawers that sat on her kitchen counter in plain sight. They had paper inserts with the contents' names written on them. Mom and I had worked on the project together, but as with practically everything, she didn't remember. She also wasn't able to process printed, written words as informational. I hadn't quite figured that out yet when I added, "See? It says *Stamps* right here, Mom."

She had gotten up off the couch and was standing by me as I pointed to and tapped (with frustration setting in, I was probably jabbing) the word *Stamps*. I caught the bewildered look on her face, though, and backed off. I lowered my unproductive, escalating voice. I was curious. "What does this say, Mom?" It was a real question without attitude.

"Stamps," she answered, but she didn't move. She didn't reach forward to open the drawer. She couldn't connect the printed words on the drawer with the contents inside. She couldn't connect reading the words aloud with being the items she wanted. Another lost connection to the ravages of dementia. I turned my head away from her to suppress my tears. I hated this disease! I hated what it did, what it was doing, and what it would continue to do to her, and others. With a fingertip grip on the little drawer's knob, I pulled it open to reveal the stamps.

"Oh. There are the stamps," she said. "Thank you."

Her voice mimicked a child's, excited about a new toy. She took them out of the drawer and walked back to the couch, content. I went into her bathroom, turned on the fan to camouflage any telltale sounds, and disintegrated in a puddle of tears. I cried so hard that my shoulders shook and my chest heaved in and out with every forced gulp of air. This sucked! It was crushing to see her slip away, and I loathed myself for my despicable behavior. It wasn't her fault. When I pulled myself together and wiped away the makeup mess, I went out, opened the little drawer marked "Envelopes" and offered my help.

"I don't know Mary Agnes's address," Mom said.

"It's in your address book. I'll bring that over too."

With that I guided her through the process. Old memory afforded her some letter-addressing skills, and I helped with the rest. Mary Agnes was the resident across the hall from number 342. When Mom went to the bathroom, I scanned her letter, curious about the tone and content. It was relatively benign. So Mom could write coherently if the thoughts originated with her, but she could not read and process the printed word reliably. I made a mental note and tried not to break down again at the loss of a great mind ravaged by dementia. Her disease was not just smoldering; it was a blazing inferno.

There were occasional glimmers of lucidity when reasoning

and judgment prevailed. She thanked me for all I did for her; I smiled. She recognized that she couldn't remember things. She liked seeing me more often. I smiled at that too. At least she could remember that she was seeing me more. That memory would dissolve too. I dreaded the day that she might not know me.

A week later, Stephanie called to tell me my mom had lost her processor. *Crap.* Stephanie had alerted housekeeping, residents, and other staff. They all had an idea what it looked like, and would watch out for it. I wasn't optimistic, though. When I got there, I opened the safe and handed Mom the backup processor, and she put new batteries in it. Able to hear again, I asked if she had any idea when she realized she didn't have sound.

"I thought I was here," she said, referring to her apartment.

"Okay, so let's start here."

Mom was surprisingly together, and her search-and-rescue skills were impressively systematic, not random and scattered. We pulled off all of her bedding, one layer at a time, smushing the pillows and shaking the pillowcases. No processor. She opened every drawer and lifted every stack of clothing. I shook her towels, went through every item in the laundry basket, and checked the bathroom drawers. No processor. We looked under the bed and behind the dressers with a flashlight. No processor.

As Mom continued looking in the bedroom, I went into the living room, removed the couch cushions, and stuffed my hands deep down along the seams. Then I checked every kitchen cabinet. Nothing. I opened the bifold closet and peered in; nothing on the floor either. Now I was ticked. With my hands planted firmly on my hips, I looked up and said aloud, "Will you guys stop laughing at me and help me find this damn thing." I was not insane, yet— just frustrated and invoking Jerry's and Wendie's help. I actually could picture them laughing, and I was really miffed. Then, at that exact moment, I saw it! The processor was wedged under the bifold door itself at the hinge. It blended right in with the carpet and moved with the door as it was opened or closed.

"Really." I said aloud again. "Okay. Thanks." I brought this innocuous-looking but incredibly valuable lifeline of sound to my mom.

"Look, Mom. I found it."

"That's wonderful," she said. "Where was it?" I showed her and then slowly looked upward again. Had they really just helped me find it? I shuttered for a moment, the hair standing straight up on the back of my neck. I *was* a believer in metaphysical powers. That was not the first nor would it be the last time I would sense Jerry's or Wendie's presence. It helped me not feel quite so alone in the long, tragic journey accompanying my mom to her death.

# CHAPTER 35

## *Petite but Perverse*

Wednesday, August 4, 2010

My "Hi, Mom" was met with "I have a bone to pick with you!" She was standing in the lobby. Before I knew it, Mom rotated her left hip, leaned onto her left leg, and hurled her right foot into my butt and kicked me. I felt instant anger but suppressed it. There were a number of people around, so I just said, "Let's go to your room." Quietly we walked back to her place. I wanted to drag her back by her hair, but she didn't have enough. I wanted to put her in a time-out, but she wouldn't remember why she was there. I wanted her to get better, but that wasn't going to happen either.

"What was that about?" I asked.

"You take me back, right now!" She was actually shouting at me.

"I can't do that, Mom," I said. "Friendship Village won't take you back." My repertoire of nonconfrontational responses was kaput, as my mom would have said.

"I called them, and they said I can."

I was miffed at being kicked, but then I had to suppress a chuckle. She called them? Not likely. I should have been impressed that she still maintained the equilibrium skills to pirouette on one leg and wallop me with the other. The conversation recycled for some time. I buffered the best I could that afternoon, but other than brief periods of calm, I had to acknowledge an increase in her agitation and hostility. Stephanie saw me in the hallway when I finally left. I visited Mom about three days a week and received regular phone calls from Stephanie with updates—some good, some not.

"You might want to consider a psychiatric consultation," Stephanie volunteered. "Perhaps there are medications that could better manage your mom's behavior." I could only assume she had witnessed or heard about my ass whoopin'. I took contact information from Stephanie for Dr. Reddy and his psychiatric nurse practitioner, Cindy, and thanked her. Cindy returned my call a few hours later and set up an initial appointment in my mom's apartment for the following Wednesday morning.

Friday, August 6, 2010

My fortieth high school class reunion was the first weekend of August. Originally I had no plans to attend, what with all the "mama drama," the new collective title in the subject box of e-mails to friends. However, my old neighborhood friend and sometimes date in high school, Richard, was flying in from Texas and nudged me into coming. I drove out to Napier before heading on to Portage for the social evening.

When I pulled into the parking lot about three thirty, two Napier police cars were there. For a second I wondered if they had been called because of my mom. Just as I stepped out of the car and shut the driver's door, my cell phone rang. In the bright sunlight, juggling my phone, my purse, and Mom's laundry, I could not make out the number, but when I answered, it was the receptionist, Mary. Her voice was tense and she spoke fast, running a few sentences together. I caught something about my mom being threatening.

When she finally took a breath, I said, "Mary, I'm literally walking in right now."

As I entered, I felt like I was walking in slow motion, with deliberate, cautiously placed steps. Like a detective canvassing the scene, I was instantly assessing events as they unfolded in real time. What threats lurked, yet to be revealed? The Napier police were straight ahead as I entered the lobby. One was talking to an employee. His partner was standing right next to him, silent but writing something, a complaint form, perhaps. Mary was to my right, behind the reception desk, turned in profile. She appeared to have just hung up the phone, probably with me. My mom was not in the lobby. I could hear the voices of other people to my far left, but they were not in my visual field. Mary was not engaged with either officer. I approached her at the desk.

"Hi, Mary. I couldn't make out everything you said, so what happened?"

"Your mom asked me earlier today to call you at the lake. I told her I didn't have that number but I could call you on your cell." Mary rambled on a little longer, repeating the account. She was still unsettled and speaking fast. "Betty came back just a little while ago and demanded again that I call you at the lake." Mary slapped her hand on the counter for effect. *Had my mom done that?*, I wondered. "When I tried to explain that I didn't have a phone number for your cottage but I could call your cell, she got loud and angry and said, 'Well, then, I guess I'll just slit my throat!' and left."

I was more than dismayed about what had just happened, but also surprised that my mom would reference the cottage. It was a small place on a beautiful inland lake in Brighton and belonged to Joe and his brother. Mom had only been there a few times. I glanced subtly in the direction of the police, but if they were there for my mom because of her threatening words, it was not apparent. They were busy talking and did not even regard us.

"I'm very sorry, Mary. My mom has been increasingly agitated and vocal, and I have an appointment next Wednesday with the psychiatrist. She probably can benefit from some different medications. You *know* the person who said that is *not* my mom."

We talked a little longer. Mary was understandably on edge

but was not inexperienced with handling people. Knowing this affirmed how brutal Mom's behavior must have been. As Mary relaxed a bit and got busy, I listened in on the policemen's conversation. I could pick up enough to know they were dealing with another resident issue, so I went down to Mom's room. As usual she was sitting on the couch. Soon I confronted her with Mary's account, the short version anyway.

"I said that?" she replied. "I don't remember saying that."

I couldn't get anything more out of her. If she had wanted something specific, she couldn't remember any longer and seemed very subdued. When the escort came to take her to dinner about five o'clock, I left for the reunion. Wednesday couldn't come soon enough for me.

---

Dr. Reddy and his psychiatric nurse practitioner, Cindy, arrived at Mom's apartment at eleven. Dr. Reddy had a commanding presence, a cross between Sigmund Freud and Albert Einstein. He was a pleasant and knowledgeable, but his speech pattern was slightly labored. His mustache, soft voice, and tendency not to project his words worked against my mom. She couldn't understand him at all. Cindy, however, had excellent diction and made direct eye contact with my mom, thus serving as Dr. Reddy's interpreter.

For at least a half hour, Mom pleaded her case repeatedly, denying, accusing, and negotiating. In the end Dr. Reddy started her on Seroquel and increased her anxiety medication dosages. They would see her every other week initially, but I could call Cindy with questions or concerns anytime. I almost asked Dr. Reddy if he carried any Seroquel samples so I could start my mom on them *immediately*, or if he had some extra Valium in his pocket for me.

Within a week after starting the Seroquel, Mom did settle down noticeably. I had a flashback to the New York World's Fair and the Dupont Pavilion Exhibit. "Better Living through

Chemistry" was their advertising slogan. I was certain it referred to advances in technology and not pharmacology, but the colloquialism *wonder drug* applied here. My mom was calmer on subsequent visits and I was grateful that her escalating negative behaviors seemed to be resolving.

### Early September 2010

I was leaving for Germany around Labor Day for ten days. As time for the trip neared, I meticulously compiled a notebook detailing every physician, every phone number, the pharmacy, Mom's insurance information, her Social Security number, and other vital information—everything Joe might need in my absence—in a color-coded notebook.

Stephanie called me the Thursday before I left for Germany. She wanted me to know that my mom's wanderings outside were increasing. Mom was found across the circular drive at the mall entrance and became disoriented. A resident spotted her, and an employee escorted her back. More recently, Mom tried to get into the locked assisted-living side. The staff let her in, and she spent the better part of the day there, playing bingo and having lunch.

"Really? I didn't know that," It sounded charming that Mom was finding some fun activities and people to eat with, even if they were in the assisted section. And then it hit me: she needed assisted living. Mom couldn't remain in the independent section. She had to be moved, again, twice in less than two months. How did I screw up so badly, thinking that independent living with an enhancement package would be sufficient?

"Stephanie, do you think my mom should be in assisted living?" I asked.

Her reply was, in a word, "Yes." With that, I was on board as well. I had lived in denial or ignorance in the past and would not make the same mistake again. We agreed that Mom would be moved after I got back from Germany. In the meantime, they would house her in assisted during the day and return her to her apartment in independent at night.

I was actually on the golf course the Thursday that Stephanie called me and quite grateful that I had such a great excuse to just scoop up my ball and carry it over the water hazard while she and I talked on the phone. Good timing Stephanie. My golf group friends were humorously suspicious, however. They graciously granted me a bogey on that hole in exchange for having shown them my mother's very skillful putting techniques. Mom didn't hit a long ball, but she was deadly accurate around the green. We all had sunk some very tricky putts because of her.

I went over the notebook with Joe and recapped Stephanie's phone call. When I returned home from Germany, we would pack Mom up and move her yet again. It would not go as planned, not even close. Joe would have to step up for his mother-in-law and me well beyond what most people would or even could handle.

# Chapter 36

## *An Assisted Journey*

September 2010–March 2011

September 5, 2010

"How's my honey?" My husband called me from home on my first full day with my grandbabies, Isaac and Lillian, in Wiesbaden, Germany.

"We're good," I replied. "Just got back from a picnic in the park with the kids. They're headed down for a nap and maybe me too." I had adjusted pretty well to the toll an eight-hour, mostly night flight across six times zones could take, but it still took a few days to completely acclimate. Normally I shared my mom's assessment about naps and felt groggy afterward, not rested, but jet lag was totally different.

As I was on the phone with Joe, it suddenly occurred to me what time it was at home. "You're up early," I said. There was a six-hour time difference. When it was 6:00 a.m. in Michigan (EST), it was noon in Germany.

And then the drama unfolded. "Yeah, I just want you to know that everything is under control, so I don't want you to worry or even think about coming home early, but Hunter Place called at five thirty this morning. Apparently your mom wandered outside sometime during the night, fell, and couldn't get up. The paper delivery guy found her on the sidewalk near the parking lot. There are several abrasions but no deep cuts. They got her into bed, and I'll go out later and check on her too."

Poor Mom. Obviously our decision to move her to assisted was the correct one, although it was unfortunate it couldn't have been arranged earlier; the timing was just off. Joe had Mom's notebook and would take it with him when he went out there later. I filled Christie in and then took a short snooze before narcolepsy had a chance to set in. Christie was on child-care leave from work for the first semester with baby Lillian, then ten weeks old, and Isaac was two and a half. I was in Grandma heaven. Poor Joe, however, was about to take on son-in-law hell.

---

Surprisingly, Joe was up again early on Monday. *Odd*, I thought as I saw the caller ID indicate our home number at 6:00 a.m. EST. "Hi, hon," I said. "Are things okay? What's up?"

"I have some updates on your mom." He was upbeat, so I didn't flip out, yet. "Again, I don't want you to worry. I can handle this. That notebook you prepared has been great. As usual, my honey is on top of things. Your mom was taken to the hospital last night. When I got there, I could see her face was badly bruised and purple. I wasn't comfortable removing the blankets to check her over myself, so I had one of the caregivers do it. Her entire body was discolored, completely black and blue, and there were several spots of dried blood on the sheets, so they called EMS and admitted her. Apparently, your mom's Coumadin level was in the life-threatening range, which of course explains her severe bruising."

"Wow," was all I could muster as I absorbed the information he was giving me. Slowly we went back to the beginning and reviewed all of the events again in greater detail. I started to offer to fly home but didn't even get the words out before he shushed me. He told me to have a great time and enjoy the grandkids; he could handle the rest. I did make him promise, though, that he would be totally transparent and tell me everything. If I knew he wouldn't camouflage the facts, I would stay put. He promised he would share everything, and he kept that promise as increasingly more drama unfolded layer by layer. Good man.

Gradually Mom became alert enough to recognize Joe and chat with him a little. She could not fully explain what possessed her to go outside literally in the middle of the night. The only glimmer of insight was her disconnected comments about "going back for groceries" and "putting the car in the garage." Dementia is devious, indiscriminate, and ruthless, invading the mind and distorting fiction into one's reality.

Although her skin bore horrific discoloration, Mom was medically stable for discharge by midweek. However, Dr. Tashka was adamant that Mom could not return to independent living. Dr. Tashka's observations and casual remark from our first meeting in July were completely accurate. Although Stephanie and I had already agreed on relocation to assisted living, absolutely nothing was in place for a specific move and I was still overseas. The complete operation fell entirely on Joe's mighty shoulders. He had to scramble to arrange for twenty-four-hour-a-day sitters for Mom, at a hefty price, in independent living while her room was being readied in assisted. Then he had to hire movers for the big stuff, get boxes for the little stuff, and physically juggle it all. And he did.

I was overwhelmed and appreciative beyond words for what he accomplished efficiently and selflessly. Every time we talked, he brought me up to speed on his progress and reassured me over and over that I could relax and enjoy my grandbabies. While I literally sat on the floor playing with the kids, he was plowing ahead with another move.

"Anything else I should know?" I asked Joe. I was flying home the next day and, with the time change, it would be our last opportunity to chat by phone.

"Well, I didn't want to tell you, but since you asked, your mom's processor is missing."

"Again?"

"Yes," he replied. "I didn't mention it before because I was sure it would turn up in the repacking and move, but it hasn't. I got the one out of the safe and followed the instruction sheet that you prepared so she can hear."

"Okay. Thanks again for everything you've done for her. Maybe it will still show up."

When I returned, although her new place still needed another round of sorting and reorganization, Joe had successfully moved a small mountain.

## Mid-September 2010

"Oh, Elaine, it's so good to see you." Mom's smiling face, complete with ugly, greenish-yellow bruises and healing abrasions, welcomed me. It was my first post-Germany visit with my mom. She struggled to move comfortably and was still very tired. Several people remarked how fortunate Mom was to have been found in time with such dangerously high Coumadin levels. She "could have bled out and died," which my mom would have been fine with, actually. "It was God's will," she would have said.

"I don't know," she answered when I inquired what had happened that night. "I thought I had to get groceries out of the trunk, but that doesn't make any sense, does it?" No, it didn't make any sense. Not much did anymore.

I met with Dr. Tashka at my mom's place in mid-September. We reviewed her medication changes and recent hospitalization test results. Mom sat on the couch and participated initially but then leaned her head back and nodded off. I took advantage of Mom's "absence" to express a significant area of concern to Dr. Tashka.

I looked right at her pretty face and attentive eyes. "We don't know each other very well," I began, "but after what's happened recently, I need you to know that my mom has very clear end-of-life wishes. Mom and I may not agree—she's a 'God's will' person—but it's my job to be her advocate and make sure her desires are carried out. If she had bled out from high Coumadin levels, she would have been okay with that. If she could see how much she has deteriorated through more lucid eyes, she would be appalled and humiliated." I was singularly focused on this perfect window of opportunity to discuss potential future issues with my mom's new but philosophically unproven internist.

"Although my mom worked full time for a while, it was my dad who was the investor and who amassed a comfortable financial estate. My mom would be appalled if she depleted it for herself. The black-and-white decisions are easy. It's those that fall into the gray area that I want to be certain are handled the way she would want."

Dr. Tashka listened intently and never broke off eye contact. She nodded her head when I was done. We would explore this area again, but I knew she had really heard me and would support decisions in my mom's behalf as it became necessary down the road.

There was one more area I wanted to explore. "Do you think my mom has Alzheimer's?"

"That's a very good question." Dr. Tashka replied. "An MRI would yield helpful diagnostic information, but we can't do one because of your mom's cochlear implant. She does have dementia, but I don't think she has Alzheimer's."

---

The rest of September and October were relatively stable. Mom was almost always sleeping on her back, ankles crossed, with a throw over her when I arrived, but she woke up quickly. Her room took shape with each box I sorted through. In one of the few remaining boxes, I found several pairs of pants and miscellaneous other things probably thrown in together in haste to expedite her move.

Mom pulled out one pair of pants at a time, and I put them on hangers. She could no longer coordinate pressing on the hanger clips and keeping them opened while simultaneously putting the pants under the tab before it sprung closed. This simple, everyday chore that I could do with my eyes shut was too complicated for her. I wondered which neurons were still firing and which were already dead, never to return. As the last pair was hung, I heard a thud. Something had dropped to the floor. I looked down to find her missing processor on her bedroom carpet. She must have put it in her pants' pocket before her nighttime grocery shopping adventure. I put it in the safe.

Mom's new place in assisted living, ironically, had a floor plan that was very similar to that of both of her previous two apartments, but she didn't even notice. Her ability to discern familiar from foreign, her things from those of others, was virtually gone. Mom beamed, however, when I asked her about her mom, my grandma, Lillian Oberle. Occasionally I thought I heard her mumble comments about taking care of her mom or seeing her, but my mom's voice was soft at times and her remarks were incomplete. She described her mother as very kind but firm. Grandma sounded exactly like my mom.

---

Colleen, one of the caregivers in assisted, had been assigned to my mom when she first moved over. One day, when Colleen spotted me in the hall, she said she had a story to tell me. Colleen had been completing bed-check rounds every two hours when she entered Mom's room. She heard my mom talking to someone in very clear, purposeful sentences. Colleen overheard, "I'll take care of you" and "I'll be there for you." Colleen stepped further into the bedroom to see whom my mom was talking to, but no one was there.

Mom turned and spoke eloquently to Colleen, saying, "You don't see her, do you? I can see her, but you can't."

Colleen answered, "No, I can't." Just as Colleen was about to reveal the identity of the invisible person to me, I said, "It was *her* mom."

"That's right," Colleen affirmed. "She said it was her mother."

I knew it! My mom had always described her mother as "a saint." I was not surprised to learn that she was the person that my mother would offer to take care of. It made my day that Colleen shared such a touching story with me. It was a charming tribute to both wonderful ladies. I regretted not knowing Grandma Lillian longer, but I had a sense that she lived through my mother.

## 1978–1984

Jerry and Wendie opted not to have children. In striking contrast, I hit the jackpot with twins. My girls, Christie Ann and Angela Lynn, were born January 14, 1978; they were six weeks early, weighing in at only three pounds, eleven ounces and three pounds, fifteen ounces, respectively. Hospitalized for just under three weeks, they came home days before my twenty-sixth birthday. They reminded me of shar-pei puppies, with their signature rolls and folds of wrinkly skin. Being a mom of twins during their first year was exhausting, but from the toddler years on, it was filled with fun; new adventures; laughter; some tears, of course; and twice the unconditional love.

My daughters and I did everything together, but it was my mom who taught them how to cross-stitch, and they, in turn, taught me. Mom's talent for handcrafts like tatting, blind-hem stitching, black work, Hardanger, and ribbon embroidery was exquisite. As first graders, my girls cross-stitched recipe card holders for their teachers with the words "Bon Appetite," under my mom's tutelage.

"Grandma taught us that the back of your cross-stitch project should look almost as good as the front," Angie informed me as she flipped her project back and forth to show me how the ends of the embroidery floss were hidden under the stitches.

"And if you make a mistake, you have to take the stitches out and fix it," Christie added. "That's what makes it perfect when you're done."

My daughters' collectively professing my mother's meticulous techniques did not surprise me. I had three pairs of big shoes to fill as I tried to come from behind and learn what they already knew. The girls were very good teachers and modeled my mom's instructions and style beautifully. I will never forget the treasured moments when the four of us were all cross-stitching together in our living room or hers.

### Mid-October 2010

"You moved it again," Mom said when she came out of the bathroom.

"Yes. I'm looking for the perfect place to hang it," I replied. "*The Angel* has always been my favorite."

"Mine too."

"I remember the very first time I saw it finished and framed."

"It hung over the server in the living room," she said, a surprisingly accurate recollection.

"And beautifully I might add." We were having a rare but wonderful conversation, and I savored every word. "Where do you think it should go?" I asked.

"Oh, I don't know. Whatever you think." I was hoping for a more detailed response. Then she added, "It looks fine where it is."

Then so be it. *The Angel* hung in her bedroom and could watch over her; Mom was spending more time in bed anyway.

"Is this good?" I asked. Mom didn't answer. As I turned around, I could see that she had dozed off on the bed in her usual position, ankles crossed, snuggled under the warm throw. I stepped back, admired the magnificent angel, and reflected on the first time I had seen it. It had been majestically displayed over the server in their dining room. It was perfectly framed and elicited profound emotion. Very few things were truly works of inspiration like *The Angel.*

### 1992

"Like it?" my mom had asked with a smile. On visits to her place or ours, I had watched her work on it, but to see it finally finished, framed and hung left me breathless.

"It is truly exquisite, Mom. Just beautiful," I said.

Mom had cross-stitched many amazing pieces over the years, but nothing had embodied such elegance. It was impossible to really describe the angel's soft, flowing gown, meticulously accented in gold filament threads; striking, deep crimson ribbons trailing down her white petticoat; and the subtle hues of teal and underlying olive accents in her dress. Her blush face, in profile, projected calm and reverence. In her hand she held a single, glowing candle, casting its protective light over the miniature town below. The angel's dramatic, white wings were adorned in soft touches of blue, and her golden locks bore a wreath of holly. In the tiniest of stitches, which required a magnifying glass to decipher, Mom had worked in her initials, "BW," and the year it was completed, "'92." It was overwhelming.

The Kalamazoo Institute of Arts had displayed *The Angel* circa 2000 along with additional works of my mother's and of other local artisans. Someone told me that *The Angel* had been insured for ten thousand dollars during the exhibit. To her, to me, and to my daughters, however, it was priceless!

### Mid-December 2010

I was anxiously awaiting our Germany family—Christie, Chris, Isaac, and six-month-old baby Lillian—at the international arrival area at the McNamara Terminal. I had prepared myself for the possibility that my then two-year, nine-month-old grandson, Isaac, might be a little shy around Grandma Elaine as it had been three months since I had visited. As soon as he saw me, however, he ran ahead of his mom, who was pushing baby Lillian in her stroller, and into me with his little boy arms extended, knocking me over with his big, full-bodied hug. Christmas was made for me right then and there. I was so thrilled to have them with us that I repeatedly said, "Your presence is my present."

## Christmas Day 2010

I was a little anxious about what kind of disposition Mom would be in on Christmas Day. Her alertness fluctuated constantly, and I said a silent prayer for a decent holiday for everyone. On Christmas morning, we contemplated our gift clues and tore through the presents amid laughter and great fun. Then Joe headed out to get my mom.

When they returned and Mom came in, her face lit up brightly when she saw her granddaughter Christie. Mom's blue eyes still sparkled, and her smile exuded warmth and comfort. Christie was very happy that her grandmother had recognized her. Mom did fairly well at my house that Christmas Day. She was quiet and only able to participate in a few, simple tasks. Christie tried to get more information about her daughter's namesake, but my mom was sadly beyond detailed recall of her own mother. Mom asked frequently for Isaac's and Lilli's names and how old they were. She smiled a lot about seeing the grandkids and great-grandkids and appeared to be engaged—visually, anyway.

I was concerned again about Mom transitioning back to her place, but she was so exhausted when we got to her room on Christmas evening that she crashed on the bed. She smiled as I kissed her good night, and I said, "I'm glad you were with us for Christmas."

"I'm glad too …" she began, but her voice trailed off. I filled in the blanks in my head the way I wanted to hear it, "… that I could be there." *I love you, Mom. Good night.* It would be our last Christmas together, forever.

# CHAPTER 37

*Mom Is My Angel*

January 2011

Not long after New Year's, I was reviewing with Mom the 2011 calendar and the girl's impending birthdays on January 14. From out of nowhere, she said, "I told God I was ready to go anytime."

Her frank comment had me scrambling for an appropriate comeback. "And what did he say?" I asked.

"Oh, you know, He doesn't really answer you."

I released her with "I will miss you terribly, Mom, when you are gone, but I will be okay. Your boys—Dad, Jerry, and David—are ready for you when you are."

"I appreciate everything you do for me, Elaine," she said. "I'm so grateful to have you."

My eyes welled a little, and I replied, "And I am glad to be here for you, Mom."

She continued in clear and coherent detail. "I know my memory is very bad. I get upset when I try to remember things ..." She paused; I waited. "And I can't. It's very hard." Then, she tilted her head back and closed her eyes. My mom was nearly completely ravaged by a brutal, mind-zapping disease with a voracious appetite for brain cells. Until her dementia had gobbled up every last one of them, she would continue sinking farther and farther until nothing was left. It was hard to watch, but I did anyway. She deserved as much.

### February 2011

Joe and I took my mom out to dinner one weekday evening in February. She had been fairly stable for a few weeks, so we got adventurous. "Oh, how nice," she said when I told her what we were doing. I helped her order from the menu, but overall the evening went well.

I was totally blindsided, however, when we got back to her room and she suddenly experienced unabridged emotional collapse. Without warning, she became hysterical, streaming frantically, "Where are we? Why am I here? What is this place?" She ran her words together in one long, verbal assault without pauses. "Will you be back?" she asked. I couldn't respond to one question before she launched another one. She was very distressed and disoriented. Her body trembled, and she looked mystified by her surroundings. She grabbed at my hands as if seeking security from my grasp.

I wanted to wrap my arms around her tightly as she had done to me so many times, so long ago, calming me with her strength, but I didn't dare move. Her verbal onslaught continued, quickly becoming random and disconnected. When she finally relaxed her grip, I was able to guide Mom to sit down on the bed with me. I put my arm around her waist and pulled her toward me slowly. My other hand was still in hers. Gradually I ventured a few comforting words, speaking with a slow, calm voice.

"This is your room, Mom, at Hunter Place." I paused. "I don't live here." I stopped, not wanting to overwhelm her. Her breathing had slowed from the rapid, hyperventilating speed of earlier, but she was still trembling. We sat there for several minutes before I asked, "Are you okay?"

"It's terrible to feel like this," she answered, still staring into oblivion.

"I'm sure it is, Mom. I'm sorry you feel this way."

"Are you going to leave me here?" she asked.

I wanted to fall apart. I wanted to make her anxiety go away. I wanted to make her better. I wanted answers, but there weren't any good ones. I did keep it together for her, though.

"This is your room, your bedspread," I said, patting it for effect. The trance that held her captive was fading, and she looked downward as I tapped the bed. Then, as if inspired, I knew what to say next.

"Look up there, Mom. That is the angel you stitched." She was following my hand as I pointed toward her striking artwork. "It's my favorite."

"Mine too," she replied. We stared at it for a minute. Her breathing returned to normal, and a smile broke through. Then she said, "I want you to have it when I'm gone."

"Thank you, Mom. I would be honored to have it."

"She looks peaceful and comforting," Mom said. I completely agreed with her, but was surprised by her thoughtful description. Then she sighed and said, "I'm so very tired."

"Well, why don't you lay down, and I'll get the throw and cover you up," I offered.

"That sounds good."

She laid back, securely snuggled under the warm, ivory throw, and closed her eyes. I kissed her good night but waited in the threshold of her bedroom doorway for several minutes to make sure she remained calm. I didn't want her to reescalate after I left. I glanced over at Mom's angel and then back at her. Mom was my angel.

## Mid-March 2011

After three years of grueling law school, my daughter Angie would finish her course work in April and officially graduate in May

2011. Mom continued to experience a downward slope of waning orientation and memory skills. When she actually did remember one day, though, that her granddaughter was in law school, I took advantage of my mom's fleeting lucidity to remind her of a promise that I had made to her a year earlier.

"I want to acknowledge Angie's finishing her law degree," Mom had said to me definitively in the late spring of 2010. I knew she meant a financial recognition.

"That's very generous of you, Mom, but you'll have to wait until next spring."

"Oh, she's not done yet?" I shook my head. "Well, promise me that if I forget, you'll remind me to write her a check."

"Okay, I will," I had said. Sadly I knew it was likely she would not remember.

As we sat together on the couch, I reminded Mom of our brief conversation from the previous year. Of course, I did not expect her to recall it. I wrote the check to Angie but had Mom sign the card. I noticed that my mother's once consistently beautiful penmanship had deteriorated significantly as she attempted to sign her name. Her grip on the pen was weak. Her face grimaced, presumably from concentrating, and the letters were very compromised by her wobbly hand. Just as I was about to seal the envelope, I caught that my mom had signed the card "Grandma Oberle," her mother's name, not "Grandma Ward." *How weird*, I thought. It was a prelude to the next chapter of her life.

Elaine and Betty. Circa Christmas 2006

# CHAPTER 38

## *Houdini Mom*

Monday, March 28, 2011

The caller ID said "Hunter Place." It was Marcy, the director; I had not met her yet. Marcy explained that on Saturday afternoon, during their open house, my mom had been hovering around the lobby doors and exited along with the guests. An employee astutely recognized my mom, however, while she was still under the overhead canopy and promptly redirected her inside.

"Maybe it's time to consider Memory Care for your mom," she said frankly and went on to tell me that my mom's agitation and wanderings were on the rise again. We faced yet another move, her third in nine months. I had overheard Mom utter a few times that her mom was "across the street." I wondered if my mom's twisted memory had woven the illusion that her mother lived close by. My mom's reality was anything but real.

Hunter Place's fee structures were competitive with those of the other facilities except for their Memory Care wing, which was exorbitantly out of line and out of the question. I wasn't sure what factors catapulted the cost, but Joe and I would be doing some serious looking at comparable options and quickly. Mom would never approve of her estate being drained by the high cost of Memory Care if a respectable alternative were available. I didn't really want to move her out of Hunter Place as they

231

had provided stellar care and transparent communication. I knew my mom's stay had been very difficult at times. Despite this, however, staff members told me how much they enjoyed working with her, how they delighted in her spitfire one-liners and honestly humorous antics. They were able to see beyond my mom's agitation and occasional refusals to dress or eat and patiently redirected her through those behavioral shutdowns to more productive conduct.

With my professional background as a therapist, I knew firsthand what I should and, equally important, should not see, hear, or experience in a quality assisted-living center. Unbeknownst to the staff, I was always listening in on employee conversations, among themselves and with residents, watching for eye rolls and observing their touch when providing physical guidance to a resident. Nothing that occurred within my line of sight or earshot escaped me.

## Tuesday, March 29, 2011

"So, what did you think of it? How does it compare to the others we saw?" Joe asked.

Joe and I had toured two potential alternative facilities together, and I had visited one on my own. Armed with brochures, room options, and price sheets, we could make a final decision. I was leaving for Germany again in late April and thus had a month to make this happen. Joe was not going to be saddled with an emergent move a second time, plus he was accompanying me for part of my nearly three-week stay.

"Well, at least I understand why these places are less expensive," I said. "They all offer companion rooms with two residents in each, rather than private only."

Attempting to replicate a floor plan or room colors was no longer relevant. Mom had already crashed in other residents' rooms, wore what was handed to her, wasn't able to recognize her surroundings, and hadn't shown much awareness of family photos in some time. Joe and I hashed out the pros and cons of each facility, location, sense of professionalism, availability, and every other significant option we could think of. Basically it came down to a gut sense.

## Wednesday, March 30, 2011

Joe and I took a quick tour of Hunter Place's Memory Care wing for comparison and then had an appointment with Dr. Reddy and Cindy in my mom's apartment. Dr. Reddy's Einstein/Freud insight was incredibly revealing. I wanted to employ the Vulcan mind-meld like Mr. Spock on *Star Trek* so I could expeditiously soak up Dr. Reddy's extensive knowledge in order to better understand my mother's demented brain.

In a few, succinct sentences, Dr. Reddy spoke volumes. He was already aware of Mom's sleight-of-hand trick over the weekend, trying to slip out through the main doors undetected, her petite physique camouflaged by the crowd of guests.

"Your mom is unable to avail herself of the care provided in assisted as she can't identify what she needs assistance for, nor does she mingle with other residents intentionally in activities unless she is brought there. Her fluctuating behavior is unpredictable, but not unusual. It is only a matter of time before she will need Memory Care, and relocating her while she still has some ability to adapt to new routines would be best. Betty no longer takes ownership of her personal belongings versus those of others," proof of which was the fact that, like Goldilocks, she had been found sleeping in another resident's room. And then came his amazingly prophetic final remark: "Her flight-risk behavior could result in more serious injuries should she manage to get out again anyway."

With that, we were done. I was both listening to and hearing every word he said and already had the wheels in motion for her next move. I just had to make the final decision.

"It will all work out," Joe reassured me on the drive home. He was right. It would work out, only we would be totally blindsided by how.

Sunday, April 3, 2011, 7:25 a.m.

I was up early Sunday morning, strategizing that maybe while Mom was at breakfast, I could start packing in anticipation of her next move. I didn't want her to dissolve at seeing her things boxed. My thoughts were interrupted when my cell phone rang. It was Porcia, the nurse, and Marcy, the director.

"Your mom was found outside early this morning," Porcia began, "and has been transported to the hospital."

I was taken aback, of course, and asked, "How did she get out?"

"We don't know yet. It is still under investigation, but when she's discharged she *has* to go to Memory Care." Porcia was emphatic.

*It's okay*, I thought. *No one has to cram it down my throat.* "I would love to keep her in Hunter Place, but Memory Care is cost prohibitive. We have toured other places already." Virtually instantly I made a final decision to move her to Sunrise.

Marcy spoke up. "We are reviewing the tapes to see how she got out and will let you know what happened."

Immediately I called the hospital ER. Mom was still being assessed, but they confirmed a urinary tract infection and severe hypothermia. *Severe*, I thought. *What's going on?* I filled Joe in. Periodically throughout the morning I called Providence Hospital for updates until she was admitted. Then I called Sunrise and set up an intake assessment for Monday morning at Providence. Joe was up to speed on Mom's great escape and overheard me as I finished my call.

"You decided?" he asked.

"Yes. I know my mom can't capture ambience anymore, but for reasons I can't fully explain, I feel better about seeing her at

Sunrise than the other places we visited, even though they were all quite acceptable."

"And that's as good a reason as any," he reassured me.

Just the idea of my mom being outside in the cold, alone at night for a couple of hours was disturbing. I wondered whatever possessed her to exit the building. Was she trying to find her mom? If so, it was sad but very sweet just the same. I accepted that wandering was a characteristic of dementia, but I didn't really understand why. I could only assume that in her fragmented, logic-depleted mind, she was looking for someone—her mom, my dad, or Jerry maybe?

Mom was finally transferred to a room by midafternoon Sunday. At three, we headed out first to Hunter Place to get her cochlear device and meet with Marcy for an update. Marcy introduced herself and shook our hands. I mentally noted that Angie would especially have appreciated Marcy's firm handshake, a gesture Angie would have interpreted as indicative of confidence in a female administrator.

Immediately Marcy offered her sincere apologies for the circumstances surrounding my mom's exit. She said she was "still reviewing videotapes and interviewing staff, but since the records indicate Betty was in her room at the 3:45 a.m. bed check, she exited sometime between then and when she was found. Caregiver reports indicate that at 5:30 a.m., Betty was not in her room. An indoor search was started immediately. Another staff person went outside and found Betty around the building."

Mom was dressed only in her red flannel pajamas, with no robe and no slippers. She had nothing to protect her from the night's twenty-five-degree temperatures. I tried to keep my composure as I fought back overwhelming emotions. The visual image was difficult. They still didn't know which exit Mom had used, but Marcy said she would be there all day until she knew.

Marcy acknowledged that Memory Care's fee structure was more expensive than other facilities' because they didn't offer a companion-room price option. She had already been in contact with the regional director, and they were considering offering that feature. I volunteered that I had set up an intake assessment with Sunrise in preparation for Mom's eventual discharge and that I could postpone it for a day, but obviously it was a time-sensitive matter.

At Providence, we found my mom nestled in the hospital bed. She was extremely drowsy and didn't open her eyes. Her nurse informed us that the hypothermia was resolving and the infection was being treated. They had used several warming blankets in the ER to help raise her body temperature and still had them on her bed. I smiled a bit at the thought of my mom snuggling under a warming blanket. If Mom had been aware, she would have loved it.

I explained my mom's total deafness, showed the nurse the cochlear device and how it slipped on, and left a copy of the very simple instruction sheet. We grabbed some dinner and drove home. Marcy called me about eight o'clock that evening and told me that the regional director had approved a companion room comparable to the cost of Sunrise. "That's great, and thanks," I said. Marcy still hadn't interviewed everyone involved, but she should have those conversations completed soon. I would meet with Marcy and Kushbir, the assistant director for both Assisted and Memory Care, at eleven on Monday.

Monday, April 4, 2011, 9:30 a.m.

There wasn't much change in Mom or her condition the next day. I had put her cochlear processor in a drawer the night before, and when I went to get it out, I saw a business card from the State of Michigan, Adult Protective Services. *Who called them?* I wondered. It was an intriguing question. I would call the contact person later. I was hopeful that my upcoming meeting with Marcy would shed more light on the details on my mom's great escape. I pulled the blankets up higher on Mom's shoulders, tucked them in around her neck, and kissed her good-bye.

Marcy and I sat opposite each other in the two chairs in front of Kushbir's desk. Marcy looked at me and jumped right in with the facts. Pen in hand, I was ready.

"A review of the videotape clearly shows that Betty pushed on the inside door, setting off the alarm about 1:30 a.m. Sunday night, and then she is redirected away from the door. She's off camera for a few minutes and then the video shows her walking back to the lobby area and sitting down off to the side (1:40 a.m.). Betty approaches the door again but does not touch it and steps back. Then the doors open automatically, but the alarm does not go off, and the video shows Betty exiting the building at 1:45; she goes right and then is off camera. She was found around 5:45, sitting on the ground by the doors on the east side."

I made a few notes, but mostly I just sat there. I felt numb and sick and was still absorbing the information when Marcy continued. There was more?

"I've completed staff interviews, and the caregiver who signed off that Betty was in her room at 3:45 didn't actually see her but assumed that Betty 'had to be there; where else could she be?'" Marcy quoted the caregiver. "She was supposed to be checked on again, but that staff person skipped the bed check completely. They have been fired." Marcy still didn't know why the doors had opened. The alarm company had been contacted and still had to come out and check the integrity of the alarm system. "All staff already have or will be in-serviced on exactly what a physical check entails," she added. It involved actually seeing the resident's face and not just presuming the lumped-up covers had a person underneath them, which had happened in this case.

There was still the door mystery to unveil, but otherwise I had the entire, awful story. My ninety-five-pound, four-feet-eleven-and-a-half-inch, eighty-six-year-old pixie of a mother was outside in twenty-five-degree temperatures for four hours in just her pajamas! She had no robe, no hat, no shoes, no gloves, and no help because a minimum of two staff people had screwed up big time. Anger hadn't even begun to set in. I felt everything from outrage, crazed fury, and disbelief to complete and paralyzing numbness. I was amazed by Marcy's candidness. It was impressive. She never broke eye contact with me, not once. She never sugarcoated the facts and never excused—like she could have anyway—any of her employees.

I took a breath. "I can't imagine how difficult it is to sit across from me, look me straight in the eye, and tell me honestly that at least two of your staff are responsible for my mom getting out." I clearly saw the moisture build up in Marcy's eyes as I spoke. "But I appreciate your transparency."

Then Kushbir showed me the apartment they were offering my mom. The room was more than adequate, with a large bathroom separating each resident's bedroom and two closets, one for each person. I felt an incredible sense of relief. I still had to wrestle with the dichotomy of keeping my mom in the same facility that allowed her to escape in the first place, but my friend Jill helped me reconcile that quandary. Basically, Jill offered that in the previous nine months, I had had no concerns about Mom's care at Hunter Place and that this was an unacceptable but isolated incident and not reflective of the facility's genuine intent or integrity.

Tuesday–Friday, March 5–8, 2011

Heather called on Tuesday to say that they would move Mom's things from the assisted-living section to Memory Care at no charge. *No shit*, I was thinking. *They owed her at least that.* By Friday, when Mom was to be discharged, her room was set up and functional. This time Joe didn't have to juggle everything by himself. Mom was more conversational with each subsequent visit, but she had lost ground that she would never regain. When my dad was still alive, he had been hospitalized a few times but never returned to his preadmission level of abilities either. Mom collectively referred to those setbacks as "death by feet," rather than inches. The same applied here.

Over dinner, Joe asked me, "What exactly constitutes hypothermia?"

I realized that I didn't know exactly what distinguished mild from moderate from severe, so, naturally, I Googled it. I found a wealth of resources, all with the same consistent information and shared the highlights with him.

"Hypothermia is a severe drop in internal body temperature," I summarized, "that can cause death if untreated. Normal body temp is 98.6 degrees. Mild hypothermia occurs below 95 degrees, but a core body temperature below 93 degrees constitutes severe hypothermia. I do remember the ER nurse telling me that Mom had 'severe hypothermia,' but I don't recall and can't find her actual core body temperature in my notes."

"Maybe no one told you," Joe suggested.

"Well, that stone won't go unturned." I sounded like my mom with her colorful expressions, only I had a different selection in my repertoire. I made copies of a few articles, all saying the same thing, and carefully placed them in Mom's black binder.

I was at the hospital Friday morning for Mom's scheduled noon release. I asked at the nurse's station if they possibly had the ER notes from my mom's arrival. Not only did they have those, but they also had the EMS run log. Awesome. I signed for both. I scanned the EMS sheet first for the times and vital signs. The call came in for an ambulance at 6:27 a.m., paramedics arrived at 6:32, and at 06:35 Mom had a body temperature of 89.8 degrees. I was sitting straight up now, carefully perusing the EMS notes. I dragged her big, thick notebook out of my bag and furiously searched for the hypothermia information I had tucked inside the night before. The critical number ranges indicated only a couple of degrees separating mild from moderate from severe, which was below 93. Mom's was more than three degrees lower than that—well into the dangerously life-threatening range!

I could feel the steam building within. I wondered what core body temperature I would rise to as I continued to digest the EMS log regarding Mom's condition. The handwritten notes were fairly legible, and I could make out "shivering, covered with lots of blankets," "per staff, patient found outside at 6:30" (*not* 5:45), and "abrasions feet and left elbow."

The original picture in my head had been ugly enough. The amended version was even uglier, and then it got worse. Suddenly it occurred to me that my mother could have died. It was clearly within the realm of legitimate possibilities, and if she had, it would have been negligent homicide! Firing two people was nothing compared to their being arrested.

Mom was being readied for discharge. She would still need antibiotics, but her abrasions were healing, her vital signs were normal, and she still knew my name. We got her settled in her new room, but she didn't even realize it was different. That was both good and bad—good that she wasn't distressed by yet another environmental change and bad because she didn't recognize yet another environmental change.

Staff started coming in to meet her. The first person was the nurse, Tammy. My mom wouldn't remember her, but she smiled weakly anyway. I admired how pretty Mom still looked despite the recent, heinous incident. I ran my fingers through her hair to rearrange it. Her beautiful blue eyes were still bright. More staff came in—new caregivers, Kushbir, the medical technician. It was a circus. I felt annoyed that they might perceive my mom as the center stage, feature attraction: "Come and see the Amazing Houdini Woman!" I could envision it on an advertisement placard. I couldn't help but wonder if any of them had the potential to be as neglectful as their two former coworkers had been. The energy in the room rose every time someone entered. Every new face was a reminder of what had happened to my little mom and how we had gotten there. By the time Jeff, Director of Operations, and Marcy arrived in the afternoon, I was seething, but fortunately, I accepted Jeff's apologies.

They were there to meet with the alarm company representative. *Finally*, I thought. If *I* owned the alarm company, *I* would have been there on Sunday, well before the resident's daughter got there. Jeff and Marcy returned about two fifteen and informed me that the alarm had not malfunctioned. It needed to be manually reset once my mom had tripped it the first time. When it wasn't, the doors opened automatically as she walked by. Resetting it had been the responsibility of one of the two already-fired staff. They had *really* screwed up, and it was my mom who had paid the terrible price, which had almost cost her her life. No one should have to literally freeze to death, especially due to negligence. Mom would *not* have labeled that scenario as "God's will."

After the five days of hell, the chronology of reprehensible events had become transparent. I wasn't sure my mother would have approved of my acting like a piranha in her behalf, but she would have moved mountains for her husband, her children, and her parents. The apple didn't fall far from the tree, and I was proud to be her apple.

# CHAPTER 39
### *Final Passage*

April–July 2011

My Houdini mom recovered physically from her abrasions, hypothermia, and infection. Her room looked great, I thought, but sadly she didn't notice. I had spent some time deciding where to hang Mom's precious angel. In the new room, *The Angel* could look down on Mom and from any location. Finally I decided on the wall adjacent to her bed, centered over her matching pair of dressers.

Mom's responsiveness fluctuated from visit to visit. Sometimes she could help me put her clean blouses on hangers, and other times she just fiddled with her shoelaces or blanket. It was always a mystery as to what level of alertness I might find her in when I arrived. I distinctly recall one late-morning visit when I found her nicely dressed, hair coiffed, and sitting in a chair in the common area chatting with a few staff people. As I walked closer, I became aware that she was looking at a piece of paper. Apparently one of the employees had written out a math problem, and Mom was trying to figure it out. *Interesting*, I thought as I got close enough to realize what was happening. I couldn't help but wonder what my math-major mom was computing in her head, a precalculus problem maybe? I sat next to her on the armrest of the chair.

"I'm trying to do this," she volunteered with an upbeat tone, glancing at me with her beautiful smile. "I know it, but ..."

"She got the other one," one of the staff people offered.

My moment of elation burst when I saw that the math problem on her paper was literally "2 + 2." The one she had been able to answer was "3 + 1," I was told, but this basic equation eluded her. Two plus two was almost a math joke. There were songs and commercials emphasizing the simplicity of adding two and two, like the ABCs. How sad.

## May 5, 2011

I went to Germany for a longer visit than usual with the grandkids, from late April through early May 2011. Joe joined me for a ten-day stint and was there when I learned that Dr. Tashka's office was trying to reach me.

Apparently on the morning of Thursday, May 5, Mom became quite unresponsive, slumped over, and was transported to the ER. A chest X-ray revealed fluid around her left lung and low oxygenation. Her internist, the stylish Dr. Tashka, and I talked a few times via the wonders of voice-over-Internet technology since I was still in Germany. Mom's lung was partially collapsed, so it was recommended that she have a procedure called a thoracentesis to remove the excess fluid. I gave the appropriate consents over the phone. Neither Joe nor I could be there, but her internist, the floor nurses, and I kept in touch both pre- and postprocedure. Joe would be returning to Michigan on Friday and would visit her on Mother's Day, Sunday, May 8.

I felt so bad that my mom was alone in the hospital with no visitors. At least at Hunter Place, there were staff and residents talking, even if she didn't hear all of it. There were activities and community meals, even if she didn't participate much. People bathed her, clothed her, and brushed her hair so there was frequent human contact.

On Mother's Day Sunday, Joe took a card and flowers out to his mother-in-law, and I called the hospital to get an update. Mom was medically stable, I learned, but not eating which Joe confirmed, as her tray had not been touched. My return trip was scheduled for Wednesday, May 11. With the time difference working in my favor since I would be flying west, I would be home the same day I left. How cool.

By Friday, Mom and I were both back to our respective homes. She had been discharged, and I had flown in. During my visits, Mom was usually subdued and wasn't particularly alert or coherent, but she did come around for a few minutes each time and smiled. After a long life of nearly eighty-seven years, her last chapter was about to unfold. On some level, Mom was preparing herself for her final passage home, and I would be with her.

---

"The chest X-ray taken Monday (May 16) shows the fluid is building up again around your mother's lung." I listened intently to Dr. Tashka's information. "I think her condition is treatable, though, and would like to arrange for a slightly more invasive procedure, if you are agreeable."

I knew what Dr. Tashka meant by "if you are agreeable." I had made my mother's quality-of-life issues crystal clear to Dr. Tashka. She, in turn, had made it equally clear about circumstances that were not on or near the line. She felt the proposed surgery was appropriate, and at that point, refusing interventions was not in Mom's playbook.

She went on. "A thoracic surgeon will drain the fluid again and then use a paste-like compound to help the lung adhere to the chest wall, thereby closing off the pocket. I just need your consent."

"Okay. Yes," I said. "I understand."

Yes, I understood what she was saying. Yes, I understood the medical necessity. Yes, it was premature to say no. Or was it? I didn't want Mom to suffer, but I didn't want Mom to suffer. The lines were starting to blur. I was confident about some decisions but waffled about others. How much of my own philosophy was drifting in like storm clouds, rolling over my judgment? Events were about to collide, and I could feel it. Mom's journey was going to make some very defining turns, only I seriously underestimated how much control she still owned.

The surgery was scheduled for Thursday, May 19, and I was there all day. It was almost eight o'clock that evening before I was finally escorted back to the ICU to see her. I traversed the lengthy hall toward her room. With every step, I felt like I was moving in slow motion, plodding forward under the weight of uncertainty. My body tensed as I rounded the corner toward Mom's room. What would I see? What would she look like? The physician assistant had already prepared me that Mom would have a chest tube and be intubated and sedated. I loathed the hospital setting and couldn't wait to scamper out of there.

My petite, white-haired mom was dwarfed under the covers in her hospital bed, connected to a multitude of instruments that were wheezing and beeping in rhythm. Only her little face poked through the blankets. The atmosphere was eerie, the room lit by the waning sunlight of a very long day and glimmers of colored lights from each machine. Her vivacious spirit was absent. All the energy, kindness, and other qualities that defined her were completely obscured by the wonders of modern science. And for what? I wondered what my mom would think if she could view herself this way. Would she have agreed to this surgery? I sort of doubted it looking at her, but it was done, and all I could do was be a buffer through the fallout.

The bed was too high for me to reach her, so I pulled over a chair and knelt on it. I stroked her face with the back of my hand, kissed my fingertips, and placed them on her cheek. No response. A single tear crept down my face. This breathing body was *not* my mom. I returned to the ICU every day, but Mom's recovery from surgery was painfully slow. She just couldn't wake up even though all of her sedating medications had been stopped. Her first audible words to me didn't come until Sunday. "That feels good," she mumbled when I rubbed lotion on her face, but her voice was raspy and weak.

"She might not turn it around." Dr. Tashka's voice came from behind me as she stepped into the room. I suspected as much.

---

"How do you handle it?" Mom's nurse for the day, Carol, asked me.

"Handle what?" I honestly didn't know what she was referring to.

"That your mom doesn't know you?"

Unbeknownst to me, Carol had overheard me on several occasions ask my mom who I was. Mom's responses had been either absent or inaudible. Carol offered that her father had early-onset Alzheimer's and that his not recognizing her was the worst part of the disease. It was my biggest nightmare too. Mom had known me, but since her surgery, I hadn't gotten anything.

The next day, after applying lotion to Mom's pitifully dry skin, I tried again to jump-start her recollection of my familiar face. This time, however, when I asked Mom who I was, she finally answered, "Elaine." I smiled and was reminded of Carol's question just the day before. So far, anyway, I was still accessible to her fleeting and failing memory.

Mom was still not drinking or eating. Food just pooled in her mouth. She had been started on IV nutritional supplements, and end-of-life decision lines were starting to blur. I knew she would never approve of a stomach feeding tube. That one was easy. Would she have authorized nutritional IVs? I wasn't sure, but under the circumstances, I seriously doubted it.

"Nutritional supplements are used only for a few weeks," Dr. Tashka said when I inquired. "Let's see how she does weaning off of them and transitioning her back to real food."

I nodded my head and added a generic, "Okay," but we would revisit this.

By Thursday, Mom was transferred out of the ICU to a regular floor, her eyes were opened more, and she knew me regularly. I had a very nice, new photo of Angie taken the night of her graduation ceremony from law school in May. It was among a few select pictures that I had brought with me and showed Mom every day. Angie looked very pretty in her sleeveless sundress and curled, shoulder-length brown hair with her hands resting on her hips. When Mom looked at it, she said, "That's you."

I beamed. Angie and I did resemble each other. I was flattered that my mom thought this picture of my thirty-three-year-old daughter was me. *Thanks, Mom*, I thought, and I smiled at the unintended compliment.

It had been five months since my mom had startled me with "I told God I was ready to go" after New Year's. Remembering that, I pulled my chair closer, looked right at her, and said, "You don't have to fight so hard for me, Mom."

"Maybe I do," she replied.

Perhaps I was triggering her maternal button, so I rephrased: "I just want to do for you what you would choose for yourself." Her eyes were still open, looking at me. She tried to lift her left hand. Her wrist and fingers shook slightly and she was only able to elevate them a few inches off the blankets. "I think you would not want this for yourself," I added.

Then she spoke very distinctly, shaking her head for emphasis. "No."

"I feel you're ready to meet God."

"Yes. I am." She smiled and then slowly closed her eyes.

Was she really lucid enough somewhere inside that this conversation was reflective of her wishes, or was it a meaningless fluke? I contemplated her words over and over on the half-hour drive home. My default afterlife connection was Jerry, so I began a ping-pong chat in my head. Was she telling me something, or was I looking for guidance that wasn't there? My rhetorical conversation with myself went on for a while.

Normally, because I am intolerant of commercials, I played radio roulette, always searching for my favorite tunes, but this time I was oblivious to the music. Then, eerily, as if by Jerry's hand,

I became aware of an advertisement on the radio for hospice. "Thanks, Jerry," I whispered as I pulled into the driveway. Perhaps just an inquiry call could provide some direction for me.

Midwest Hospice was well known in our area to have an excellent reputation, so I called them first. The receptionist connected me to Lori, one of their hospice nurses. Lori's astounding insight was quite validating. Mom wasn't eating because she was asserting control, Lori offered. It wasn't funny, really, but it was *so* my mom. I conjured up a visual image of Mom as a little girl, clamming her mouth shut, crossing her arms tightly in front of her, and clenching her teeth to avoid some perceived foul-tasting food or medicine. I know I had done it—apple and tree.

"Your mom is leading her own journey." Lori advised. "Let her guide you. From what you've told me, you know each other very well. She will show you the right passage at the right time."

I relished her words of comfort and direction. I would replay them in my head again.

Friday, May 27, 2011

On my Friday morning visit, I learned that my mom failed repeated swallow studies. The report said that she held the "food bolus in her mouth for more than ten seconds. Patient is not safe to eat." That statement also applied to oral medications. I pondered the next step. Nutritional IVs were temporary, she doesn't eat, I won't sign for a permanent feeding tube nor would she ever want me to—so now what? I knew Mom was ready for hospice and a peaceful end to the volatility of the past several months.

Joe and I went out to dinner Friday evening at a favorite local pub, he for the all-you-can-eat fish and me for the draft Blue Moon. My cell rang; it was Dr. Tashka. I stepped outside to hear her better.

"I've seen your mom, reviewed the swallow studies and nursing notes. I want to make absolutely sure you know there are a few options," she began, "but your mom is not eating enough to sustain her and is pushing or taking the medications out of her mouth." Then she finally said it. "It's time. I support hospice, if that's what you want."

With those words—words I will never forget—it was done. I burst into tears. Mom's eleven-month downward spiral since the original move was nearing the end and, as promised, I would be there until it was over. When I was finally composed, I stepped back inside the restaurant. Joe could see the expression on my face, and he knew. More words were not needed.

# CHAPTER 40
## *Joining Her Boys*

In typical fashion, Mom had highs and lows that were confusing and brought into question the hospice decision, at least for me. Nursing notes from Saturday night indicated that my mom had been very alert and had eaten dinner. I could feel my chest tighten as the nurse updated me. Was Mom actually getting better and hospice was a terrible mistake? By Monday, however, Mom's lows returned, as she was difficult to arouse, it took three requests before she knew my name, and she was irritable.

Cautiously, I offered to brush her teeth. "I'd like that," she said, but she didn't open her mouth. I imitated the action of opening and closing my mouth, my jaw going up and down as I tried to stimulate the same response from her. "I know what to do, but I can't," she admitted. This was another strange combination of events. She could verbalize what she knew to do but couldn't execute the movements. I would never grasp the intricate complexities of a mind eroding away from dementia.

Mom was discharged from the hospital on Tuesday, May 31, just after Memorial Day weekend. I reflected on the irony a calendar year had brought. In 2010, I was making final decisions to transport her to Napier. A year later, while I waited at Hunter Place, a transport team was bringing her back, albeit for the last time.

Thursday brought more unexpected events. I stopped by at dinnertime, but she was not in her room. Where could she be? Puzzled, I walked out and was about to ask when I caught a glimpse of the back of her head. The annoying hair cowlick she referred to as her Red Sea part was clearly evident. She was in the dining room, dressed, talking and eating. Stunned couldn't even begin to explain how I felt inside. Were we going through this again? The ups and downs were playing with not only her head but mine as well.

"Hi, Mom." I tried to project an upbeat tone.

"Oh, Elaine. Hi." Then, out of the blue, she asked me about Dad. "Have you seen Wayne today?" I had not seen that question coming.

"No."

"He's dead, isn't he? I haven't seen him in a while."

*Like seven years. Yep, that's a while, Mom.* "Yes," I responded honestly.

"I thought so. How is it that you know that, but I don't know that?"

How did she suddenly string fifteen words together in two separate statements, with appropriate voice intonation, when she had barely spoken for weeks? I told her that she had known once but that her memory was not always reliable.

Then Mom started to push herself up into standing using the chair arms. I hadn't seen that in weeks either. We returned to her apartment. Almost immediately she reached for her cochlear device and said. "I hear it beeping." I was certain she was accurate about hearing the battery warning beep, but it had been over six months since she had identified that sound. I changed the batteries for her. I was a wreck inside, barely holding it together, and just needed to dash out of there. Stephanie, the hospice worker assigned to my mom's case, and I were scheduled to meet on Saturday for the first time, so I would be back then.

It was another crappy drive home as I pondered Mom's yo-yo alertness levels and a cornucopia of other absurd notions. Where was my brother through all of this? If he hadn't already been dead, I would have killed him. What a ridiculous thought. Clearly I was coming unglued. Jerry wasn't controlling Mom's alertness like a puppeteer working his marionettes with strings. I knew that. I just needed to vent, and he wasn't there for me.

Saturday, June 4, 2011

Stephanie from hospice was a gem, a lovely, genuine and articulate woman. In another time, my mom would have loved her. I liked Stephanie's analogy regarding "benefit versus burden." Essentially, if it helps my mom, whatever *it* is, then great; if not, that's fine too. I asked Stephanie the indelicate question of a time assessment as one of mom's granddaughters was in Colorado, preparing for the bar exam, and the other was still overseas. I told her I was not asking for myself but for them, but I lied. I was struggling too. Stephanie suggested a month or two *if* Mom's fluid intake remained suppressed but longer if my mom started drinking more.

We also met briefly with Kushbir and Tammy who had heard about my mom's incredible rally at dinner, only Tammy's Thursday morning with Mom had been completely different.

"She had been very lethargic all day," Tammy offered. "I tried to do a medical assessment, but she was so unresponsive that I couldn't finish everything." I felt an immediate but strange sense of relief and validation that Mom's upbeat moments were exactly that—upbeat moments, not a dramatic comeback.

Angie's Visit, June 11–12, 2011

I updated my girls regularly on Mom's status. Angie was taking the Colorado bar exam in late July. Her bar prep course and studying would increase as the exam approached, so she decided to come out June 11 and 12 to see her grandmother. I was touched.

Angie looked stunning as she exited the airport terminal,

dressed in sharp, navy blue pants with a vertical array of decorative buttons at the hip, complemented by a crisp navy and white blouse and coordinating silver jewelry. She and I chatted nonstop on the drive out. We would visit with her grandma for a while, and then Joe, who was at the cottage in Brighton working on the dock, would drive in to meet us for dinner at a restaurant nearby. I said a prayer that Mom would at least be aroused enough that we didn't just sit and stare at her sleeping.

Mom was in the bathroom with two caregivers when we arrived and looked very nice when they wheeled her out. I said, "Hi," gave her a kiss, and made sure the processor was working. Then we pushed her back to the empty room near the sunny window. Mom never did get a roommate. Angie pulled over a chair to talk to her. She reminded her grandma who she was, that she was studying for the bar, about her kitty, Cleo (Mom was a cat person too), that she had flown in to visit, had made some travel plans, and so on. Angie spoke very deliberately and in short sentences. Her voice was strong, and her words were well enunciated. Mom would have been proud of her granddaughter for her thoughtful prosody. I know I was and admired the effort Angie put in to maximize her grandmother's comprehension. Mom didn't definitely acknowledge Angie by name, but she recognized her granddaughter as someone important. Mom's smiles had become her communication lifeline, and I could discern the subtle differences between them.

We kissed her on the cheek and said we'd be back tomorrow. Our dinner with Joe was very fun, and then we drove home and he returned to the Brighton cottage. Sunday's visit with Mom was the same, and then I drove Angie to the airport for her evening flight home. We were both quiet in the car. I suspected my daughter was absorbed in thought.

"Does it feel strange to possibly have seen your grandma for the last time?" I asked.

"I'm trying not to think about it," she answered, but it would be.

## Christie's Return, June 19, 2011

For weeks Mom hadn't acknowledged me by name until one day in mid-June when the caregiver was walking her out of the bathroom. The staff person had a firm hold on Mom, who shuffled her feet slowly but purposefully as she moved forward, but my little mom was getting there. "There's my daughter," Mom said when she saw me. It made my day.

Christie, Chris, and the grandbabies flew in from Germany on June 19 to stay for five weeks. As it was Father's Day, Joe spent the day at the cottage with his sons and had taken the dogs with him. I got several calls that Sunday from Hunter Place. At ten o'clock that night, I also received a call from Julie with Midwest Hospice. She had been called out to Memory Care in my mom's behalf. Mom was unresponsive, had labored breathing, and, based on Julie's experience, would not rally again. They had given Mom one Ativan and someone would call back if Mom's circumstances changed. Christie and Chris were busy getting their kids settled in bed so I would update Christie in the morning.

*Oh, my God*, I thought, *this is how it will end*. I called Joe at the lake.

"I think this is it," I said. I started to cry as the words tumbled out of my mouth aloud for the first time. He offered to drive in immediately, but I assured him I really was okay. I just needed a phone hug and someone to talk to. He provided both.

## June 20–July 6, 2011

The next morning, Christie and I went out with Lillian, almost a year old. Mom was on the couch, writhing and restless. It was an ugly scene. She had *never* looked like this. I saw Christie tear up, and I averted my gaze lest I start crying too. It was so unfair that on Christie's first visit since January, she had to see her grandmother that way. Two of the staff people offered to transfer my mom into her room, which I graciously accepted. Mom's condition would not change because of it, but we could visit more comfortably in a private setting.

Consistent with Mom's unpredictable side, she rallied some after hospice's projection to the contrary. The emotional investment I had made preparing myself for Mom's end had taken its toll. The endless ups and downs were exhausting. I didn't wish for anything in particular—just a peaceful, quiet passing without pain for everyone.

Christie, Lillian, and I went out again midweek, and Mom was much more alert than on Monday. Christie talked to her about their last six months in Germany, their plans for the summer, their efforts to relocate back to Michigan, and how much she liked being a mom. Lillian cooed, waddled, played, and scooted around on the floor. She was frickin' adorable. Lillian's first birthday was just four days away, on the twenty-sixth of June. Mom's soft voice only mumbled inaudible words.

Then slowly, subtly, a very distinct, bright glimmer of awareness came over Mom. She sat up, leaned forward, and looked purposefully at Christie with Lillian sitting on her lap. Mom's piercing blue eyes had not shown so brightly for some time. I shot Christie a quick glance and smiled. There was absolutely no doubt that my mom recognized Christie or, at the very least, knew Christie was an important person to her. It was so validating to see Christie be acknowledged after Monday's frightful morning.

Subsequent visits were flat, but I had come to expect the unexpected. Then Joe and I went out together to see her at the end of June. Mom was in rare form, alert, funny, still picking at her food but drinking regular coffee with cream. Unbelievable. She had taken only black decaffeinated coffee for as long as I could remember, but whatever.

Then Mom called Joe by his name and added, "He's the head honcho." Seriously, where did this come from? And they called me spunky! Joe had pulled up a chair at the end of her bed, and she was looking right at him.

I got brave and asked, "What's my name, Mom?" I wasn't sure if she could tell me. It had been several weeks. "Elaine," she said, smiling. I smiled too, inside and out.

## Late Afternoon, July 7, 2011

Christie and I were sitting at the kitchen table with Lillian, who was enjoying a snack, when the phone rang. It was Stephanie. She had just left Hunter Place and called to tell me my mom had taken a dramatic downward turn. Her breathing was labored, she barely opened her eyes, and her fluid consumption was nil. Stephanie told me she would be back early the next morning, and in turn I said I would make a run out that evening. Christie looked to me for more information as I hung up the phone.

I summarized Stephanie's call and then added, "It was so completely draining last time to prepare myself for Mom's end and then not have it happen. It's not that I want it to end; I just know that it's coming." I felt like I didn't make any sense at all as I tried to put my raw emotions into articulate words. "I'll go out after dinner. So far, Grandma's spunk has carried her through."

Christie squeezed my hand and offered to come with me. When Christie and I arrived, Mom was flailing some, her breathing was slightly labored, her eyes remained closed, and I didn't hear even mumbled sounds. Christie caressed and cradled her grandma's hand between both of hers, and I ran my fingers through Mom's hair. We just sat quietly for a while, sharing the time with her. Then we made a plan to return in the morning.

## Friday, July 8, 2011

Christie and I drove out Friday about nine. Despite our brisk walk to Mom's room, I felt a sense of déjà vu, trudging forward in slow motion in an emotional quandary, only vaguely aware of the sights and sounds around us. I set aside the likelihood of Mom's eminent passing after preparing myself once before on

Father's Day night. What would we see behind her bedroom door, I wondered, as we slowly pushed it open?

It was apparent that Mom's breathing was even more labored. Her exhale was hard and forced, and her chest caved in and heaved out with each breath. Mom's skin was pale and cool. She was motionless except for a few random jerky movements, and her eyes stayed closed. She did not mumble a sound. Stephanie was there; she had been there since eight. Christie and I stayed to spend some alone time with my mom. Occasionally a familiar staff person would gently push the bedroom door open and peer in. I motioned to them to please come in, and most did. They offered their sympathies. A few skirted in and out quickly to avoid breaking down in tears in front of us. Word was traveling fast throughout the unit that, this time, Mom's end was definitely close, a day or two at best. I had asked Stephanie the indelicate question, again, about a time frame, but it was impossible to tell—a day or two, a few hours, perhaps.

We had a houseful of people at the time. Joe's son Chris and his family from Florida were there, plus Joe's other sons, Ron and Joey, were headed over to spend the day with Chris. They would be leaving for Florida very early Saturday morning, so this was a rare opportunity to have everyone together. Christie and I spent about an hour with my mom, and then I made sure Tammy had my cell phone number and we headed back home. My plan was to take Christie home, visit for a while with everyone, and then come back. I would grab my toothbrush, contact lenses case and glasses, and return in the early afternoon for an indefinite vigil. It was important to me to be there through to the very end of Mom's final journey. I had been fortunate to be at Jerry's side when he took his last breath and wanted to be there for my mom also.

Christie and I had only been home less than an hour when Tammy called. It was just after noon; I remember hearing the wall clock just finish the twelfth chime as the phone rang. Tammy indicated that I should return immediately. Christie and I scurried out of the house and jumped in the car. Silently I prayed for

Mom to hang on just a little longer until I was at her side. We were buzzed in and headed toward the Memory Care Unit just as Nicole was readying her key to unlock the door.

As she held the door open for us, she said, "I'm so sorry about your mom."

My face must have said it all, although I think I also mumbled, "She's gone?"

"I'm so sorry. I thought when Tammy called, she told you."

"No, but that's okay," I said. "I knew it was coming. I just wanted to be there with her. It was important to me."

July 8, 2011, 12:35 p.m.

We opened the door to her room. Mom looked exactly like she had earlier except her breathing was silenced. Tammy was standing next to her holding her hand.

"I'm so sorry," she said.

"I just wanted to be here," I managed to spew out as tears rapidly filled my eyes. They clouded my vision, and I blinked constantly to see through the wet haze. I could still make out Mom's petite body and walked toward her. My lip quivered. I gave her a kiss on the cheek and stroked her face with the back of my hand as I had done so many times before. Christie cupped her hands over her grandmother's. More staff came in, but they were no longer able to contain their emotions any better than I was. There were hugs, tears, condolences, and accolades. "She was the best," one said. *She was*, I thought. "I will really miss her," said another. *Me too.* "I can't believe she's gone." I felt that also.

It had been almost a year to the day (July 11, 2010, to July 8, 2011) since Mom had arrived at Hunter Place. I imagined that no previous resident had ever left such an indelible mark, with multiple escapes and a cornucopia of attitudes, including sarcastic one-liners and outright verbal assaults from one of the sweetest women on earth, now in heaven.

The kitchen graciously prepared sandwiches for Christie and

me while we waited for the Napier police, the coroner, and finally the transport team who would take her to the funeral home for cremation. I called my husband, Joe. Christie called her husband, Chris. I asked Christie to call Angie also, as I knew I couldn't talk without crying. Angie and I would talk later.

My mother's journey to join her boys was finally over. I felt relief for her and overwhelming sadness for myself. She would have said she had a great, full life. With the tragic exception of outliving her two sons, I would have agreed. The priceless, memorable highlights of our life together from long ago flashed across my mind and made me smile.

During the couple of hours that we waited there, Christie referred to Grandma's calendar, the one my daughters had made for her every year with a collage of family photos, and we picked a day for her memorial service and entombment in Kalamazoo: Wednesday, July 20. It would be small and private; so many of Mom's friends were already gone. The following day, Thursday, July 21, would have been Mom's eighty-seventh birthday. Christie and I decided on and arranged for a moment of silence at exactly twelve noon for friends and family who wanted to participate but resided too far away to attend the service in Kalamazoo.

I took down *The Angel* that had watched over Mom in her final months; I would take it home for safekeeping. Everything else could wait. Mom's battle was over. Peacefully, she had rejoined her boys in heaven. I would miss my mom terribly, but I would be okay because of her unconditional love. And despite my fear that she might forget who I was, she never did. I was very happy for that small but genuinely priceless recollection.

With Christie living overseas and Angie in Boulder, I had prepared myself for the unlikelihood that either of my daughters could be physically present with me during my mother's final moments. As Christie and I walked out together, our arms entwined around each other, I felt so unquestionably grateful that I was not alone. I both needed and wanted at least one of my girls with me. The closing chapter of Mom's final journey was on my mind as I smiled softly.

It had been a genuine honor for me to give back to her after she had given so much to me. Just as my mom had said "I have no regrets" about the care she selflessly provided to my dad, I was proud to say that I had no regrets either.

"The dead are not buried in the ground but in our hearts. They will be there for you when you need them."

(Paraphrased from *The Count of Monte Cristo* by Alfred Dumas. Read at the memorial service on November 26, 2011, in Rochester, Michigan.)

# I Will Never Forget

I don't remember where I am.
I really can't add two plus two.
I don't recall what you just said.
I'm sure it's sweet, if I just knew.
You ask me what I did today, but
I just don't have a clue.
Yet still, I Will Never Forget
How very much I love *You.*

I don't know what clothes to wear.
I need Depends to hold the pee.
My hands tremble when I eat.
My hearing's gone, though I can see.
The apartments here all look the same.
If I'm in your bed, just let me be.
Yet still, I Will Never Forget
How very much you love *Me.*

I don't know what season it is.
The days all seem to be the same.
I told God I was ready to go and
Soon I'll join my Boys and Wayne.
I think your face is familiar to me,
But I don't always recall your name.
Yet still I Will Never Forget
That *you* are my daughter, *Elaine.*

Elaine C. Pereira

CPSIA information can be obtained at www.ICGtesting.com
Printed in the USA
BVOW081731140513

320696BV00001B/1/P